T0320347

Artists, Writers and Philosophers on Psychoanalysis

Artists, Writers and Philosophers on Psychoanalysis presents eclectic interviews with leading figures in their fields, focusing on the impact psychoanalysis has had on their lives and work, and the place of psychoanalysis within culture.

Mariano Horenstein's intimate discussions with figures including Hanif Kureishi, Anish Kapoor, David Cronenberg, and Slavoj Žižek—among many others—bring insight from the therapeutic space to bear on their broader experiences. The first-person testimonies presented here delve into the links between life, art, and psychoanalytic experience, shedding new light on their work. Bringing together interviews with artists and intellectuals from the vibrant fields of cinema, music, visual art, and architecture, *Artists, Writers and Philosophers on Psychoanalysis* identifies the common psychoanalytic thread between them.

This book provides fascinating insight for anyone interested in interactions between psychoanalysis and the arts. It will also be of great interest to psychoanalysts in practice and in training, and to academics and scholars of psychoanalytic studies and interdisciplinary studies.

Mariano Horenstein is a training and supervising analyst who belongs to the IPA (International Psychoanalytical Association), FEPAL (Latin American Psychoanalytical Federation), and the international research group Geographies of Psychoanalysis. He is based in Argentina and lectures internationally. He is the recipient of international awards, has published three other books, and was the first chief editor of *Calibán-Latin American Psychoanalytical Journal*.

Artists, Writers and Philosophers on Psychoanalysis

From the Couch

Mariano Horenstein

Routledge
Taylor & Francis Group

INTERNATIONAL
PSYCHOANALYTICAL
ASSOCIATION

LONDON AND NEW YORK

Designed cover image: Luis González Palma. "Portrait of a Half Body Priest (Retrato de medio cuerpo sacerdote) Serie: Hesiquía (2016)

First published 2025
by Routledge
4 Park Square, Milton Park, Abingdon, Oxon OX14 4RN

and by Routledge
605 Third Avenue, New York, NY 10158

Routledge is an imprint of the Taylor & Francis Group, an informa business

© 2025 Mariano Horenstein

The right of Mariano Horenstein to be identified as author of this work has been asserted in accordance with sections 77 and 78 of the Copyright, Designs and Patents Act 1988.

All rights reserved. No part of this book may be reprinted or reproduced or utilised in any form or by any electronic, mechanical, or other means, now known or hereafter invented, including photocopying and recording, or in any information storage or retrieval system, without permission in writing from the publishers.

Trademark notice: Product or corporate names may be trademarks or registered trademarks, and are used only for identification and explanation without intent to infringe.

British Library Cataloguing-in-Publication Data
A catalogue record for this book is available from the British Library

Library of Congress Cataloging-in-Publication Data
Names: Horenstein, Mariano, author.
Title: Artists, writers and philosophers on psychoanalysis : from the couch / Mariano Horenstein.
Description: Abingdon, Oxon ; New York, NY : Routledge, 2025. | Includes index. | Identifiers: LCCN 2024030657 (print) | LCCN 2024030658 (ebook) | ISBN 9781032708355 (paperback) | ISBN 9781032708584 (hardback) | ISBN 9781032708591 (ebook)
Subjects: LCSH: Psychoanalysis.
Classification: LCC BF173 .H76165 2025 (print) | LCC BF173 (ebook) | DDC 150.19/5--dc23/eng/20241108
LC record available at https://lccn.loc.gov/2024030657
LC ebook record available at https://lccn.loc.gov/2024030658

ISBN: 978-1-032-70858-4 (hbk)
ISBN: 978-1-032-70835-5 (pbk)
ISBN: 978-1-032-70859-1 (ebk)

DOI: 10.4324/9781032708591

Typeset in Times New Roman
by KnowledgeWorks Global Ltd.

The project of which this book is a part has been supported by the International Psychoanalytical Association.

Contents

Profiles

Paul Auster (USA, 1947–2024) Writer, screenwriter, and film director. He is one of the English language's most relevant writers, with works translated into over forty languages, esteemed by critics as well as a broad community of readers worldwide. He has received recognition in France and Italy and has obtained, among other prizes, the Premio Príncipe de Asturias de la Letras, the Prix Médicis, and the Faulkner Prize.

Alain Badiou (Morocco, 1937) French philosopher, playwright, and novelist. With strong influences from Maoism and psychoanalysis, his multiple areas of interest range from mathematics to history, from left-wing movements to love, and from ethics to politics and ontology. Indispensable for his thinking on the contemporary, he has written several dozen books and actively participated in academic life, in France and across the globe.

Sophie Calle (France, 1953) Conceptual artist, writer, and film director. She has explored contemporary intimacy—by way of different projects and languages, such as performance and photography—like no one else. She has received numerous prizes, such as those awarded by the Hasselblad Foundation and the Royal Photographic Society. Her work has been exhibited throughout the world, from the Centre Pompidou to the Venice Biennale, even including the Freud Museum in London.

Javier Cercas (Spain, 1962) One of the Spanish language's most influential narrators. His work cultivates testimony, crossing over between genres like essay and fiction, and it has been translated into over thirty languages. He has obtained, among other prizes, the Independent Foreign Fiction Award (UK), the Grinzane Cavour Prize (Italy), the Athens Prize for Literature and the Premio Planeta (Spain). He has written over twenty books and has been an educator in England and the United States.

J-M Coetzee (South Africa, 1940) South African writer, nationalized Australian. He was awarded the Nobel Prize for Literature in 2003, in addition to having received the Booker Prize on two occasions. He is the author of some twenty novels that are widely translated, one of the English language's most indispensable bodies of work; a uniquely insightful observer of contemporary reality.

David Cronenberg (Canada, 1943) One of today's most relevant film directors, in addition to being a screenwriter and novelist. Truly a contemporary classic, he has directed forty-seven films. He has received recognition at the Venice, Cannes, and San Sebastián festivals for his career achievement, and obtained seventy-seven international prizes over the course of his career.

Arnaud Desplechin (France, 1960) In addition to being an actor, he is also a screenwriter and producer, having been awarded prizes on eighteen opportunities, including at the Cannes, Chicago, Venice, and Gijón festivals and at the Viennale. He is a member of the Academy of Motion Picture Arts and Sciences in the United States and has received recognition in France. He is a prolific film director and a lucid interlocutor with psychoanalysis, in his life as well as in his work.

Georges Didi-Huberman (France, 1953) Philosopher, art historian, and curator. He is an academic who has been widely recognized with prizes including the Adorno Award and the Aby Warburg, Humboldt, and Walter Benjamin Prizes. He is the author of sixty essays on images, a field in which he is the most important contemporary thinker. He is Director of Studies at the École des hautes études en sciences sociales, and teaches in numerous countries, always maintaining a fertile dialogue with psychoanalysis.

Peter Eisenman (USA, 1932) One of the greatest architects on the international contemporary scene. Outstanding among his works are the Holocaust Memorial in Berlin and the City of Culture of Galicia. He collaborated with Walter Gropius and was an interlocutor with philosophers like Jacques Derrida and artists like Richard Serra. He has taught at Yale, Cambridge, Princeton, and Harvard Universities. He has been awarded recognition for his entire body of architectural work at the Venice Biennale of Architecture, in addition to receiving distinction from the American Academy of Arts and Letters, and the Wolf Prize in Arts.

Andrea Fraser (USA, 1965) Contemporary artist who works fundamentally in the field of performance. A pioneer in institutional critique, she teaches at the University of California, Los Angeles. By way of her work, she investigates conflicts and structures in the institutional art world, greatly inspired by psychoanalysis. Her provocative work has been exhibited at the Venice Biennale, the Whitechapel Gallery (London), the Centre Pompidou (Paris), the Museum of Contemporary Art, Los Angeles, and the Museu d'Art Contemporani de Barcelona, among others.

Luis González Palma (Guatemala, 1957) Visual artist. He is one of Latin American photography's most referential figures, and his work engages in a fertile dialogue between photography, painting, and architecture, in addition to poetry, oriental philosophy and psychoanalysis. Among the prizes he has received is the Gran Premio PHotoEspaña "Baume et Mercier." His work has been exhibited internationally since the 1980s, and has been featured in the Venice, Vigo, and San Pablo Biennales, among others; it can be found in the collections of the world's most prestigious contemporary art museums.

Siri Hustvedt (USA, 1955) Novelist, essayist, and poet. Her sensitive, fertile work moves between different genres and themes with ease, with her interest most often focused on the mind and the brain. She has been awarded the Premio Princesa de Asturias and the Prix Femina, among others. She is frequently invited to speak in psychoanalytical circles and has been a guest lecturer at the Freud Museum and at the International Psychoanalytical Association.

Sudhir Kakar (India, 1938–2024) Essayist and novelist, he is India's most renowned cultural psychologist and psychoanalyst. With a European educational background in Engineering, Economy, and Psychoanalysis, he has been considered the great interpreter of Indian mentality for the West. He is a lecturer at the Institut Européen d'Administration des Affaires and at Harvard, Chicago, Princeton, McGill, Melbourne and Berlin Universities, and author of over twenty books. He is referred to as one of the century's most important thinkers.

Eric Kandel (Austria, 1929) Neuroscientist from the United States, awarded the Nobel Prize in Physiology/Medicine. He is the author of indispensable publications in the field of memory—both inside and outside the field of biology—and has been Director of the Institute for Brain Sciences at Columbia University. His range of interests and activities includes history and literature, science, and art.

Anish Kapoor (India, 1955) British artist, one of the world's most relevant sculptors. In a career that spans an infinite array of materials, scales, and geographies, his sculptures constitute true landmarks in cities such as New York, Chicago, Bilbao or London. He has been awarded countless prizes, with the prestigious Turner Prize among them. In a fecund dialogue with psychoanalysis, his work traverses different disciplines and also entails a fluid exchange with writers and architects.

Joseph Kosuth (USA, 1945) Multi-faceted artist and pioneer of conceptual art. His work implies a profound investigation into language, thinking, and art. He has received recognition in numerous countries and has been distinguished at the Venice Biennale, in addition to participating in many editions of Documenta in Kassel. Powerfully influenced by Freud, he initiated a collection of contemporary art at the location where he lived and worked almost his entire life, today converted into the Freud Museum in Vienna.

Julia Kristeva (Bulgaria, 1941) Philosopher, linguist, writer, and psychoanalyst. She is the author of some thirty books, between novels and essays. Her work has unfolded over the course of over fifty years, renovating the fields of semiotics and feminism. She is Professor Emeritus at the Université Paris Diderot and teaches in the United States as well as in Europe. She has received the Hanna Arendt and Holzberg Prizes for her work on the intersection between linguistics, literature, and culture.

Hanif Kureishi (London, 1954) British novelist, playwright, and screenwriter of Pakistani origin. His internationally renowned work has been translated into thirty-six languages, and some of his stories have been made into films. He maintains a rich dialogue with psychoanalysis in his novels and essays, but above all, it is a practice that he has cultivated on a daily basis for decades. In late 2022, he suffered an accident that left his mobility severely impaired but had no effect on his sharp, lucid thinking.

Daniel Libeskind (Poland, 1946) North American architect of international prestige, educated in England and the United States. With a humanistic educational formation focused particularly on music, he has been awarded many prizes and received numerous distinctions. His works have left their mark in cities around the world, with museums designed in Berlin, Copenhagen, London, Toronto, San Francisco, and Denver, in addition to powerful urban interventions in public spaces in Asia, Europe, and North America. He was selected winner of the competition to redesign the World Trade Center in New York following the September 11 attacks.

Caetano Veloso (1942, Brazil) Musician and singer/songwriter. One of Latin America's most relevant popular artists, he was one of the founders of the Tropicalism movement, and through his extensive production of recordings, he has been part of millions of people's lives. Considered one of the 20th and 21st centuries' most important musicians, the Universidad de Salamanca awarded him a Doctorate Honoris Causa. He has obtained numerous prizes, including several Grammy Awards. Throughout his life, his psychoanalytical experience has always served as a center of gravity.

Slavoj Žižek (Slovenia, 1949) Philosopher and cultural critic, is one of the most relevant figures in contemporary thought. He has published over fifty books, translated into more than twenty languages. He was a presidential candidate in his country and is currently International Director at London University's Birkbeck College. Considered an intellectual celebrity, he has achieved the aim of combining psychoanalysis, philosophical thought, and popular culture in interventions that reach vast and diverse audiences.

Acknowledgments

I owe this book to the complicit community that I form part of, and my immense gratitude goes to each and every one of you.

To all the people from different geographies who willingly colluded with me in getting to the place that needed to be reached: Jessica Von Lehsten Goes, Pablo Goldberg, Silvia Gadea, Pablo Arana, Miranda Salt, Monika Pessler, Hugo Aveta, Adriana Carrizo, Federico Ossola Piazza, Bernardo Tanis, Tenório de Oliveira Lima, María Teresa Andruetto, Roger Koza, Cecilia Rodríguez, Fabián Martínez Siccardi, Jorge Bruce, Cali Barredo, Lorena Preta, Bill Glover, and Heribert Blass.

To those of you who offered such decided support from the institution to which I pertain: Virginia Ungar, Sérgio Nick, and Andrew Brook. And particularly to the former Latin American members of the IPA Board, who made this project their own, with the enthusiastic leadership of Abel Fainstein: Sérgio Lewkowicz, Jorge Kantor, Cláudio Rossi, Silvia Resnizky, Pablo Santander, and Álvaro Nin.

To the people who patiently transcribed and translated the texts: Tamara Stuby, Kelly Frame, Mariana Díaz Bringas, Karen Delamuta, Nicolás Garibaldi, Gabriela Levy, Ana María Olagaray, Carolina Raso, Laura Verissimo de Posadas, Aline Wageck, and Constanza Molina.

To my tireless friends, Raya Zonana and Carolina García, and the Calibán team. To Gastón Sironi Luis González Palma, who are always so generous with their friendship.

To my family, for their endless patience.

Without every single one of you, this book would not exist.

Chapter 1

Introduction

From up close, nobody is normal

Eminent and fervent analysands are nothing new. The case of Woody Allen, for instance, is so paradigmatic that it might be hard to come up with anything to say about it that he has not already said in his books and films. Not long before his death, Bernardo Bertolucci confessed to me that, though he was exhausted from his long career as "Freudian patient," some of his films would not have been possible without his analysis (in fact, he included his psychoanalyst in the credits for one of them). Similarly, at a Louise Bourgeois retrospective, I found the name of her analyst mentioned as if he were the coauthor of her work—in it, the influence of psychoanalysis is patent. Frank Gehry's analysis was so important to his life that his analyst appears in the documentary about it. The list is endless and marked not only by light but also by darkness: Though Hollywood studios foot the bill for a full-time analyst for Marilyn Monroe, the tragic end to her life was not avoided. Clint Eastwood, like his friend Jane Fonda, was analyzed in California by Wilfred Bion; Robert de Niro, in New York; and Isabelle Adjani, in Paris. The list includes as well writers like Philip Roth and Emmanuel Carrère, and filmmakers like Nanni Moretti—the figure of the psychoanalyst appears in the work of them all. In the cases of other public figures, the presence of psychoanalysis in their lives has been kept from public scrutiny. In the case of politicians, the experience with psychoanalysis left a lasting influence on their lives—think of French President Valéry Giscard d'Estaing or Pope Frances's.

Countless testimonies of celebrities contain moments when they needed or wanted to lie down on the analyst's couch to talk about their troubles. It might not be necessary to wait for biographies, so many of which are posthumous, to find the veins of precious metal in the quarries of the testimonies of individuals who have made the world a bit more livable, interesting, or intelligible.

A psychoanalyst hears things many wish they could hear—and a good many other things no one wants to hear, but that is another matter. At play in a psychoanalytic, session is a particular sort of secular confession where the one speaking tracks what himself or herself says like a bloodhound on its own scent. Thanks to the analyst's attentive ear, the one who speaks listens to him or herself as never before.

DOI: 10.4324/9781032708591-1

What is true for the common person is doubly true for the public figure. Visual artists and writers, intellectuals and singers, actors and filmmakers, eminent architects and scientists, and even politicians turn to psychoanalysts. If an analyst is always bound by discretion, that is even more the case when the analysand is even a minor public figure. If the one seeking the analyst's care has not fled after the first encounter, if he or she comes back to that place they went to talk out their troubles, that is because the analyst has been able to take that persons in, to listen to *them*, not to the public person they are.

A true analyst, one who honors the ethics of the practice, can never speak of what they have heard. Indeed, unlike other professionals, analysts cannot even mention who has sought their care. Whereas others build their reputation on the prestige of their clients, psychoanalysts are vigilantly silent. Patients, famous or not, are not bound by such discretion; however, they can say whatever they feel like. They are, then, the ones I have asked about their analysis, about their own experiences lying on the couch, about how the Freudian experience, that intimate laboratory of words and emotions, has affected their work (which enriches us) and the course of their lives.

For someone who knows how to make the most of it, a well-acquainted analysis has consequences. There are myriad of past and present accounts of how an experience virtually unrivaled in what it requires of those who embark on it affects what they produce. After all, perhaps no practice asks patients to put themselves on the line as much as psychoanalysis.

The names of the analysts of those interviewed are not included in this book. I did not, generally speaking, ask their names, and when they were mentioned by chance, I decided—with only one exception—to ignore them. I like to think that the analysts of celebrated figures are not themselves infected by celebrity; I believe that the art of being able to help someone weighed down by the public nature of their life through a practice intimate like few others lie, in part, in the ability to relegate him or herself with any hint of celebrity. It means disappearing, turning into a mere listener, a valet, a secretary who takes notes on lives that are, at times, the stuff of legends.

And here I attempt to disappear even more than we psychoanalysts usually do. I set out to do away with any narcissistic whim, to resist the temptation of the fan or the autograph hunter. I reduce my presence to enable something new to be said, and for it to be said as intimately and as true to the experience of the other as possible.

In pursuit of these testimonies, I have traveled halfway around the world, from Buenos Aires to New York, Córdoba (Argentina) to New Delhi, London to Paris, Madrid to Berlin, Teheran to Ljubljana, Rio de Janeiro to Trieste. The conversations have been held in more languages than I speak (Spanish and English, but also French, Portuguese, Hebrew, and Italian). My encounters with these remarkable informants have taken place in bars and restaurants, museums and studios, publishing houses and hotels—mostly, though, in the places where they live, dream, and work, where their public images fade and they appear with none of the trappings of their celebrity. I have, then, set up what might be called a field psychoanalyst's office in many different cities, paving the way for encounters that, I am not afraid to admit, did not always come to succeed. But what did happen at a number of these encounters more than justified the effort.

I met personally with most of the people interviewed, though in some cases my long journeys were in vain. The interviews were preceded by feverish exchanges of phone calls, text messages, and emails, often deeply resonant with what I would later hear in our rich conversations. The scheduling and logistics for each interview took a long time—never less than a year. Many celebrated personalities appear inaccessible at first—and who couldn't understand their desire to protect their privacy? But something else might be at play as well: they understand, whether consciously or not, how important it is to keep an air of mystery. Nobody idealizes someone who can be found by simply opening the phonebook—domesticity spoils any spell.

Reaching many of the interviewees has been a veritable obstacle course around, among other things, watchful bodyguards. My preference has always been for direct contact, not the usual mediation with agents, representatives, editors, gallerists, and personal assistants. Sometimes that was possible, other times it was not. It is not the same to reach a famous singer through their agent as to reach them through a childhood friend; the willingness to open up and utter greater truths changes radically.

I strictly followed a self-imposed ethical rule: not reaching any of the interviewees through their analyst. Analysts rarely speak of the patients they see, and if they do so it is just as clinical cases, always altering identifying details. There may be those who, driven perhaps by veiled narcissism, brag about the stature of their patients—I cannot say that that never happens. To keep the record straight, I have only found out that a given writer or artist has been in the analysis if that person— or a third party, not the analyst—has told me so.

For that reason, this book would not have been possible without an intricate network of friends and contributors in a number of countries who have acted as informants, facilitating personal contacts in whose absence this series of interviews would not have taken place. If I had set out to write a book of interviews with spies, Freemasons, or lovers of some perverse practice, the task would have been no less difficult. While engaging in psychoanalysis is not as shameful as it was at other historical moments, it is usually not something one declares publicly. And that makes sense. There is reason to mistrust those who boast publicly of what happens in a space whose power lies largely in its intimacy.

Indeed, the mere mention of the fact that I am a psychoanalyst sparked the most disparate reactions imaginable. Some of them agreed to the interview only for that reason, while others rejected it on the very same grounds. When I did manage to pass the keepers of the gates, when I was able to reach the one I sought, my petition was not discarded as if coming from a fan obsessed with his idol, a terrorist in disguise, or a yellow-press journalist, I often found a candor and openness uncommon in people with many fewer credentials.

While I was at first surprised that some of the potential interviewees were interested in conversing, I had, after a few interviews, grown tired of listening to myself. The interview device was honed as a result, and at times—not always—the conversations were, in their power and uniqueness, more like sessions. Hence, they were prone to slips of the tongue, unexpected apparitions, jokes, and so forth, that is, the whole range of phenomena that let analysts know we are before the incandescent experience of the unconscious—sometimes *my* unconscious. There is nothing worse than beginning an interview with a slipup, to start by putting your foot in your mouth or misspeaking—so much for painstaking preparation! Sometimes, though, the interviewee was the one to slip up—and the effects were often surprising. They have, at times, even wanted to pay me as compensation for an auspicious intervention. In any case, I have the sense that in many of the interviews there was a real connection.

The purpose of this book is not to discuss the work of the individuals I have interviewed—plenty has already been written about that. Nor does it attempt to delve into their private lives in order to quell the public's thirst to learn about the personal experiences of stars. If repetition is eschewed as avidly as the morbid gossip that a situation as intriguing as psychoanalysis promises, what is the reason for gathering these voices? There are as many as the reader wishes to find, but there is one primordial meaning that this interviewer has encountered in testimonies that cross oceans, languages, and disciplines—and that is a new version of what happened at the very origin of psychoanalysis.

If, back then, something like the analytic device came into being, it was thanks to the truth uttered by patients—original in both senses of the word—like Anna O., Elizabeth von R., Emmy von N., and Dora. Psychoanalysis emerged not only from the truth unleashed by their symptoms, symptoms that, when voiced, burst free from the bounds that tied them to their neurosis—no, that was not the only thing that allowed psychoanalysis to come into being. Equally important was the inverted *didascalia* that Freud was able to mine with unknown finesse, following like none other the instructions his patients conveyed to him between the lines.

One of them, a woman sick of the suggestive laying of hands on her forehead, told Freud, "Enough already. Let me speak." Another explained to a friend that at stake in her work with Freud was less a cathartic method than a "talking cure." The psychoanalytic method was thus constructed with the help of those who experienced it. There was not a single major methodological innovation that was not the result of a passing remark from a patient, a sort of clue left for the clinician willing to heed it. It is fair to speculate that theoretical advances were born of dilemmas in clinical practice, of the resistance of patients to a cure, of their determination to make heard something more than the theoretical bias of the time. Psychoanalysis, from the very beginning, has been a collaborative project.

An eminent architect who has two analysts at the same time swears that psychoanalysis was what broke up his family but also gave him a degree of freedom he had never known before. A director of art films who wanted to make a film showing all the people who, one after another, lay down on the same analyst's couch, suddenly decides to replace the analyst's office with a cab. A pair of famous writers discuss how much psychoanalysis changed—or did not change—one of them. An author of note reports that his analysis—he has ridden his bike to his analyst's office twice a week for thirty years—is where the greatest conversation of his life took place. A Nobel prize-winning neuroscientist states, in all likelihood to the horror of his colleagues, that psychoanalysis is the most encompassing theory of the psyche there is. A couple of French intellectuals—once a writer of fiction for the few, now he is a bestseller; she is a semiologist accused of being the spy who came in from the cold—live together, but they choose to speak to me individually; thanks to the magic of champagne, they agree to let me in on their secrets. A very famous singer and songwriter dreamt about psychoanalysis before he knew what it was. In listening to himself talking to me, the name of a future album comes to a folksinger who travels the world. An Israeli filmmaker talks to me in his attic apartment in Paris; he uses his body as much as his mouth as he speaks in four languages at the same time. Another filmmaker, his hair still wet from the shower, tells me how the analyst's couch has colored his entire life. A bankrupt Mexican writer pays for his analysis with manuscripts that are worthless until he becomes famous, at which point his analyst returns them to him. A Brazilian artist who exhibits work around the world welcomes me to his home along with members of an Amazonian tribe. A Slovenian philosopher who had been in analysis long before deciding to run for president converses with me in a coffee shop in Ljubljana, surrounded by the local intelligentsia. Another philosopher who has spent his career in England is a steadfast analysand and chief advisor to many Latin American presidents. Yet another philosopher, this one based in Paris, informs me before the interview that he would like psychoanalysts to get more involved in public matters; their voices, he says, must be heard. An artist who had stopped painting remembers how he started doodling while talking to his psychanalyst; the analyst jealously kept the drawings until, almost half a century later, they ended up in a homage to the man who listened to the painter and enabled him to return to his art. An artist questions the art system from within using the tools of psychoanalysis, among others, such as filming herself having sex with a collector and then selling the prints. Another artist makes works depicting emptiness that go for millions...

Looking through the interviews, I find dozens of micro-stories that evidence the woes and discoveries of men and women who have, with good reason, earned a place for themselves in the history of our culture and contributed to the advancement of the species. The intimate side of each one surfaces; they let the cloaks and shields of their public persona fall away so that each one of us can identify with each one of them. They expose that place where fame is useless to dealing with the trials life puts before us: As one of them puts it in a song, "From up close, nobody is normal."

I was not able to interview some of the people I would have liked to; some of those with whom I did converse and whose testimonies I keep are no longer with us. My work has, at times, been a fight against time, against death, and the interviews collected here do not deny the harsh reality of the lifecycle, which is revealed sooner rather than later in all analyses.

The encounters are at least partly the work of chance, that is, they could well not have happened, and the ones that have been lost at the very instant they occur, leaving behind a certain remains, a certain unconveyable quality. Maybe that is why face-to-face conversations have a special charm or aura—like the psychoanalytic encounter. For that reason, I have resisted using Skype or Facetime, email, and WhatsApp, opting instead for actual physical encounters with those I interviewed even when that meant traveling some fifteen thousand kilometers to converse for just one hour. While there are a few exceptions, I have attempted to preserve those real encounters in the written versions of the interviews in order to salvage that reserve of presence essential to psychoanalysis, something that at times seems to go against the contemporary era.

The travels themselves were more than an obstacle to overcome, more than an annoyance necessary to reach an interviewee. They became the thread that held the interviews together like beads on a necklace. The particular wisdom at play in traveling, which is so different from simply going from place to place or from endlessly tedious tourism, is central to the life of the interviewees as well as a recurring theme in their works. This book can, then, also be read as a travel log. If I have not, generally speaking, documented the interviews in photographs, I have kept the recordings of the conversations. When I listen to them, the evocative power of the voice is patent—proof that I did not makeup what I later wrote down as well as a testament to a practice—psychoanalysis—that foregoes looking for the sake of listening. As Eliot said, "ears go deeper than eyes can see."

I have, at times, sensed a secret network between those interviewed, an iridescent fabric wherever I go. Together, the interviews draw a spiderweb, and psychoanalysis works its way into the elusive community of this cast of characters. I look at their names as if they belonged to rogue cells in a conspiracy where each one interacts with the others fleetingly, seemingly by accident, even though they are all bound together by a greater intelligence. At play, perhaps, is bias in the choice of people to interview—something that has to do with my own world. I feel, at times, like the paranoid prey of a collusion of old analysands stalking me wherever I go.

The list of interviewees in this book might actually be the cartography of an invisible but sovereign nation always on the verge of disappearance. This register is an accounting of its survivors, and I act as a sort of anthropologist who salvages experiences for the explicit purpose of capturing them before they fade away, secretly hoping that, by registering them, I will help them survive.

Why have these individuals agreed to be interviewed by me when I am certain they reject more requests than they accept? Not out of a desire for publicity—none of them needs me for that. I sense that it is a way for them to get to know each other as if the full list of the passengers on this ship were unknown to everyone onboard—each one knows only their cabinmates. But through me, they have a way to get to know the others as well. I am a sort of medium that enables them to connect even to those fellow travelers who are no longer with us.

The meetings are not by chance, but highly premeditated: I personally choose all the people to be interviewed. And I now realize that I choose them because each one ventures to the edge of a cliff in their experience, each one dares to go to a place where there is always a risk of teetering and falling. And it is that very risk that joins the experiences of literature, film, art, and psychoanalysis that I find so captivating. All of them are, as Leiris insisted regarding the first, forms of tauromachy.

And it is for that reason—and herein lies another justification for including the voices of my interviewees—that I have undertaken this testimonial labor. It is an attempt to take note and hear what these privileged subjects have to say about the construction of the analytic method, its implementation, the theoretical conjectures of their analysts, and the modern rituals we invent. Here the analysands speak to build not their own micro-stories—that are reserved for themselves and those who take them in with their attentive ears—but a discipline. They are not the objects of a sort of psychoanalytic entomology, but lucid subjects, privileged beneficiaries, crafters of vital, and efficacious testimonies.

I make them speak not, for the most part, so that they might say who they are, but rather who we, the analysts, are. My aim is not for them to speak of their literature, music, or art—though they do speak of that as well—but for them to speak of our art from their foreign gaze as lucid as it is candid, indeed lucid insofar as candid.

That is a reason, just one of the many, I am publishing these interviews.

Thanks to how they resonate with those who read them, these interviews are important to both skeptics, and the devout, to those who have experienced the analyst's couch—its practitioners, that is, the "gild" of psychoanalysts of which I form part—and those drawn toward it. But the purpose of the interviews is not only heuristic or illustrative. To demonstrate what I mean, I will share an anecdote:

In his speech after being awarded the Nobel Prize, Joseph Brodsky cited the great English poet Auden, who had generously taken him in after he was released from prison in Siberia. Auden and his stateless guest could barely converse (Brodsky spoke next to no English at the time). In Stockholm, Brodsky—still a Russian-language poet, though now also a distinguished writer of prose in English—said, "I am a Jewish poet, my language is Russian. I only write in English to be with him, to do the only thing that can be done for a better man: to keep the conversation going. Of that, I believe, civilizations are made."

Forn, Juan, El amigo imaginario, Los viernes, Tomo Dos, Emecé, Buenos Aires, 2021, p. 219

The psychoanalytic dialogue is, above all else, a form of conversation. A fertile conversation without precedent, a conversation rife with effects. It is not the only form of dialogue—art, literature, philosophy, and architecture also formulate conversations—but no other is immune to its effect. There is no discipline that has not been questioned by psychoanalysis in the one hundred and twenty years since its birth; similarly, psychoanalysis has been enriched by countless fields of knowledge.

This book may, in the end, be no more than a small testimony to an ongoing conversation with some of the most brilliant conversationalists of our time.

Chapter 2

Paul Auster and Siri Hustvedt, the flip side of a monster

I visited the three-story house in Park Slope in Brooklyn on two occasions. The first time, it was for a conversation with Siri Hustvedt, a writer who had just published a stunning novel and was known—as an essayist, as a lecturer, and as an analysand—for her intense relationship with my discipline. We spoke in the sitting room, beneath a painting by an abstract expressionist that went well with the light in the space and with Siri's interests, also closely linked with contemporary art. As we spoke, two people wandered in and out: a housekeeper and her husband, Paul Auster.

Aware of the habitual misapprehension that consisted of considering Siri, a subtle, seasoned feminist, as merely "Paul Auster's wife," I paid the same amount of attention to him as I did to the housekeeper.

A few years later, when we met again in order to continue our conversation, they were both already seated at the table. In the meantime, Siri Hustvedt's prestige worldwide had grown vertiginously. It was notable how the uneasy woman who had welcomed me the first time, with whom we had exchanged quite a few written messages via e-mail—a woman who had even imagined becoming a psychoanalyst and was on the verge of finishing an analysis without which part of her work could not have been written—had become a different person. Her aplomb, her lucidity, and her self-confidence were remarkable.

We spoke at length about psychoanalysis and literature, and about what a matrimony is, something that they both—laughing over misconceptions and sexist visions—have been capable of constructing over the course of forty years.

You have been interviewed many times. I don't want to repeat the same things that you have ever said... you can help me saying one question that, in your opinion, the other should be asked, and never has been asked.

Siri: that is a good idea. I can say that there's one very obvious thing you can say. It's that... because you've been living with me during the ten years that I've been in therapy, that you must have a sense of what that's meant from your point of view...

DOI: 10.4324/9781032708591-2

Paul: That's true. Do you want me to talk about that?

Siri: Not yet.

Paul: Ok. (Laughs)... Now what question should I say that you need to be asked? I guess, maybe, no one has really addressed this about Siri, because your novels tend to be read by people in the literary world, and then they ask you questions about your art. And then your other work tends to be read by psychoanalysts, psychiatrists, neuroscientists... and they ask you about that aspect of your work but they don't ask you about your novels. So, a good question for you to ask is where these two activities join, and how do you integrate them in your life? How do you make a unified inner life out of these different interests? Cause on top of that, Siri's written a lot about art, too. So, you actually do three things. The novels, then the intellectual work, and then the art criticism... there're three prongs to your writing life.

You have all the questions now.

Siri: Paul is right. Where did these things come together, I have thought more in my work that there's profound crossovers between what I'm thinking about in my scholarly and intellectual work and what happens in the novels. The difference is that the freedom or the possibilities when you're writing a novel are much greater than when you're writing a paper. Even though, the process of writing itself is always a process of discovery. But when I write novels, Paul has this feeling too, the book has an organic reality that begins to make itself in ways that are deeply surprising. And you know there's a parallel between the work of psychoanalysis and the work of making art, it's that the unconscious, the things that you don't know you know, appear.

Yes, and you have written that psychoanalysis is a creative experience, as writing...

Siri: that is true. The strange thing about psychoanalysis and writing is that it's extremely hard to explain how you came upon it. So, in an insight, something happens to change you. You understand that the change has happened, but if you try to go back to the moment that it happened, in an analysis, you can't find it.

    I would find sometimes that my analyst would say something and I would understand it, but it wasn't until it was repeated in various configurations, that it really took on a kind of embodied value. Like a deep understanding, not a superficial understanding of what the situation was. This is very interesting, and there's a connection for me between the study of the mind or even the study of the brain, at a very physiological level, and philosophical questions about the brain-mind, and then the experience of psychoanalysis and reading about psychoanalysis, as well as making art. These are not bounded activities in my life, but are deeply related one to the other.

Paul: I see in your books all three of these strands I was talking about. Because many of your characters in your novels are artists, and you make up, imagine pretty art in your novels, it's extraordinary. I always wanted to see it.

Siri: Well, you know you have a good reader if people want to see it.

I'm not the typical reader that Paul said ... because I enjoy fiction and sometimes I learn more reading your essays about art or your fictions rather than your scientific papers, they teach a lot about psychoanalysis ...

Siri: Novels are hugely about human interaction. This is the form that's most deeply about encounters between and among human beings. There are profound insights in reading novels in general, that can't be argued. The form of the novel makes it possible to explore ambiguities that some kind of reason-paper where you are talking about ... you're making some argument, just won't do that.

Paul: In a sense, the reason why we are compelled to read and listen to narratives is because they are not reality. Reality is a big mass of confusion, and narrations help us organize them and think about them in ways that normal experience doesn't allow us to.

Siri: Right. I'm working on a book that has memories in it. And I'm trying to write the memories as they are visually remain in my head, which means that there's huge amounts that are just missing. I can still tell a story about this memory, despite the fact that I can't remember the people who were there, that there's all this fog around the memory. I remember a few things. They're usually emotionally potent things. The things that have emotional meaning are what we remember. But then, these fuzzy memories, with a few markers, you can make them into a narrative in which nobody knows how much is missing from the actual memory. Narratives are usual a kind of causal mechanism, moves, in actual lives, they're quite hidden.

Paul: You have said to me, emotion consolidates memory. And I think this is definitely true. And the things that I seem to be able to remember best are when something emotionally significant happened. But I don't remember what I had for dinner...

One of your characters said "I will find a place to rewrite me."

Siri: Yes, it's Mia, who says that, in "The summer without men."

If that's true, it doesn't matter if memories are true or not, because we are always rewriting.

Siri: We're rewriting ourselves. This is fascinating that memories change even at a molecular level, every time you pull it out. So that goes all the way down to the molecules in our brain, that we know there's no original engram. But I think in psychoanalysis, it's a question of discovering a story about the self that is more habitable and plastic. Most people who suffer from neurosis, most of us, that it's what Freud said about these unconscious patterns that just keep repeating themselves and they create unhappiness. And becoming conscious of those patterns is the road to liberation. I think very much about psychoanalysis, of my own psychoanalysis, as liberation.

Your season doing analysis worked for you?

Siri: Yes, hugely, but I'm winding down.

Paul: Well, you're still doing it, but you're coming to the end.

Siri: We're setting a date to terminate...

Paul: Let me answer the question you posed for me, cause it's an interesting question. I always had the idea that when we go to a doctor, a shrink, a therapist, whatever you want to call it, if life became unbearable, then either you find yourself unable to get out of bed in the morning, you were depressed, you hated your life; or you felt suicidal or self-destructive, or you were acting in such ways that scared you, any number of real difficult situations that human beings could find themselves in, then you would have to go and try to get help. And, whereas with Siri, I never felt that you were in that kind of situation.

Siri: Fortunately!

Paul: Yeah. So, ten years ago, when she said she wanted to start going into analysis, I was a little surprised. And then as it went on, and listen, we don't talk about what she talks about with her doctor. But I have heard enough to get a feeling of how important this has been to you, how you really feel it has changed you in really significant ways. And so I've taken a much more nuanced view of the whole process, not only a desperate cry for help of someone on the edge of the window about to jump off the building, but actually someone weighed down by certain tendencies in their personality, your own character, your own behavior, that are upsetting to you and you feel that you have to address them, that they have deeper causes and you're not able on your own to find out what they are. And I think that's what happened to you. And it's been one of the biggest adventures of your life.

Siri: Definitely.

It's like an intellectual adventure, too.

Siri: It is. It's both

Paul: There's always this myth, too, that artists shouldn't go into an analysis cause they will ruin their creative...

Siri: No. For me it's completely... a freeing...

Paul: One of the first of the great writers, besides Italo Svevo, who we know went into analysis, was Samuel Beckett.

Siri: Yeah, with Bion.

Paul: He did it in the early 1930. Beckett was deeply depressed. And he was non-functional. He couldn't get out of bed. And his mother, with whom he had difficult relations, but nevertheless they were close, paid for him to go from Dublin to London for two years, so he could get better. Apparently, it really changed his life.

Siri: I think it was liberating for Beckett.

Paul: It made it possible for him to become the artist that he became.

Siri: Absolutely. And I think what's interesting, I remember when I was reading Bion and thinking about Beckett, and I thought you can see how these two personalities would work very well together. There's something fascinating about the match. Especially when you have two people like that Bion, who wrote a lot, and Beckett. I could see how they would beautifully function together. That there could be this wonderful overlap.

I love this essay by Beckett when he wrote about failure... fail, fail again, fail better. And, arriving to the end of your analysis, don't you find that there is nothing connected to "success" at that point? That word, "success," doesn't mean anything in true psychoanalysis...

Siri: It's a very strange thing, because it's the patient who has to get out of it. I mean, the analyst is not telling you anything about what to do. It is not something successful. I feel, infinitely freer. This is what I feel, this is what this has been about for me. And our daughter had the most brilliant thing about therapy. She too has an analyst. But she's at a different stage. She was saying, mom, you've always been outspoken, you've always said what you think... But you know what's changed? It's that you no longer feel guilty about it. It's brilliant! That's exactly... You know, I think it's, what Paul, you're talking about is that, it's as if you're living with a different woman.

Paul: No, you've always been the same. And you're still who you've always been. I mean... But you have a different attitude about this...

Siri: But my internal reality is different. And that's the thing.

You have a deep and genuine interest in psychoanalysis. Could you tell us more about your early wish to become an analyst yourself?

Siri: I thought I would make a good analyst, but I couldn't afford the training. At the time, the New York Psychoanalytic Institute took one or two candidates without an M.D., so that didn't bode well for me at the time. A part of me wishes I had had the luxury to train then, if only because I would have gotten myself an analysis earlier than I did. It was never a question for me of not becoming a writer and becoming an analyst instead. I made the decision to write when I was thirteen and started doing it right away. The problem for me was how to write and make a living so I could eat and pay rent.

It seems strange that you study psychoanalytical texts, since it's usually analysts who study artistic texts or works...

Siri: I am fascinated by this question: How does a person become or continue to become who he or she is? Certain scientific psychologies, for example, evolutionary psychology, which is founded on neo-Darwinian evolutionary theory, does not include the story of individual development. That which is so significant in psychoanalysis, is missing. Evolution over millennia is important, but the story of one person has no significance because neo-Darwinian employ a static model of an evolved but mostly fixed mind. If the mind is not dynamic but merely a genetically determined entity, it becomes merely a question of calculating heredity vs. environment. If you lose a developmental model, a narrative for subjective reality, then you've done a fundamental injustice to the nature of human experience.

You speak from a foreigner's place, living in cosmopolitan New York, with a Scandinavian origin and speaking Norwegian, working as a writer... The role of an outsider, the one you played before psychoanalysis can be the best place to observe...

Siri: I completely agree. I've often thought about what it has meant to me to grow up in two languages, to have a Norwegian mother and an American father. He also grew up speaking Norwegian. I think two languages allow you to have two different perspectives because words delineate one thing in one language that are not necessarily delineated in the other. I'm sure you feel this with Spanish and English all the time, that you suddenly recognize how perception shifts from one language to another. And even though I could never have articulated that division as a child, I grew up with a sense of "here" and "there." I had a "there," Norway. And when I was in Norway, I had the other "there," the United States. There are many writers who, for one reason or another, find themselves in the position of an outsider. They write to the other, but from a marginalized point of view. I definitely have a sense of being perpetually outside, yes. But marginality as a perspective is often more interesting than holding court at the center of things.

To what extent has psychoanalysis, as you have written, changed our way of conceiving ourselves?

Siri: Freud's greatest legacy may be the incontrovertible value of two people sitting in a room while one listens intently to the other, sometimes for years, and the astounding fact that from those years of talking and listening, the patient can leave the room at last feeling better, freer, more courageous and wiser than she was when she began.

How do you see psychoanalysis at present, and how do you the place that it will occupy in culture in the future?

Siri: Let me put it this way: my hope is that psychoanalysis will again be part of what I think of as the reform of psychiatry. Psychoanalysis has a lot to offer what has become, at least in the United States, a very biologically oriented form of psychiatric treatment that has yet to define what it means by psyche and soma. Patients are collections of dispersed symptoms, not beings with pasts. Because psychoanalysis includes the idea of narrative, the developing narrative of the patient; because it cares about infancy and childhood and their relation to maturity; it can broaden what has become a narrow psychiatric approach. Also, people in psychiatry are getting sick and tired of static models of mind and the brain and primitive ways of thinking about treatment. Psychoanalysis can be part of the resurgence of a dynamic model of the mind-brain.

Susan Sontag called our attention to some aesthetic features of the analytical session. She also said that psychoanalysis was a form of art not recognized as it. What do you think of that? Could psychoanalysis be at least at the same distance from art as from science?

Siri: The actual work of doing art or science is not nearly as different as people like to assume. Doing good science also involves intuition, imagination, and emotion; these unrecognized aspects of science *are* essential to science. But psychoanalysis is an art in the sense that analysts who are good at what they do are able to call on deep unconscious places inside themselves that are extremely hard to put into words, and making art is also generated from the unconscious. Unless an analyst is able to play with these unconscious forces, he or she is not going to be proficient at what he or she does.

I don't understand why my own analysis works. I can't say what has happened. There is a beautiful essay George Perec wrote about his analysis called "The Scene of a Stratagem." He was in analysis with J-B Pontalis, and he says nothing about the content of his analysis. He traces its arc. Endless talking to himself, endless, boring. And then he says, which is exactly what I have felt, that he doesn't understand how it happened, but suddenly finding his voice, his ability to write. And the strange thing: the experience of it is how change happens, but you can't track the course of it. Perec's essay is one of the most wonderful pieces ever written about analysis. And then there's Hilda Doolittle, the poet. She was Freud's patient and wrote a lovely little book called "Tribute to Freud." She also says very little about her life. Neither of them detail the content of their analyses. They talk about the movement and the form. If you could track the course of an analysis, there would be a certain formal quality to it, a shape. The difference between making art, writing a novel or making visual art, and doing an analysis, is that in an analysis there is a real other. All art is made *for* another. It's always dialogical, but the other is imaginary. In the analytic space, there is a real other who can intervene, interpret. This is not true of the novel.

You could say the analyst is also an imaginary creature. Because the nature of the transference includes a kind of projection onto the analyst, the relation changes. One day he or she is your mother, another day your father, sister, brother, or some other intimate person. Nevertheless, the reason why a person can change through analysis is that there is a "real other" who intervenes at crucial moments, or maybe intervenes over and over again, and then a time comes when the interpretation hits. Even if you've heard an insight a thousand times before, suddenly the words have meaning. That meaning has to have a bodily meaning as well as a semantic one. An emotional, physical meaning must be present. We can all intellectualize. I'm very good at that. You take an idea, you spin it around, and see it from different angles, but real change has a deeply emotional, physical quality to it. It's amazing.

The art of the novel is the art of the particular. It's the art of specific human experience and how that experience is understood. That in itself links the form to psychoanalysis. Even though analysis is theoretically guided, it is always about an individual's story. In that way it's novelistic. I don't think psychoanalysis is about dredging up objective truth, or finding the real story. This is an absurdity. The nature of memory simply doesn't bear out that possibility. Even if you've had a film crew with you every day of your entire life, you might know "the facts," but you would be in the wrong perspective. You'd be looking at your life from a third-person point of view. Both novelists and psychoanalysts have a profound concern for the first-person narratives of human beings.

Let's back to you...what's a couple?

Paul: A couple is two people that make a third thing between them. And whatever that third thing is, that is the couple.

Siri: Remember I said that at the beginning of an essay.

Paul: Did you?

Siri: Yeah, but I said it, that we all know that two perfectly nice people can create a monster between them. That's the worst.

I'm interviewing that monster!

Siri: I think that.

Is it possible to know the other, or there is something always missed?

Siri: I think there's always something mysterious. I feel that about you. I feel that I know you very well.

Paul: Yeah, I feel the same, but I don't really know you. But I don't know myself either. So, if I can't even know…

Siri: Neither do I…

You never did an analysis, right?

Paul: No, I never did.

You see, that's the reason you don't know yourself.

Paul: Maybe, maybe…

Siri: You'd get to know yourself better…

Paul: I was never in that desperate situation that I thought you needed to be in to go for help. I never felt that I couldn't just go on from day to day, reasonably.

Siri: I always thought you could have done very well with an analysis, that it'd be good for you, but you decided not to, and that's your business. I think there are real parallels between writing and psychoanalysis. But I also think that what makes psychoanalysis what it is, is that there's also a real other, in the room. It makes all the difference. You can think about yourself till the end of time, and you will not have the experience that you have in an analysis because there's a real other. Whatever you are projecting onto that real other, nevertheless, there's a real other there. And that, for me, I don't know what they are, moments of truth, working through that's probably the best expression… I never would've gotten there alone.

Paul: I don't agree exactly but when I'm writing, and it's not always fun, it's a lot of hard work. But having done it now for more than fifty years, I understand that it does give me pleasure. The difficulty of it is what makes it interesting. If it were simple, why bother? When I'm not working, then I feel that I'm just an ordinary every day neurotic. But when I'm writing…

Writing saves you…

Paul: I'm better than that. I am inside myself of course, but also outside myself. And I had this revelation. It finally occurred to me only about two months ago, what it is and why I do it. And it's taken me all these years to figure out. Here's the thing. The first thing I can remember writing, I was about 9 years old, I started writing early. It was the first really pretty day of Spring, after a long cold winter. And it was Saturday, so there was no school. I lived in a little town in New Jersey, and I got up and I went and took a walk. Just by myself. It was early in the morning and I wondered around and went into this little park that was in the town, and I remember feeling so happy that the birds were out and the sky was warm, and the air was pleasant, and I felt so good about it that I said, I have to write a poem about it. I remember I walked on through the park and into the little town and I bought a little notebook and a pen, and then I went back to the park and I wrote what probably is the worst poem ever written about Spring.

Siri: But you remember it, right?

Paul: But I remember how happy I was. And I realize this is what writing did. It made me feel more connected to the world, to things outside of myself, that I felt that I had a connection to the things around me, which I could never feel under any other circumstances. And maybe that's why I keep doing it, so it's just the opposite of what people think. I'm not going into that room to isolate myself from the world, I'm there to connect myself to the world.

It's a paradox but it's true.

Siri: Absolutely. Or that strange thing that I've observed for a long time, is that when I'm writing, I feel more alive than at any time.

Paul: Well, that's it. Me too.

I would like to speak about the father... Your symptoms, Siri, began after your father's death...

Siri: yeah, the shaking...

And I have read your "Invention of solitude," Paul, where you wrote a lot about your father. What's a father?

Siri: Isn't that a strange thing? I guess I'm thinking about these questions now with these memories. What has been said, the difference between fathers and mothers, is that we really do come out of our mother's bodies. This is a difference. And most of us we don't remember our infancies. It's infantile amnesia. But in the world we grew up, there was—I think this is changing by the way—much greater intimacy with the mother, and that the father was more like a distant being. Now, women really do give birth to their children, and there's a cord that is cut. I mean, this is a pretty deep and profound connection as someone who is also a mother...

Paul: Yeah, most mothers are really connected to their children on a very intimate physical and emotional level. The fathers are generally not as connected.

Siri: No, no Paul. Now it's changed.

Paul: Now it's changed, but I'm talking about back in the old days...

Siri: Young fathers are much more involved in the grooming of the bodies, at least in some cultures. I see this all the time that that's changed.

And what's a father in your opinion?

Paul: I don't know. I think in my own case, if I can indulge a little amateur psychoanalysis, well I had a distant father, as you know. It wasn't that he was cruel or didn't like me, but he was, for his own reasons, his own unfortunate history, he was a man who had trouble connecting. Especially with the people that he should have been most connected to. It was easier for him to be warm to strangers than to his own family. So, because I didn't feel that masculine presence in my life, from early on, I started looking for it elsewhere. And I think there were a number of older men who became friends or mentors throughout my young days, particularly in literature, who were very helpful, very kind to me.

But you said that a child has been part of the mother's body. You, Paul, wrote that a son invents his father, gives birth to his father…

Paul: It's a Kierkegaard quote. He gives birth to his own father.
Siri: And that's true. That's like an ideal father. This notion that fathers are "out there" and mothers are "in here" is also reflected since the Greeks, that women are and occupy domestic space, and men occupy public space. And this is changing somewhat but it's still rooted in our ideas about the paternal… and also Lacan says this—I have problems with Lacan—about the paternal as the law. And Kristeva, of course she changes this a bit, she also locates what we think of as the law and the symbolic in the paternal, not the maternal, which is sort of speechless. I think this can be taken too far, but certainly are ideas about fathers. The fathers we give birth to have some kind of authority that locates in the world in a different way from the way we locate mothers.
Paul: Yeah, this is in our culture, our western culture. I guess in eastern cultures too, but there must be cultures in which it's different.

Yes, there are. There are some Chinese cultures…

Siri: Yes, there's also… Did you read that book my sister translated about the culture without fathers. It still exists, it still goes on. It is complicated, because it's matrilineal. But the fathers of the children were never recognized as part of the essential group, which is I think the mother's uncle was sort of the head male in the way the families organize themselves, and bizarre thing is the way they couple… It would be men from other groups who would be allowed entrance into—this was all ritualized of course—into a woman's bed, essentially for a night, or a few nights. And he would go back to his own community. There's a whole different way of organizing things. You still had forms of male authority in the uncles.
Paul: But what about love, did that exist?
Siri: Well, they certainly had sexual passion. The guy wouldn't get into the woman unless she liked him. He wasn't forced on her. She got… She was either available to that particular guy or not. So, she chose. They didn't send them… It wasn't like a kind of rape thing where… No, there are different ways of organizing. If you look also at pre-Columbian cultures.

I've been interested in the fertility... you know there's one little guy very famous with like a penis about this big, but they also have the female fertility symbols, with the enormous breasts and the swelling belly, so they had both sides if you will, were hugely important. I think Lacan makes a little mistake with the phallus, that's it. And what happened to the other part?

Paul: Yes, it's both and it's equal.

Chapter 3

Alain Badiou, the power of thought

We meet in an apartment close to the catacombs in Paris. I would ask him questions in English, or, from time to time in French. He would answer in French, or, from time to time, in English. The words of one would condition the language of the other's response and I had to tell him several times that I could understand him perfectly in French. His friend Isabelle—our host—would occasionally translate a question but for the large part, the conversation took place in that space between languages that is so propitious to enabling something truthful to be heard. The interview had begun over a year ago, when I received a message from this wise octogenarian with youthful eyes, in which he not only rejected the proposition but urged all psychoanalysts—whose teachings inform his thinking—to take a stance regarding the problems of today. After insisting, we agreed upon a meeting that he had to call off due to the tragic disappearance of his son Olivier in a mountain accident. From that moment on, he would sparingly tell me that his schedule was overloaded.

If this great thinker, born in Morocco and having become one of the most eminent contemporary philosophers, with faith in the young and harboring a discreet confidence in the future, is able to overcome this unspeakable loss, it is thanks to the purest power of thought. I witnessed this strength when I found myself face to face with this figure at last, handsome despite the heterodox garb of advancing age. There I was certain that if this affable man was able to bear a loss that would leave anyone without words, it was due to the pure power of his thinking, in which the role of love is by no means a minor one.

What has been psychoanalysis' contribution to the world? A small question...

I believe it has been a very large one. At a particular point, in my process of becoming a philosopher, in the early sixties, I found myself in a contradiction: my philosophical formation was in Sartre's existentialism, and at the same time, that era's current philosophy, structuralism, was opposed to existentialism. I was caught up in that contradiction, in which the question of the subject was the crucial point. In existentialism, the subject was central; in structuralism, the idea of the subject's absence predominated. For example, my teacher, Althusser, would sustain that the "subject" category was a bourgeoise, ideological one. And I accepted the developments in

DOI: 10.4324/9781032708591-3

structuralism, but didn't want to abandon the notion of the subject. The solution was proposed to me by Lacan and psychoanalysis. It was in the possibility of erecting significant structural constructions in relation to the subject, without suppressing the category, but on the contrary, renewing it instead. Psychoanalysis also enabled me to maintain a structural concept of the subject, a synthesis. From this standpoint, then, I owe a lot to it. Contemporary philosophy should remain in permanent dialogue with psychoanalysis. That has always been my position.

I've asked in an overall sense and you've answered in a particular one. I appreciate this manner of arriving at a response. And you have spoken about your experience, and further yet, to say that philosophy should maintain ties with psychoanalysis.

I believe that the philosophy of our time absolutely needs psychoanalysis in order to renovate, but not in a metaphysical way, the question of the subject, which is an old philosophical question that predates psychoanalysis.

Psychoanalysis has a short history—one hundred years—while philosophy is thousands of years old.

Contemporary philosophy cannot continue to talk about the subject without a very complete and precise dialogue with psychoanalysis. No modern philosophy can exist today that is not closely related to it. By that I don't mean to say that psychoanalysis is part of philosophy. No, it's an independent discipline, with an independent practice. But philosophy must have close ties with this independent method, as, on the other hand, it does with mathematics, with aesthetic production, with political action. I think that psychoanalysis is a modern necessity for philosophy in general. And I don't believe that any acceptable philosophy can fail to completely recognize psychoanalysis.

And what can you say about the philosopher's place in society these days?

In the first place, it is not a necessity: we know of societies without philosophers. Philosophy is a cultural, social, and human singularity. It has a long history, but it is not universal. Philosophy began in Greece in the 5th century BC, along with mathematics, and it has developed in a certain number of countries, but not all of them. For example, I don't believe there have been Chinese philosophers. Philosophy is a singularity, and as such, it is impossible to sustain that it is a necessity. People can live without it. It is, however, evidently beneficial. It is better that it does exist. But its place in the world is not an established one, it is uncertain and always yet to be invented. And all philosophy and all philosophers reinvent the place it has in society. There are philosophers who accept being great university professors, which is the case for the majority of the Germans: Kant, Hegel. On the contrary, there have been those who have rejected this figure outright and are first and foremost men of opinion, of ideological and political combat. In France, this tendency was initiated by Voltaire or Rousseau, fulfilling a critical function within society. And deep down, I believe that for every era, philosophy (which is never necessary) reinvents and reconstructs its place in society. As always, there are more established, more serene figures, generally speaking academics. And there are more rebellious, non-conformist figures, which are usually political figures. And this began long ago, because society condemned Socrates, our principal ancestor, to death, while other great philosophers have been celebrities, with worldwide acceptance. Such is the history of philosophy, a discipline which, as I say, is always extra in some way. Hegel would say: "Philosophy always arrives too late." It doesn't share the same place of the rest of the disciplines, with life, the State or politics. It arrives later.

As I understand while reading you, it seems as though there is something foreign, or a sort of foreignness, in philosophy's critical place (rather than that of the philosophy professor).

Yes, absolutely. I coincide. A philosopher is perhaps a stranger in the night, or something of the kind.

Something like that... Because a psychoanalyst is also a stranger.

Absolutely.

"Strangers in the night" sounds very good. That could be the title for this interview. I like it. You agree that psychoanalysis' place in society is also a sort of foreignness.

Yes, there is something of that. I believe we can make a comparison between the psychoanalyst and the philosopher. The former's place is more on the side of medicine, while the latter's is more on the side of teaching.

In both cases, however, they are marginal practices.

I agree with you. A psychoanalyst is a stranger, a stranger for the medical field, even though he or she is also a doctor. And a philosopher is not truly a professor, even though he or she may be one. And so their place is always on the margins.

You have quoted Plato, identifying yourself with his words: "He who does not begin with love will never know what philosophy is." Could we paraphrase and say: "He who does not begin with love will never know what psychoanalysis is"?

Yes, I think so. To dominate the dubious question of transference—or counter-transference—a psychoanalyst must have a clear idea of their own desires and experience of that which takes place in love, that is, as Lacan said: "The relationship with the Other's being."

We are used to think that love is blind, and to believe in (always imaginary) symmetries, but you conceive of love in relation to "difference"...

Precisely, love is exposed to the absolute "difference" in the face of another "subject." If we imagine the contrary, which is that that difference does not exist, we are speaking about love as fusion. But, as can be seen in Tristan and Iseult, fusion-love only comes to its realization in death. Living love should accept difference and transcend it without dissimulating it.

I also know that you like art, and have written much about it. Do you think that an artist's place in society is also marginal?

Artists tend to have greater ties with social activity. They have to sell their works, and so make portraits of powerful people: if you are an architect, you construct palaces; and if you are a musician, you play in front of a large public. An artist has a more defined place in society, because it is truly a necessity for many activities. All power surrounds itself with painters, sculptors, architects, musicians, or writers. But not philosophers. No official place exists for a philosopher, as it does for artists. An artist may reject them, but then a difficult destiny awaits them. And a philosopher, in turn, can speak with anyone.

What relationship do philosophers and psychoanalysts have with power?

I believe that a true philosopher and a true psychoanalyst are independent with regard to power... to the extent that it is possible.

You have to think against power...

When you really think, you encompass all of the world's possibilities. You mustn't be on the side of power, because all power is, by definition, conservative. Power wants to conserve power. Accordingly, it wants to conserve the society that makes that power possible. This is why a philosopher cannot be a man of power. Nor can the psychoanalyst, who works with the unconscious. But the unconscious is rebellious, the superego is power. A psychoanalyst fights against the superego in an attempt to reach the true unconscious, that which is not dominated or falsified by the superego. In psychoanalysis, then, there is a fight against power, and in philosophy, there is a critique of power. This is also a link between them.

In that sense, speaking about a conservative philosopher or analyst is an oxymoron...

A conservative philosopher is a strange sort of beast.

You write philosophy and you write literature. Which of the two practices comes closest to the unconscious?

Literature, surely. An artist fabricates forms. And should also fabricate them with the unconscious. They should not fear it. On the other hand, a philosopher distrusts the unconscious somewhat. They prefer that which is conscious, although, given that they recognize the unconscious' existence, they should have some relationship with psychoanalysts, but their task is to perfect that which is conscious. Not to probe into or enter the depths of the unconscious.

A psychoanalyst should not forget that they address an individual subject. In reality, the question is not so much about the relationship between philosophy and psychoanalysis, but between psychoanalysis and politics, which always hinges on symbolic figures: because the symbolic is collective. The symbolic has a personal impact, but transformations of the symbolic are collective ones. When Freud wrote Civilization and its Discontents, he clearly showed that any analysis of the symbolic is also a cultural matter. An issue for society. Today, there is a discontent in civilization, and this discontent in culture has considerable effects on the unconscious that require psychoanalysis.

You wrote: "In the field of the psyche, I believe that only psychoanalysis is capable of saving us."

If the symbolic enters into crisis in those subjective, unconscious aspects, psychoanalysis should enlighten us. Then, that will have side effects in psychoanalytical treatment, and in those effects, and in young people's relationship with psychoanalysis, there will also be political consequences. Effects that are organized, effects of transformation. When I say that psychoanalysis can save us, what I refer to is that it should enlighten us regarding contemporary subjective discontent. It should explain to us why these situations exist, why there is such subjective, essential disorientation in contemporary young people. Today's cultural discontent must be written about. And this is going to touch on the theme of the significance of the father, of relationships between men and women, sexual relations, all these questions are psychoanalytical issues. This is why there should be an alliance, not only between psychoanalysis and philosophy, but also between psychoanalysis and politics. Because I believe that there are aspects that are dealt with today, such as feminism, sexual relations between men and women, youth's discontents, etc., but in a way that is insufficient, because the thinking is weak. And for this realm of thought, I truly believe that psychoanalysis has something essential to say. And one sign of that are the attacks made against psychoanalysis.

If I have understood you correctly, you say there is a lack of thinking from a psychoanalytical standpoint in power, and you say that one sign of that is that psychoanalysis is under attack.

I believe that discontent in culture is a necessity for our contemporary order. It is the price to pay for modern capitalism. Our teachers and our bosses want to protect the status quo. They fear that psychoanalysis will come along and say: "No, there is a real discontent that needs to be transformed." And that is why psychoanalysis is attacked. And psychoanalysts are too afraid of being attacked...

In a way, risks are implied by being a psychoanalyst. In my opinion, it is, at times, a risky profession.

I agree with you. There is a professional risk, absolutely. If I go back in my life to, shall we say, thirty years ago, I used to feel alive in psychoanalysis, I was present in the overall discussion. Many philosophers took up positions regarding it, either in favor or against, but it was most certainly important. Today, psychoanalysis is a specialty. It is absent from general cultural debates. Marx is attacked for a reason that is evident, attacking him is to defend capitalism. Darwin is attacked because he is the thinker of change and evolution. Evolution is not liked in the least, because the desire is to conserve the laws of the world exactly as they are. And Freud is attacked because psychoanalysts hold an independent position regarding the state of the symbolic crisis and the state of subjectivity.

Is it true that, many years ago, you swore not to become a psychoanalyst?

Yes, it's true. I never wanted to be one. Psychoanalysis is necessary for a philosopher, but it isn't necessarily good for a philosopher to be a psychoanalyst. When someone is a psychoanalyst, they have a close mutual understanding that is practical and professional and a personal commitment to their patient. The relationship established is absolutely particular, and I don't believe that having such a close mutual understanding is either necessary or productive for a philosopher. I think they should have a close understanding with what I would call the intellectual aspect of psychoanalysis: its concepts, its way of thinking. But the practice is something else. I like psychoanalysis, I think it is fundamental, a great invention in the history of humanity, but I have no need to become a psychoanalyst. I can find all the teachings I need in the discipline's history. I can read Freud, and Lacan, but for a philosopher, engaging in the practice would be an obstacle, a disturbance. Because the resulting priority would be the practice, and psychoanalytical practice is very demanding, very particular… and just as Lacan used to speak about philosophers a lot, about Hegel, Heidegger, Descartes, etc., but was somewhat anti-philosophical, that is my manner of speaking about psychoanalysis…

… being somewhat anti-psychoanalytical…

(Laughs) Exactly!

It is a vengeance of sorts…

When in very close proximity to subjectivity, as is the case for a psychoanalyst, there must be a certain degree of skepticism. Philosophical skepticism. Psychoanalysis is a discipline in which a determined number of intellectual constructions refer back to a root neurosis. Not always, but often. Psychoanalysis has the ability to see the little detail in everything that is larger, while the philosopher achieves seeing that larger thing in all of the small details. It is not the same thing, not in the least. And confidentially, I want to tell you that I understand how psychoanalysis is able to see symptoms at work in an important, intellectual, creative construction. There is a reductive side to it, but in a rational sense. And it is interesting. But in philosophical terms, with respect to how I function, the direction taken is quite different: I manage to see a promise of grandeur that is there in the small things.

Not skepticism, but promise.

The promise. And it isn't a criticism of psychoanalysis. I think it is normal for it to be that way. What I dislike is that some people attempt to play on both game boards at the same time. To be psychoanalysts and philosophers at the same time ... and suddenly, no one really knows ... there is disorder.

You have said that hysteria is revolutionary and that the reaction is obsessive. Following along with that idea, is melancholy a form of lucidity?

I rather think that lucidity is linked to a form of patience. Rimbaud comes to mind, who states that "armed with a burning patience, we will enter the splendid cities." In effect, melancholy can be patient, it can have the lucidity of patience, but it is not a "burning patience," its degree of pessimism is exaggerated.

What is passion, honorable Alain? What place do passion and desire have in our current experience?

Passion is a devotion that is in some way global, an insistent form of desire, whether it has to do with a person, an activity, an idea... Passion has by no means disappeared today; what happens is that the big market attempts to utilize it, to divert it toward goods that are profitable.

From your point of view, can we think of psychoanalysis the way we do of an impassioned, amorous experience (even when all explicit sexuality, except in speech, is prohibited)?

It certainly is a tender, sometimes passionate experience, but the fundamental objective is to go from an (imaginary) impotence to a (real) impossibility, and so I believe that the dominant subjectivity should be—as is the case of politics—a "burning patience."

One last question. How do you conceive of the future, the future in general, and the future of psychoanalysis?

I am optimistic, I am not skeptical. But I do think the current situation is a very difficult one, because we are headed toward war. If things continue as they are now, we are heading into confrontation. Inevitably, the third world war is in preparation. Between the United States and China, both have been preparing for a long time now. There will be two blocks, this can already be seen: the United States and the West will align, and on the other side will be Russia and China. For the moment, on a worldwide scale, that's how it is. And nothing can prevent this conflict unless massive brakes are applied to the contradictions of global capitalism. This is what we should be working on, it's what I call the new communism, but you can call it whatever you like. Although a war like that... I don't know. Maybe it will be a limited war. It has already begun, in some way. It has begun in Syria, and in the

China Sea. The whole world is re-arming, raising new armies. Statements by Russia and China worry me a great deal, by confirming that they now have weapons that would allow them to penetrate the United States' defense barrier. But no one pays attention to them.

Is this an objective analysis?

On the one hand, there are forces, above all young people, who are working against this. Even when these forces are a bit blind. Demonstrations are produced, and protests are held. There is also a very surprising crisis in the political system, a confusing, complicated situation, and that favors war. Because when problems don't manage to be resolved, war is a temptation. People can even now say "yes to war." What needs to be thought about is uniting all the forces which, for one reason or another, are able to work on a new figure of peace, but there are no givens, and the positive political forces, the carriers of a future, have never been as weak as they are right now. They haven't been this weak since the 19th century. I can compare the current situation to that of 1914, prior to the First World War. It was the same. On the one hand, there was rivalry between France and England, and with Germany on the other. No one could find a way to regulate the problem. The forces of the Left were very weak, something that the explosion of the October Revolution would dissimulate. But in fact, two years before that, no one was seeing communism in the world, it didn't exist. I recall a sentence by Lenin, by 1914 or 1915, which said: "Either revolution will prevent the war, or the war will trigger revolution." The second hypothesis occurred, twice. The First World War led to the Russian Revolution; the Second World War, to that of China. How I would have preferred to have the other hypothesis occur: that revolution would prevent war... but that doesn't happen very often.

Chapter 4

Sophie Calle, a character from a novel

For quite some time I didn't manage to contact her. Finally, when I least expected it, I received an e-mail in French in which she said that psychoanalysis was not her territory but, she pointed out in English, if I was headed to Paris someday, we could have a drink.

So naturally, I did. We spoke in Malakoff, the suburb of Paris where she lives and works—in her case, it is the same thing—in an old industrial complex that she bought together with Christian Boltanski and Anne Messager over forty years ago.

After passing through a tropical patio with trees that she planted herself, she receives me in a small church of sorts made of glass and steel, plagued with objects elevated to the category of ex-votos, small paintings, books and photographs, and the unsettling presence of dozens of embalmed animals, each one with a name that has to do the artist's emotional relationships: a giraffe who looks toward the door with its neck peering out from the wall is her mother, a Bengal tiger alongside some foxes and bears is her father, a recently purchased otter is a friend, and so on... In an endearing kind of animism, Sophie's house is populated by friendly ghosts.

Although she does not "believe" in psychoanalysis, her life itself functions like an itinerant analysis, a sharp questioning of the other, where she believes in nothing and in no one, because she knows that she is the one who carries a mystery. As her e-mail anticipated, we speak in a mix of languages—English, French, and Spanish—which perhaps shed light on Sophie Calle's slippery universe better than anything.

The gaze is central to your work, isn't that true?

My work is more about absence, about what you don't see, what is not there. Yes, it is also about looking, but I don't know whether it has to do with looking as much as being there, without reciprocity of any kind: a relationship without reciprocity. If I had to point to one line that runs throughout my work, it would be that which is not there, what is gone.

I find a contradiction in this: psychoanalysis has to do with absence, as well as with intimacy. But you have your own method of approaching both. Do you feel very distant from psychoanalysis?

I don't feel that I am distant, but I do not feel close to it, either.

DOI: 10.4324/9781032708591-4

You are indifferent to it...

Yes... I never... well, sometimes, in the work that I do... Do people undergo psychoanalysis in order to feel better?

Sometimes, but not necessarily...

Why do people undergo psychoanalysis? I think it is because they suffer, and want to feel better. When I want to feel better, I do a project. Although in reality, I don't do it in order to feel better... If I want to feel better, I don't know... I take a vacation. Once, I went to see a psychoanalyst for three or four months, by mistake. I'll tell you the story: my father was a doctor, he was the director of a hospital and he was obsessed with the fact that I had bad breath. But neither my boyfriend nor my friends thought so, so it was clearly my father's problem. He was obsessed. One day he told me he had set up an interview for me at the hospital, and since I love him and didn't want to resist, I said fine, that I would go. At that time, I often used to sleep over at the house of a girlfriend, who was a psychoanalyst in Paris. I told her I had an appointment with a general practitioner at the hospital, and she said, "But that isn't a hospital. It's a place where they specifically do psychoanalysis." I said no, that can't be; because my father seemed to be allergic to psychoanalysis. So I called him and asked him: "Did you make an appointment for me with a psychoanalyst?," and he replied: "No, no, no, with a general practitioner, on account of your breath."

A Freudian slip on your father's part.

My father thought he was a general practitioner. He misunderstood when he asked the doctor: "What do you do?." He must have replied that he was a psychoanalyst, and my father understood that he had said general practitioner... I don't know. So, once I understood that I was in a place for psychoanalysis, I told the guy: "I'm really sorry. I'm here because my father thinks I have bad breath, and he thought you were a general practitioner, it's all a mistake. I won't waste any more of your time." To which he replied: "Do you always do what your father asks you to do?"

That is a good question...

Right! And I said yes. I was twenty-six years old. I responded: "Yes, why not?" So then he asked me: "But, don't you want to stay?" Afterwards, I understood why he wanted me to stay. The man was exhausted, because it was a place for people who are really crazy. I saw the people there in the waiting room, and they were clearly not there for fun, they had serious problems. So I think that he saw the opportunity to relax a bit with someone different. And I said to him: "There's a big problem. I have no money. I can't pay you." And he answered: "Well, you're in bad shape, because this is the only place in Paris that offers attention free of charge." The cost would be reimbursed by Social Security for me. So then I replied: "Give me a good reason to stay," and he answered, "It would be interesting." That's something that you have said to me too, it's curious. I told you that I didn't want to do this interview, and you wrote to me: "You should do it because you might learn something." In a certain way, you've said the same thing that he did.

And was it?

It was, it was. But it was in a very egocentric manner. It weighed on my conscience every time I went to see him, once a week. I had a guilty conscience twofold: one was that the French Social Security system was paying for those sessions, and I thought there must be more important, more serious cases, and that, in fact, was what led me to stop after three months. But I also had a guilty conscience because I didn't do anything, I didn't prepare for the sessions. It was like hiring a woman to clean your house—as in my case—and every time she comes you clean everything beforehand so that she doesn't find the house dirty. Well, then, with the psychoanalyst I had a heavy conscience about just standing there, without knowing what to say. So I began to prepare for the encounter like you prepare for an exam. And that way, I began to write... I searched my memory for things that had left a mark on my life, and I began to put together the stories that make up *Des histoires vrais,*[1] the small...

True stories...

I did them for him. Because I had to say something when I would go to see him, I would sit down and I had to tell him stories... I understood right away that what this man needed was stories.

You've invented these stories for your analyst.

No, at first I searched my memory for them, I looked for moments from my life to have something to tell him.

It was the analyst who was more interested in receiving you than you were in going...

I think so, but when I did this, I realized that it was also interesting for me, because it obligated me to search for things in my memory. I didn't see the psychological interest, but I did immediately realize the literary interest. Now, whenever something happens to me, at that very instant I know that I can use it for a story. And so all of the stories that I tell in this book that took place before 1981 were, in some way, for him.

For him... You know that artists in general, and you in particular, always generate a particular fascination. The analyst was more interested in treating you than you were in going, that isn't a good thing for psychoanalysis.

But we didn't do a classical thing. We knew that it was a parenthesis for both of us. I didn't go for my own sake, I went because when something happens, I like to follow it up, try it out... It was an agreeable experience and the guy was a charming little old man. I knew it was something that wasn't really having any effect on my life. And being there in that waiting room, with people who were completely crazy before the session was a real experience, too. I had an exhibition once in Freud's house in London. They invited me to show my pieces, and I took objects from my life there, the ones from which those stories had emerged. For example, to tell the story of the wedding dress, I took the actual dress, not a photo of it, and for the story of the bathrobe, I showed my own bathrobe. I showed all the objects that appear in the stories in the book there, on his couch, mixed together with his things. The public that was there for Freud, fundamentally American visitors, were horrified that they had allowed me to touch his things...

A sacrilege...

Absolutely, absolutely. There was no problem with the people who came to see me, but for the Americans, it was a complete sacrilege. It was precisely because the house didn't attract many visitors that they began to invite artists like me to exhibit, and that way, many more people came to see it. For me, there were two or three things that were special there. One was the couch, because even though I don't do psychoanalysis, the couch is the couch, I know what it is. Putting my dress on Freud's couch seemed very amusing to me. They also let me go upstairs, to a place closed to the public, and I put on his coat, and I put on his hat...

You were dressed as Freud.

[*Shows photo*] Yes, I found the same coat, really the same. Not the hat, I couldn't find it. The hat is mine. But it's the same coat.

It's evident that you are very present in many of your works, as the protagonist. But you have also done fictional works about your mother, about the break-up in your relationship... We believe that we know things about you, but that isn't the case. It's fiction.

No, it isn't fiction; but everything is fiction. If I tell about my day, today, and I only tell about this hour between the two of us, without telling anything about before or after, it's also fiction, a story. Everything is fiction. In my film *No sex last night*, the story of one year is told. We had filmed for sixteen hours and we made a film that runs an hour and a half. It was fiction. We have chosen to talk about the absence of sex or of a trip, we haven't talked about the family, we haven't talked about... we could make ten films, all real, true, and all of them different, saying contrary things, all true. Everything is fiction.

But you know that you generate a sensation of intimacy that is exposed.

Of allowing the public to come to know me, yes, yes. People always tell me "Oh, you don't know anything about me, but I know everything about you," and generally... I think they know less about me than about most people, because I always turn down interviews, at least the ones that seem stupid to me, the ones where they ask you about one day in your life, or what restaurant do you like in Paris, or what do you read. I have never, ever answered such things. I don't want people to know what bars I frequent, or what I read. I did that once, but only playing with it. They asked me what would happen if a man were to come into my bathroom and find me completely naked, they asked: "In that situation, what would you hide first?" And I would never say what I would hide first, so I said: "My surprise." I would never say what part of my body I like or don't like. I mean, I can't even imagine…

You make people believe they know you, when you actually preserve your intimacy.

Well, they believe that they know me, but I don't let them.

Your work hinges on that, but you preserve your intimacy more firmly than many people who show their lives on Facebook.

I don't have Facebook, I don't have Twitter, or Instagram.

By showing yourself, you protect yourself much more.

Well, I never thought it was telling my life; I never thought my work was about that. That may be what people feel, but for me, it's not about my life. I don't have any problem with telling something about my life, if it is part of a project. I say it right away. There are stories, moments that tell a little, you know? Like the fact that my mother had a lover… I don't have any problem with telling that if it is necessary in a story, but I don't like to talk about my life. I use my life.

But there is a certain truth in your work, there is something in it that is true.

Everything is true, but…

But you have also said that everything is fiction.

It's true. And it's fiction. It's true because it has happened, so it's not an invention, and it is fiction because it is just one moment taken out. It's not my reality. Between five o'clock and ten past five… Ok, this is something that has happened, but, this is not my life.

There is something fictional about cutting out a section, a section of time, for example. But there are fictions that are powerful, that capture something of the truth, and fictions that don't say anything. There are fictions that come closer to something truthful than others.

Well, the question is how we use the word *fiction*…

How do you use it?

I said fiction because the question of whether or not something is real or fake is always there. People are obsessed with this: "Is it real or is it fake?"

In psychoanalysis, that distinction isn't important.

But when people are looking at my work, yes, it is important. They always want to know if it is real, if it has really happened. They are obsessed with that. But that doesn't interest me all that much. I make my stories. The most I can say is when such-and-such a thing has happened, but telling it means telling it without the context, taking one moment and transforming it into a story. When I did the *Exquisite Pain* work, I told my story every day and I saw how every day it grew colder, shorter, as if little by little, I was forgetting the story and it was being transformed into *a* story. In the end, I didn't know if I was telling my story or if I had fabricated my story because I had perceived how people would laugh or cry when I would say something. I have fabricated my own story by way of repetition. It was my story, the truth, but bit by bit, my story was transformed into a fiction.

Don't you think that there is also something artificial in that difference? When someone thinks that they are telling a true story, they often unintentionally lie, and when someone fabricates a lie, they often unintentionally tell a truth.

Yes, yes. For that very reason, that is why I say that it is not true, and it is not fiction. It's something in between... Because if you tell a story, you already take distance from it, it's already fiction.

But it is as if your works, in this sense, were artifices that are at the same time capable of touching on something truthful, because they resonate, they resonate like something truthful. And truthful not because it is something that has effectively happened to you, but because it touches on something true that concerns us all, isn't that right?

When I projected the film of my mother dying, everyone cried. They don't know my mother. They cried for their mothers, their absent, their dead, their I don't know what... That's why I say that it isn't about my mother, or about my life.

What place do you think you occupy for people, when you are able to generate that? To make something that generates so much emotion. In what place do you situate yourself as an artist? Do you experience it like an estrangement?

I live it. I don't know.

There's no need to explain everything.

I don't explain it. I tell my stories, I'm not an intellectual. I don't analyze what I do. I do it, which is already something.

And what relationship do you have with writers? Because you have worked in relation with Paul Auster and Enrique Vila-Matas.

Yes, but it was for specific projects. I went to see both of them for a precise project.

Was it your idea to go and see them? Was it you who sought them out? You had asked Vila-Matas to write a character…

Yes, yes. He told the story from his point of view.

Can you tell it, in addition to Vila-Matas' narration of it?

I asked him to write my life. I wanted to become a character in a novel. I had already proposed that to Paul Auster, but he didn't want to do it. I have asked it of many writers, but they have said no. I wanted to do the opposite of what Paul Auster had done in *Leviathan*, where he creates a character inspired by me. I suggested to him to do the opposite, to write a novel about a French woman named Sophie, and that he invent everything. I told him, "I give you one year of my life, and then I will do everything that you invent about me, just the opposite of what happened in your novel." But he didn't want to do it, because it seemed to him it was too much responsibility. And others didn't want to, either. It was very difficult for them to construct a story without…

To follow instructions.

Yes, and in addition, to convert that story into a novel, into a good novel, that wouldn't be a list of orders for me to fulfill.

Not a script for one year in the life of Sophie Calle.

Yes, the idea was that they would get a good novel, and I would get material to obey. So then I contacted Enrique Vila-Matas, about whom I had read something, in one of his books, about inventing fictions, which coincided with my idea. We've arranged to meet in Paris and he has accepted the challenge. Eight days later, he has sent me a small novel about me. The problem is that it was just that time when my mother was dying. So I wrote to him: "I'm sorry, I didn't know you were going to be so quick, and at this moment I cannot fulfill my part of the deal. In your book you ask me to travel, and I cannot leave now, my mother is dying." He didn't believe me… He thought I had been toying with him.

He thought that it was part of the fiction.

Right, but when my mother did die in the end, I gave him proof of it, and he saw that I had told him the truth, and he believed me. Right after that I was invited to the Venice Biennale, which was very important for me, and I had to go, I couldn't dedicate myself to the project with Vila-Matas, which was going to last a year… I had to say no to him once again, and then he became angry, justifiably so, because if I wasn't going to fulfill my part, then he couldn't continue. I asked him to forgive me and said that he should do whatever he wanted to with the story. And he turned it into the book *Porque ella no lo pidió* ("Because She Never Asked"). I understood why he was angry with me, but it certainly isn't as if I was taking a vacation. I understood him, but I'm not sure that he understood me. Later, since I was unable to make real my idea with a writer, I managed to do so with a clairvoyant. I went to see one and I asked her, "Where do you see me in the future?" She saw me in certain places, and later I went to them. So, since I couldn't use the writers' scenario, I used that of the clairvoyant. She saw me in three different places.

And you made the future that she foresaw a reality.

Yes. I would call her, go to the place where she had seen me, and I would say: "Now there is a yellow hotel to the left and a red one on the right, which one do I stay in?" She would lay out the cards and tell me over the phone: "In the one to the right." The third place didn't work out. I went to see her and the cards were saying "no and no" the whole time. She looked for results in books, but they didn't tell her anything, either. The game ended. It was very strange, because she had a method that consisted of putting one finger on a page and reading whatever came out, but to all of the questions, the book responded "no, no, no."

And did you believe in her?

No, but she didn't know that. She didn't believe that she could see my future, either, she wasn't foolish. But she saw a way of playing, between an artist and a clairvoyant, to see what would happen with the game. For her, it was interesting to do this, but she knew that it wasn't... that the cards didn't say "I see her at the Kremlin." She knew that, and so did I.

What do you believe in?

I don't know... in a lot of things, but not in clairvoyants. I believe in my friends, myself, in art, in what I do. And I don't know whether or not to believe in psychoanalysis. It's like a language that I don't know. Period.

Note

1 Calle, S. (2016) *Historias reales*. La Fábrica (original work published in 2002).

Chapter 5

Javier Cercas, without roots

I left Madrid early, headed to Barcelona for just one day, in order to meet with this incandescent writer, who is so capable of weaving complex plots that are captivating and at the same time unfold with ease. It hadn't been simple: mediation on the part of friends, over a year of delay, frustrated encounters in Buenos Aires, Montevideo and Girona, and the determination that such a figure is well worthy of all finally led me to a conversation that I enjoyed like few others.

Cercas was familiar with success—following *Soldados de Salamina* (Soldiers of Salamis)—and yet at the same time managed to navigate it with the elegance of a toreador, intelligently poking fun at romantic glorifications of failure. Perhaps some part of that may have had to do with the season he spent in analysis.

When someone mentioned to me that he had undergone psychoanalysis due to something he had written in one of his novels, I noticed that—even aside from that fact—a good portion of his books, which hinge upon the truth of fiction, constituted a treatise on psychoanalysis, whether or not that was the intention.

One afternoon in late autumn, in a studio piled with books, we spoke about these and many other personal things, such as the chip his mother left him with at birth or the difficulties of Catalonian fundamentalism, or about the truth which is always subjective and evanescent. When I left, after having conversed with an endearing man, after having laughed and thought together, it was already dark and my train back was set to leave soon.

You were saying you had been in psychoanalysis...

Like many in my generation, I was very skeptical about psychoanalysis. At the same time, I wanted to read Freud, but failed. I just laughed at all that stuff. That said, I must confess that I went to a psychoanalyst out of desperation—by then, I had no choice.

Most people go when nothing else is working...

I was at my wit's end, in a very tough family and personal situation. I went to see a psychoanalyst one day, ostensibly to talk about other things, but I realized... I was like... S.O.S [laughter]. I kept going for quite some time. At first I went a lot, three times a week. I needed to talk to someone (some people go to a confessor). I was

DOI: 10.4324/9781032708591-5

brought up as a Catholic, but I gave that up when I was fifteen. I was the perfect child [laughter]—devout, athletic, good student, but uprooted and unsettled. That explains, in part, my interest in literature. I am from Extremadura, where we were the town's wealthy folks. When I was four, my parents moved to Catalonia. I was uprooted at that very early age—I didn't understand what I was doing here. If you emigrate, you can leave everything behind once and for all and start a new life; you can go back; or you can get stuck halfway—and that is what happened to me. It's the worst of the three. I lived here, but my roots were there. And that uprooted-ness is where my interest in literature comes from. Pavese says that literature is a defense against life's affronts, and my mother, the person who knows me best, confirms it. I would never have become a writer if I had stayed in my hometown. I grasped onto literature to take the place of what I had lost.

One summer, when I was fourteen, I went back to my town and I fell in love with a girl. My first kiss! When I came back, the only thing I wanted to do was hang my-self from the lantern tower of the Girona Cathedral. I was completely desperate. It was not until I was much older that I was able to talk about any of this—and being able to talk about things I couldn't before is tied to my psychoanalysis.

With having been in analysis…

Most likely. In any case, that summer, in my desperation, I read a book by Una-muno about a priest who loses his faith—just as I did. I started drinking and smok-ing, and fell into a sort of moral chaos that has not lifted. I grasped onto literature, and started reading to find certainties I no longer had. And here we are. In literature, I have found certainties, a defense I have not found anywhere else. So, many years later, when I went into psychoanalysis…

When was that?

In 2008, I was in a very tough situation. My father had died, and I had family prob-lems. I was in a good place professionally. I was able to make a living as a writer and enjoyed recognition and prestige, but my personal life was a mess. I was taking pills—a lot of them—and was really doped up. My wife insisted that I seek help. It was, I think, during those intense years—you and I barely know each other, but since you are a psychoanalyst I feel I can trust you—that I made a major discovery that has enabled me to live much better. It was really very simple: My mother, the one guilty for everything that happens to me [laughter], had instilled in me a ruthless judge who tormented me mercilessly, nearly killing me, for any old reason. A real professional torturer [laughter]. And I call him… my superego—and what a bastard he is. He is still around, but now I am aware that whatever I do he will be there to torture me. He is a nasty bastard that my mother put there so that I would never break away from her, so that I would never go crazy. It was a kind of protection… "If I stick this judge in your life you will never do anything bad, but you will never ever be able to get rid of him." She put a microchip inside here [pointing to his head]. There is no way to get rid of it… It has to do with Catholicism and guilt, of course.

But you have learnt to live with it...

Exactly. I am against Catholicism, but I am a Catholic on an irrational level—that was how I was brought up. It is not impossible that one day, when my mother dies, I will return to the Church and start going to mass. On a rational level, I am anticlerical; I think Catholic morality is a veritable catastrophe. And yet... [laughter] Proust says that what has irrationally come into the mind cannot leave through reason. I have spent my whole life fighting against that microchip, but it's pointless. It is inside me. Psychoanalysis helped me understand that I have it there and to avoid feeling guilty. That professional torturer still torments me every single day for the silliest of things; he goes after me ruthlessly for things that happened forty years ago. But now I know he is there.

And thanks to psychoanalysis you started writing some things... It seems as if some of your work, some of your literature, were marked by psychoanalysis—you said you started to talk about things you hadn't before...

Yes, during the sessions I talked about things I had never told anyone before. When you do that, you get them out from inside and they stop hurting you. That's how it works. Psychoanalysis is, of course, a form of literature. And the fact that literature is therapy is obvious—it's a cliché.

You are saying that psychoanalysis is also literature...?

Of course it is.

A narrative...

It is a narrative where you tell things that are not formulated, that are hidden—even to yourself. What happens in psychoanalysis—or what happened to me in psychoanalysis—is that when you say things you had never said out loud before, their drama dissipates, even disappears.

They become laughable...

That's the perfect word for it! Things that were blurry or even terrifying to me cleared up when I spoke of them. How has that affected what I write? I can't say. Maybe, much later, it enabled me to talk about something very important that I never dared to speak of, namely my family background and how my family supported Franco. I have had a lot of trouble accepting that—and my experience with psychoanalysis might have enabled me to confront that very dark past. My latest book could be seen as a sort of family psychoanalysis where someone goes off in search of his origins... What I know for sure is that psychoanalysis enabled me to talk about things I had never before put into words. And to realize that I have a torturer inside me. For that reason alone, I consider the number of hours I dedicated to it a well spent time...

Was your analysis in Catalan or in Spanish?

In Spanish, that's my language. But that's a very good question—I am bilingual.

Can some things be said in one language but not in another?

Everything can be said in every language, no matter how basic that language might be—at least that's what I think, and I work with language.

You spoke of uprootedness... Anyone who is in psychoanalysis experiences a certain inner uprootedness. The unconscious turns us into strangers to ourselves.

Uprootedness is, in my case, a defining trait.

Is it, in your case, a geographic uprootedness—that move from your hometown and not being from here or from there?

Yes, that's just what it is. It is one thing to move to Barcelona, which is a mestiza and cosmopolitan city, and entirely another thing to move to Girona. Even at the height of Franco's rule, they spoke Catalan in Girona. If I had moved to Barcelona, I wouldn't have spoken Catalan. My Catalan is impeccable. In theory, I am a perfectly adjusted guy, a stellar example of someone rooted in Catalonia.

But with an inner uprootedness...

... that is now bursting forth. These recent years have been a tragedy for me, because I have been branded a traitor and lost some of my best friends. I don't want to go into that because I'll start crying. I speak Catalan to my wife and Spanish to my son. I seem to fit in perfectly, but deep inside I have a sense of uprootedness, and in these tumultuous times here I have been able to keep a certain distance...

So uprootedness can also be a refuge.

Exactly—and well put. Uprootedness can give you a certain lucidity, but that lucidity leaves you entirely alone. I am proud of my aloneness, but it hurts—it has hurt my family. We have all suffered a lot. I don't want to dramatize or to play the victim—I loathe that more than anything. Suddenly a bunch of scoundrels tell me—a Catalan who speaks Catalan—that I am not what I am. And that has been a terrible betrayal. "You are not Catalan because you don't do what we want you to." Luckily, I can write—that is the best weapon I have.

That little bastard you have inside has never messed with your writing, has he?

He might have, but perhaps it has been for the best, since he is a ruthlessly demanding... That little bastard has to be reined in—that is what I learnt from psychoanalysis.

In any case, you know you are divided, that you are not a seamless whole...

Exactly—no one is. We are many, there are other people inside of me—above all that little bastard. What do you think?

Let's get back to psychoanalysis as narrative, beyond writing as therapy.

Writing as therapy is a cliché, and to write is to write against cliché. But if we forget that clichés become clichés because they have an element of truth, we are done for. It is crystal clear: Writing is a form of therapy, and it is like psychoanalysis. With it, you bring all your demons out, you give them shape.

Sometimes writing keeps psychosis at bay—that was the case with James Joyce...

Joyce went to see Jung once, and he told him what was going on with his psychotic daughter. And then he added, "But I experience the same thing." And Jung said, "Right, but where you swim, she sinks." Writing is what allowed him to survive, but not his daughter—a perfect example of writing as therapy.

Volumes have been written about that, but less is known about psychoanalysis as narrative. The way you conceive of the novel... If the word novel were replaced by the word "psychoanalysis" it would make little difference. You have described the novel as the art of protecting questions from answers... Analysis has to do with the elaboration and unfolding of a question for which there is never a single resounding answer. Psychoanalysis itself is a range of tentative and mutable answers to that question.

That's great—that is exactly what I say about the novel. So maybe I do see the novel as a form of psychoanalysis. That is how the novel genre works—the questions are more important than the answers. At stake is formulating complex questions as complexly as possible, that is, complicating people's life.

Because, as you have said, truth is multifaceted: There can never be a univocal response.

Exactly. Responses are never clear, univocal, or categorical; they are always ambiguous, contradictory, iridescent, ironic. In other words, the response is the search for a response—and that is quite something. In the novel, like in psychoanalysis, the reader is the one who has the answer.

The reader, or the analysand, is the one who completes the work.

Exactly. What's more, if the analysand or reader is smart, the response is never univocal or categorical.

Truth changes, as you have written; it is not absolute...

That's right. There is factual truth, but there is that other truth—the moral truth—which is always complex and shifting. The encounter between the novelist and the psychoanalyst is worthwhile. I have been told that my novels are a sort of personal or collective psychoanalysis. Personally, I have the feeling I have unburied a hidden truth that I knew was there.

But you couldn't be sure of it until you spoke of it.

Exactly. You can make up an explanation to be able to live a bit better, but I honestly don't think that is the best solution. What I did was looking at reality head-on, and that is what the novel does as well. Nothing comes out of thin air. There is no such thing as pure fiction.

And so we come to the relationship between truth and fiction. Some texts adhere, supposedly, to reality but have less truth to tell us about it than a work of fiction. The idea that you can lie to tell the truth is a commonplace, but I suppose you agree with it.

One hundred percent. Historical truth is one thing and poetic truth is another thing entirely. Historical truth is the truth of facts; it is a concrete truth about certain people at a certain time and place. But moral truth, the truth of fiction, deals with all people at any time and place. Aristotle would say that literary truth is greater than factual or historical truth because the latter remains on the surface while the former goes in deep. Through fiction, through the detour it enacts by distancing us from factual truth, we get at a different and deeper truth, a truth not accessible through facts or journalistic truth alone. Comparing them is nonsense.

Without poetic truth, factual truth falls short...

I think so. I am going to put it differently. I just finished writing a novel that is completely fictional. When I finished the book where I confronted the ghost of my past, I felt the need to go somewhere else. Otherwise, I ran the risk of repeating myself, which is what usually happens to writers of my age—you have found a formula that works and you repeat it endlessly. To avoid falling into that trap, I set out to do something entirely different: pure fiction.

Pure fiction—is that possible?

There is no such thing as pure fiction, but I wanted to do something different from what I had been doing. There is no Javier Cercas character, no mention of the problem of writing, and so on. The book is an apparently conventional thriller. Anyway, I dived deep in in an attempt to do something entirely different. And when I finished the book, I realized that that was actually an illusion. In fact, the book is intricately bound to everything that was happening in Catalonia—I realized that after I finished. The sense of betrayal, of sorrow, is expressed better in that book than if I had set out to tell what actually happened, the facts. I tried to write a thriller to take some distance from everything, and when I finished the book I realized I was actually talking about what I was experiencing!

There is no way to say the whole truth because it is multifaceted and changeable. Nor is it possible to capture it fully—the best we can hope for is an approximate or fictional account of truth... It is like looking at the sun: You have to do it at an angle—if you look at it straight on, you can't see a thing. It is an impossible...

You make up a story that seems to have nothing to do with real life in order to better express real life.

You lie to tell the truth...

But there are nuances. Fiction is not exactly a lie, but it looks a lot like one. There is no such thing as pure fiction; there is always a mix of fact and fiction. Fiction is a sort of lie through which we can get at a truth—in fact, it is the only way to get at it.

Did you, in your own analysis, have the feeling you were telling truths or uncovering those lies that we tell ourselves?

I was telling truths I had no other way of expressing.

Were you sometimes surprised when you heard yourself saying certain things? Like when we say something we knew but did not know we knew it...

I did not have the sense of not knowing any of the things I said, but rather of not having dared to put them into words or of not having anyone to say them to. I am going to give you an example. At a certain point, I experienced a trauma: an unexpected humungous success...

With The Soldiers of Salamis... A book no one would have expected to sell so well, right? It is a complex book.

But also a transparent book, and that is how I aspire to write. Kundera says that great books are easy to read and hard to understand. And that's what Soldiers of Salamis was—complex, but anyone could read it. But no one expected it to be such a big hit—and that was what set off my crisis.

A consequence of the success? Success sickens, then.

It absolutely does, and that is by no means uncommon. Psychoanalysts have told me they treat a great many people with intense public lives. They are all terrified—and that makes perfect sense to me. Success ruins a lot of people. It would have been perfectly normal for me never to write again. Furthermore, what I expressed in that book was my terrible guilt for having been successful.

Guilty before other writers or those who considered themselves...

... better than me, and friends of mine. I felt deeply betrayed by them, and they stopped being my friends. Some of them are well known—I am not going to name names. I didn't understand, so instead of saying "That's normal—they are the ones that can't stand it," I blamed myself. I knew that if I didn't write another book that would be my end as a writer, and that my end as a writer would be my end as a person. Rulfo, Salinger… writers who ceased to be writers as soon as they had great success. On the one hand, I felt great. I had never imagined I would be a professional writer and that so many people around the world would read me. It's amazing—and anyone who says otherwise is lying. At the same time, I felt really bad. Hence my mistrust of the literary life. I don't have writer friends—maybe just one or two, that's it. The thing is, I felt bad, really very bad… This is starting to seem like a session! [laughter] I talked about all that with my psychoanalyst. I had never put those things into words before; I had never dared to badmouth the people who had betrayed me, who had experienced my success as an act of aggression against them. I think that's awful, so much so that I have still not said anything about it in public—I feel too embarrassed for them. I think it casts them in a very unfavorable light. Maybe it is some form of pride—I am not sure.

Success is also a sort of fiction, don't you think?

It is a total fiction—but the whole world believes it. In practice, it doesn't mean a thing.

And did psychoanalysis help you take some distance from that paralyzing idea of success?

By the time I went into analysis, I was at a breaking point, a limit. On top of my commercial success came the death of my father. There were problems in my family—serious problems, as far as I was concerned—that made me feel terribly guilty. Fortunately it has all worked out, but I was not prepared for those problems. We are never prepared for anything. I thought I had managed to become a writer, but all around me was the earth I had scorched… A writer blind to everything but his work. I even had the sense that my work and career had ruined everything, that literature itself might, in my case, be catastrophic. I was caught up in a dead-end road: Without literature I was nothing, but with literature I was destroying myself. And through psychoanalysis, I was somehow able to say things, to understand things I had never said before. I confess that now that I am not so successful I am much calmer [laughter]. I really mean that. What I like to do is write. I love being able to make a living from what I write, for my family to live comfortably and for me not to have to worry about money. But I cannot say that I want to experience the upheaval that comes with success again. If someone told me I was going to have another big hit… I don't know that I'd feel up to it! That said, I am more prepared for it now. Susan Sontag, who had been very generous in her praise of The Soldiers of Salamis, came to Barcelona, and we had dinner. She didn't know the book was such a popular success. She thought it had been a hit just in the literary circle and alike. When she found out how popular it was, she kept looking at me and saying over and over, "You should go to Hong Kong. You should go to Hong Kong."

Flee the place where you were so successful...

I thought she was kidding at first, but then I understood she was being perfectly serious... And I should have gone to Hong Kong. But now I have antibodies, I am better prepared.

And if success is a fiction, is there more truth to failure?

Well... success is not just a fiction and failure is not a temple of truth. It depends on what we mean by success. The only medals we wear are the ones we put on ourselves. Coming up with the perfect adjective is a true success—but I am the only one who knows about it. Fleeting though it may be, that is a legitimate success. Failure, on the other hand, is ruthless, and it is unquestionably what awaits us in the end. Please don't make me say obvious things like "We learn more from our failures than from our successes." I know I was able to do the best things I have done because of previous failures.

But I meant failure in the way Beckett used the word...

Do you mean "fail better"? Well, success is very good in all senses...

Of course. Thanks to success, you are writing and we are conversing...

That's true. Commercial success is really fantastic too. Being able to make a living from writing is a dream come true, as is having so many people read your books... partly because readers are the ones who complete books. That is wonderful. What I mean is that true success is writing something even you could not imagine ever having written. And then there is commercial success, where not only you do write what you want, but also people like it, buy it, and enrich what you have written with their readings. That is amazing! That said, you shouldn't get blinded by success and believe that a book is better because it sells well—that poisons your thinking and just makes you dumber. Failure is reality, it is who we are: Not only will we all die in the end, which is obvious and a failure—no one is going to solve that problem—but I also have the sense that we are more ourselves when we have failed... That said, when you are successful you feel realer somehow—and that is really something. In theory, I am against the romantic and self-indulgent rhetoric of failure...

I know you are.

But in the end, I can't help thinking that there is always something indecent about success—I just can't help it.

Not fictional, not relative, but indecent... Why that strong word?

I don't know why. The decent guys in my book are always a bunch of failures.

And are the ones who do well indecent because they do well?

It must be my inner Catholic one—that bastard... In any case, the men I have depicted in my books are their best selves when they are doomed to failure and anonymity. When virtue becomes public, it ceases to be virtue.

What we are talking about is priceless...

I have the feeling I am in a session—for free! [laughter] At the end of her life, my agent, Carmen Balcells, went into psychoanalysis. She would say to me, "Being in analysis—what an exotic delight." If it were not so expensive and time consuming, it would be great to be lying there saying all those things... Thing is, I started analysis in articulo mortis at my wife's insistence. I had money, prestige, everything, but for some reason I felt awful—I was even taking pills. I had two choices: to see a psychoanalyst or to shoot myself in the head. In other words, I was not in it for the "exotic delight."

Chapter 6

David Cronenberg, an affable outsider

I arrived in Toronto in the midst of a heavy snowstorm that made it difficult to walk. When I got out of the taxi in front of a contemporary house in a residential setting, the front door opened even before I knocked, as if I were in a film, about to suddenly disappear into a world of exploded brains, insects, and mutant bodies. Nothing of the kind happened, and the person who welcomed me—thin and healthy, wearing a dark set of sweats and casual, comfortable shoes, with limpid, light blue eyes that complement the light that invades the entire house—is, above all, an affable man.

From his very first short film—the encounter between a psychoanalyst and a patient on a frozen plain—to *A Dangerous Method*, the mythic film director had shown signs of being interested in psychoanalysis.

We spoke about this and many other things in the living room of his home, surrounded by furniture that had been produced for his film sets, a grand piano, books, and paintings like the ones that anyone would have as gifts from friends hanging on the wall. It's just that Cronenberg counts the likes of Viggo Mortensen—who played Freud in one of his films—and William Burroughs among his friends.

We spoke in stocking feet and in no hurry, in English, about his films, about psychoanalysis, and about life, about his splendid first novel—*Consumed*—which I had finished reading on the plane, and about his project to make it into a series. It was an endearing conversation with someone who had always attempted, in one way or another, "to show the impossible and to say the unspeakable" in his films.

Most of the people I have interviewed have a very strong connection with psychoanalysis. Many of them have been analyzed for many years, but there are others who have not had the experience of being psychoanalyzed, but they have been very connected with psychoanalysis. And I imagine you have not had any psychoanalytic experience, is that right?

I went with my wife, who died two years ago. For a while my wife was thinking that she would become an art therapist herself. So I have had some little moments, you know, but I myself have not ever been analyzed, no. Socially, I have had some interactions with psychoanalysts. That's about it.

DOI: 10.4324/9781032708591-6

There are many movie makers who have been under analysis... Arnaud Desplechin, a French movie maker, and Nani Moretti in Italy, like Bertolucci, have been under psychoanalysis. But I suppose that you have not been in analysis. You shot a short movie the year I was born, 1966, about a patient and a psychoanalyst or a psychiatrist. Of course, A Dangerous Method *is very present for me, but I was surprised when I was able to see your first one... you were in your twenties...*

Yes. I was fascinated by this new relationship that was invented in large part by Freud, of a stranger to whom you open up all of your inner self, hopefully. I was fascinated by this new, essentially unprecedented relationship between two human beings. And as a dramatist, of course, I was very interested in all the things that could go wrong with that, because there are many things that can go wrong, as you yourself have written about.... And so to analyze myself as an artist, I would play with that...And psychoanalysis was very much in the air in the '60s when I was at university in Toronto, and so on. The idea of analysis, even if people weren't actually experiencing it, was very prominent, it was very forceful, and the image of Freud was very present.

And what do you think about the way in which psychoanalysis has been shown in movies, from Spellbound *onward?*

Certainly dramatically, in terms of Hitchcock, it's a question of secrets really. That's part of any crime story, what is hidden, and the idea that a person could hide something from himself is just an extension of a normal suspense crime scenario. So "what is the secret?," "what are you hiding?" is a good place to start an interesting sort of detective story.

With the analyst as a detective?

As a detective. Who discovers secrets, but in this strange setting, of course, and so... and the idea, also, that the person being analyzed is coming willingly to this, as opposed to a scene of interrogation. This is a case where the person who has the secrets is not aware of the secrets.

In your opinion, are there dramatic elements in the analytic situation, like theatrical elements?

Yes, because there is theater involved, there is drama involved, and from my tiny little couple of sessions with my wife and Irvine Schiffer, you can see how there could be a huge variance in the role that the analyst plays. And obviously, somehow analysts want to be part of the theater. That, also, for a dramatist is interesting: how much is the psychoanalyst placing himself in the drama and controlling the drama? And I think even within the field of psychoanalysis there's a variation in the discussion about how involved the analyst is. Is he really just sitting and listening and saying nothing, or is he, you know, becoming part of it... in the transference, and maybe counter-transference, how much is he inventing the secrets with his patient?

But some aesthetic features of the analytic situation have never been studied, have never been appreciated, the psychoanalytic experience from an aesthetic point of view.

Well, as you can see in *A Dangerous Method*, it is very much being considered. For me, doing that movie, there's a huge consideration of the aesthetics of the situation.

Why did you choose Viggo Mortensen to play Freud's role?

He wasn't my first choice…

Christopher Waltz was your first choice…

With Christopher Waltz it was a strange situation, because he came to me and said "I must play this role."

Did he know about your project?

He had heard about it, and he's come to me. He really said, "I must play this role. My father knew Freud in Vienna" and… he had many reasons why he was perfect to play Freud, and he was physically much more like Freud. And I thought "Ok. I think he would be a good Freud." And then, at the last minute he dropped out because he got a better offer. At least he had the decency to say, "I'm ashamed to say it, but I'm worried, insecure about my future as an actor, and so I have to take this opportunity to play this other role." I called Viggo, who was a friend, because I trusted him, and I knew that for him it would be an interesting struggle, because he is not the obvious choice. So it was a challenge and I had to convince him to play Freud.

He plays a handsome Freud, and a very interesting man, witty…

Witty, strong… and when you read Freud, his letters, he could be very cutting, witty and sarcastic, you know? Viggo did his research. He had a good idea of what Freud might be like when he was not being the official Freud.

And in the movie you display different characters with very different personalities, especially regarding the psychoanalytic movement, Freud, Jung… Do you identify yourself more with any of them, or not?

Not really. I loved though the international ferment, the excitement and the confrontations and inner hostilities of the movement. As a dramatist, and seeing this, it is very intelligent, ambitious, and they were also perhaps insecure in their social settings, as Freud certainly was, as a Jew, you know. In Vienna he was certainly aware of anti-Semitism, and he certainly was very much a Jew, and so all of these things intrigue me.

He is placed as a sort of outsider in his society…

Yes, yes, which any artist can relate to, I mean.

An artist must be an outsider in a way...

Must be, and you relate to Freud in that sense. As an artist, as a creator, he was still very forceful. So ultimately, even if psychoanalysis could be completely demonstrated to have no practical worth, it still has a lot of worth as a creative endeavor. People have criticized Freud for being didactic, and being too structurally unmovable, you know, that he insists on his structure being the way it is and so on, but when you read him, you see that it isn't the case.

You read him as if you were reading a novel, in some cases...

Yes, and he's willing to be wrong, and he's willing to be proven wrong. And his empathy is very strong. You can feel that, so him receiving a humanitarian prize would make perfect sense, you know? That's why I have great affection for Freud.

I think that an analyst must also be like an outsider. But I imagine that you, first as an artist, and then as a Canadian, and then after the kind of movies you have shot, you have a lot to do with that place, where you are able to watch more than many others, an uncomfortable place, but a necessary place.

Well, I'm very intrigued by, for example, the clothing Freud wore, the suits, because first of all, as a Jew and then, as a sort of outlier in the medical establishment, he wanted very much to be taken seriously; as a citizen, and as a professional he was basically creating himself, and as a scientist, as a medical person. So he would dress to be proper, unlike, you know, the idea of an artist in Paris living in a garret, you know, with a beret, and taking drugs or something. This desire to be, in a way, in disguise, so that he could disguise his outsiderness. But underneath all that, what he is doing is very much subversive. He is a subversive in disguise, and any artist, I think, feels that they are, in fact, in some way subversive, but they cannot act out of this subversiveness.

And do you know how to be subversive?

Well... I don't. You know, it comes naturally. I don't train myself to be subversive. I don't say "No, no, I must do it the other way, so I'll be subversive." I just assume that what I'm doing, in some ways, will be subversive.

Is it more difficult to be subversive nowadays?

Yes, it is! There are many ways to be subversive and there are many reasons why subversion is a good thing. It's also a matter of balance. It's like capitalism... Capitalism, unbalanced and unsubverted, is a very destructive thing, just because of human nature. There has to be balance. If any force in human nature is allowed to dominate completely, without any strictures, it will be destructive. And that's why I like the Id, the Ego and Superego; it's a nice, you know... it's a nice sketch of things, even if structurally, medically, in terms of the human brain, it doesn't exist. It's still a very illuminating way of presenting it.

As a foreigner, because in relationship to my discipline, you are sort of a foreigner, do you think that psychoanalysis is closer to science or closer to art?

Interesting thing… I know of course that Freud, for his own reasons, wanted very much for it to be scientifically valid. For me, it's closer to art.

You told me this neighborhood used to be a Jewish neighborhood. And I realized that you come from a Jewish origin. Is there some connection between being an outsider, being a Jewish, even though you don't practice any religion? Do you feel that?

Yes, I feel that very strongly, and I feel that was a hugely strong part of what Freud was. And, without getting too politicized, it was in my movie. Because Jung brought all that forward, Jung, who ultimately became, to me, an Aryan mystic rather than a psychoanalyst. His relationship with Freud was always a sort of Christian/Jewish struggle, ultimately. And people have asked me, "Do you think Jung was anti-Semitic?" and my answer is that for his time, no; but for our time, yes, because he always talked a lot about the rootlessness of the Jew, the wandering Jew, who has no connection with the blood, with the soil, you know, that's just traditional Nazi talk. But for his time that was not considered, everybody seemed to think that about Jews. So I think he wouldn't have been considered anti-Semitic in his time, but I think that the undercurrents of his relationship with Freud came from that.

I am reading your novel, but it doesn't seem like a first novel, you know? It's a first novel written by an experienced filmmaker… I've loved some of your movies, but your book is great.

We're trying to turn it into a TV series; I don't know if we will be able to, but we are trying. I have some producers…

And will you be the director?

Yes, I would write it and direct most of it, but sometimes, if it's ten episodes, it's hard for one person to direct all of that…

That's interesting because a series, in my opinion, has something to do with what happens in psychoanalysis, from session to session, something that remains open for the next session.

That's right. That's what I like about the idea of a series. I always feel that a movie is very restrictive. I'm trying to make a series, or maybe it becomes a movie, I'm not sure, but I did like, as you said, the open-endedness, the ongoingness of a series.

I'm very interested in the difference between what you can see and watch, and what you can listen to. They are different…

They are very different. And in a movie you play with both of them, and in a novel you play with both of them, sound and sight. When I did my movie *Spider* the idea that... of hearing voices, the idea that you hear voices and that means you are insane, but of course we all do hear voices. I hear voices myself, all the time. I understand them as memories of voices. My wife is dead. I still hear her. If I thought I was really hearing her, as opposed to remembering her voice, then... But to me it's only a small movement, you know? Between being sane and not being sane.

That was Freud's idea too. There are not strong differences between insanity and health, mental health. Your movies have been watched, in a way—some of them, probably not the last, but many of them—as sort of perverse movies, and you are quite a normal person. That is also very present in Freud, that our imagination, in a way, is perverse, and a neurotic can have perverse fantasies without being perverse.

Yes, I think that's true. But it's a way of... I wouldn't say confronting, but just acknowledging all the many, the infinite variety of human experiences, including socially unacceptable ones. And I think people love this about art, because it allows them to live different lives without committing themselves fully to those lives, including the perverse things and the forbidden things. People say to me "Is it therapy for you, to make this kind of movies?" I say no, it's not therapy. It's pleasure, it's joy, it's fun, it's intriguing, you know, it's not like "I have this problem; I'm going to have to work it out by making a movie."

I mean, I'm arrogant enough to think that I actually don't need therapy. There are things, of course, in your life, like the death of my wife, for example, a horrifying, difficult, provocative event in my life, a huge event in my life and my children's. Do I need to see somebody about that? People say I should, and I'm thinking "No, I'm suffering, but I should suffer." I mean, this is something worth suffering about, and I have just to endure it.... I have to ... I analyze it myself.

You are in on friendly terms with your unconscious...

Yes, I would say so. And even without... I mean the question, I'm sure Jeffrey Masson might say that there is no such thing as the unconscious, that Freud just invented this thing that actually doesn't exist. Yes, that's where you might say that psychoanalysis is more art than science. But the unconscious has huge appeal to people because of what they feel about their lives, and about the lives of other people. To me, maybe that makes it more art. It still can be accurate, that doesn't mean it doesn't have a reality in the way your life is lived.

I agree... If it is an invention, it's a good one, a fruitful one. The Freudian unconscious is different from other unconsciouses in a way. How do you imagine the future?

In what sense? Which aspect of the future? Sometimes, I have to say, because of my age, sometimes I think I don't even have to imagine the future. It doesn't matter. I won't be alive, so it doesn't really matter. It depends on... I mean, I think if we're talking about hundreds of years in the future, it could be catastrophic for our planet. I think we really are destroying the planet. It might not happen for hundreds of years, but we are *en route* to doing that. So there's that future.

Which kind of practice, in your imagination, will replace...

Yes, because I'm not an analyst, I haven't really thought about it. I mean, more and more people ask me, "What do you think will happen to cinema in the future?" I haven't really considered what might happen to analysis. I assume it will continue to shape-shift, that it will continue to exist in some form or another because I think it's... Despite the various versions of analysis that have evolved since Freud, it seems to be attractive to at least the Western culture. And I think it's happening in Asia now, too, it's very popular. So I think there is an innate desire for a relationship that is in some ways psychoanalytic.

A new kind of relationship, you said...

Yes, that strange, invented relationship seems to have taken hold, or rather touched some nerves and proven to be pretty durable, I think. I don't think it will go away very easily.

I've asked you about the future regarding psychoanalysis. Many people ask you about the future regarding cinema. Perhaps both experiences are in a way connected, because it seems as if literature, cinema, psychoanalysis are always in danger of disappearing.

I think that's part of the excitement that's involved in being an artist, the fact of possible extinction. But if you are an existentialist, which I basically think of myself as, you understand that this is inevitable, you accept it, you accept your own extinction, and you accept the extinction of all the things that meant something to you. There's no escape. You accept that all your art might disappear, that everything you've done might disappear, and mean nothing. So that obscurity, that disappearance... for example, my movie *Crash* has just been restored! After only twenty-seven years, it had to be restored, a restoration... because of the movement of technology to digital and 4K... We've had to do a 4K. That means, you know, a higher resolution digital remaster. Now, to me, to understand that my own movie had to be restored, in just a small part of my lifetime, I said to my audiences, because we showed it in Venice and in Montreal and some other places, I say "What about me? I need restoration! When do I personally become restored?" There is no restoration for the artist.

Are you writing now? Are you working on the scripts for a series?

Not quite yet. It's actually very much like the idea for an analyst, I need to be paid for writing. There are some novelists who cannot write unless they have a deal with a publisher, and there are others—I've spoken to Don DeLillo, who wrote

Cosmopolis—who are the reverse. He does not want a deal, because he doesn't want to feel pressure. Others feel that they are not in the reality of literature unless they have a publishing contract, so I'm sort of halfway there, you know. I'm sort of in the middle of that. At the moment, just because of where I am, I feel that some of these things, if they cannot be made as a series or a movie, I will consider turning them into another novel. But I need to know, first, that they cannot be made into a series or something else, so I'm not writing now. I'm not doing that kind of writing. I'm making notes. I do make notes.

You know I have talked to many very important writers. You are completely different. You are a sort of rara avis. Because the writers I've met, like Phillipe Sollers in France among others, they live and think in an environment that is completely different than the artist's. And when I listen to you, you have something of both worlds.

Well... that's interesting because filmmaking and writing are not the same, and filmmaking, of course, has a very strong visual aspect, and writing is quite different from that. I have said that I always knew I'd be a novelist.

When you were young?

Yes, my father was a writer; not a novelist, he was a journalist and...

What kind of things did he write about?

He wrote many things, about... He was the editor of some magazines, and he wrote all kinds of... He wrote for a magazine called *True Canadian Crime Stories*.

Ah! About crime?

Yes, but he also wrote for... he was an editor, there was a magazine called *Magazine Digest*, which was a kind of compilation of different articles, but compressed for people to read.

Did he publish books?

Yes, but not novels. They are mostly articles.

Did he want to be a novelist?

No, he never wrote novels. But I used to—I've said this many times—I used to fall asleep to the sound of his typewriter. So, I always thought I would be a writer, and I thought I would be an obscure novelist. I like the idea of being an obscure novelist. Almost unknown. But when I became a filmmaker, you cannot be obscure, because you need to get money. So I couldn't, but the idea of being an obscure filmmaker is OK with me.

Which artists do you admire?

Oh, I can't… There are many, there are many. Oh! I was going to mention to you… It always intrigues me who hates Freud and why.

Who hates him now, nowadays, or…?

Whenever, because I think it's very interesting when Freud, Freudism or analysis provokes hatred in people. I don't mean… oh, well, yes… hatred. So I have read a lot of Nabokov…

He hated psychoanalysis…

He hated Freud, and I have not come across any detailed discussion by Nabokov of his understanding of Freud, and what aspects of Freud he particularly did not like, or hated, or despised. And I've invented my own reasoning for that, which is this: you could read Freud at times, as thinking that art, like the myth of Oedipus, was really a kind of primitive groping towards the truth, which was a psychoanalysis, so that an artist is really kind of making primitive attempts to come to some understanding of the human condition, which, in its ultimate form, is actually psychoanalysis, and therefore, Freud is in competition with artists. So Freud is disdaining art and saying, "Well, here's the truth of what that art actually is." For me, that's the real misunderstanding of Freud. But I have a feeling that that's what it was with Nabokov. So if that's your attitude, then yes, Freud is a threat, and then of course, if you also decide that everything Freud said was just bullshit, then you can hate Freud. I don't see it that way at all. But I wonder, if I had met Nabokov—which I never did—I would ask him: "Tell me, tell me about your hate for Freud. Is it because of your reading of Freud? Or is it because you have friends who were in analysis, or what was your experience?"

Perhaps he had a bad experience in his environment.

It could be. Or did he feel threatened by it in some way? I think he did. But it would be interesting…

Who else hated psychoanalysis?

Well, this Jeffrey Masson.

He was a former psychoanalyst, you said?

Yes, who turned against it, you know?

He probably had reasons, because he knew psychoanalysis from the inside, in a way.

It's illuminating to read, and he wrote some… I can't think off-hand of others who were as adamant as Nabokov, because he criticizes Freud, or he disdains Freud in his own work. I don't remember others, maybe because I particularly like Nabokov so much.

Do you enjoy contemporary art?

I only flirt with it, you know, peripherally. So I would say I'm just a normal consumer of art, as opposed to someone who is really following it.

And that picture? Is it someone connected...

Well, that picture? That's William Burroughs.

William Burroughs, who wrote Naked Lunch.

Yes, "Naked Lunch." That is by the artist Burns; a friend gave me that because of my connection with Burroughs. And this is a painting that my wife bought. So that's my connection to art.

Chapter 7

Arnaud Desplechin, failure and its beauty

Arnaud Desplechin is someone who has an angel, a French cult filmmaker who is able—in a question of minutes—to stir up enthusiasm and create closeness with anyone he engages in conversation. That was certainly the case for me, anyway, when I met with him in Paris one spring morning.

I reached his apartment, where we spoke in the midst of a delicious domestic disorder, in a language that was neither his nor mine, but that did allow us to capture something of the nature of the unconscious, in a spontaneous and playful expression between the lines that is hardly foreign to analytic dialogue.

When we had arranged our meeting through an exchange of e-mails, he said that the "psychoanalytical issue" was still a dark and complex one for him—one he is familiar with first hand, as a passionate analysand—a veritable labyrinth in which he might yet lose his way. And he ended the e-mail by naming his stage fright as well as his passion for the Freudian cause, even matching, perhaps, that which he feels for his true cause: film.

Listening not only to what he says, but to how he says it, clearly it is no coincidence that psychoanalysis and film—two experiences whose advent makes them contemporaries and that are always at risk of extinction—are so very present and so united, both in his way of speaking and in his films.

You have a link, an intimacy with psychoanalysis.

My first link has been through books. My father couldn't study; he had to work very young; it meant grief, a wound for him, not to be a scholar. My brothers and sisters became scholars after that. And I was the only one in my family who didn't want to be a scholar. I wanted to be just like my father, so what I did was go to a cinema school, where I learned nothing other than how to plug in a lamp, load a camera, record sounds… When I arrived in Paris, I thought, "This will be my life. I will never be a scholar. I will do stupid things, the things that I love to do." So I had to have some knowledge if I was going to cinema school, and I've read in the newspaper: "Jacques Lacan is the most intelligent man in France." So I bought a book of one of his seminars. I didn't understand a word; it took me two years to get to the end of the book, and I knew I had learned something, but I didn't know what

DOI: 10.4324/9781032708591-7

I had learned. The Lacanian studies were part of the package for film critics. It was my first glimpse of psychoanalysis. I started to read Freud at school, and I discovered a wonderful, powerful novelist. It was not just the story of each of the cases, but also the story of the narrator, and the narrator was in a crisis himself; he was in search of the truth, and sometimes he was taking the wrong way, and sometimes another way, which was better. I really loved his writing. Some of the best I've read. I learned a lot. I couldn't stop thinking about the links between cinema and psychoanalysis; they had something in common. And after that, when I started to do my own films, I started to forge my own theory about the relationship between cinema and psychoanalysis.

What's your own theory about these links?

The first is a historical point. The birth of cinema is contemporary with the birth of psychoanalysis. It's the movement between the old times, the classic and old, and modernity, something which appears and makes a break in continuity. There is a continuity between the 16th century and the 19th century, and at the end of the 19th century, there is a break, which is the birth of modernity. And you have something new, psychoanalysis. So I was struck by the fact that they happen in the same time.

The second point is that you can't reduce psychoanalysis to a science, but there is always an attempt for it to become a science. I think a good psychoanalyst is an analyst who is always trying to become a scientist, to say something that will be absolutely founded, grounded, established, logical, accepting, embracing the complexity of the human soul. So, to establish something which is a science but which will never be entirely a science, and that's the beauty of psychoanalysis. And what I love about cinema is that cinema is not an art, just an attempt to become an art. And in this attempt to become a science, or to become an art, I thought there was a brotherhood between the practice of psychoanalysis and the practice of cinema.

A brotherhood in failure...

I don't think they fail. Science would be really poor without psychoanalysis. Scientists need psychoanalysis to enlighten them, they need to have this feeling of this very strange object which is always attempting to become, and which is always accepting not to become a science, because it's dealing with human beings. There is beauty in the fact that it is not succeeding absolutely, but is always trying to attempt it. You cannot be a serious shrink if you don't give your patient this attempt, to reach the point where your art will become science, and where my practice of making cinema will be an art. So each time I'm starting a film, I have to remind myself of the fact that I'm not an artist. I always have to remember that what I'm doing is not noble. How can I say it is noble, if it's coming from popular art? It's very stupid. That's why I love cinema, because it's stupid, not noble, like painting. That's what fascinates me. That would be why I feel a brotherhood between the practice of psychoanalysis and the practice of cinema. And the third one is about dreams.

Which are very present in your movies…

Yes, but the thing is that Bazin, the most famous film critic in France, or Panofsky, the two of them were writing that the ultimate tool for filmmakers is reality. That's the solid tool that you have. Your tool is just slices of reality. In my dreams, it's incredibly real and it's not reality; and it speaks… There is an illusion which is erased, which vanishes, because of psychoanalysis or because of cinema, which is the fact that reality is boring. In my daily life, I think that what I experience is very poor. That's what grown-ups tell kids. Your life is dull, simple, basic. It's not fascinating. And what happened? Once again, I come back to the Lumière movies, you screen reality, and it's magic. It's incredible and it starts to mean, it obviously means something. And you don't know what it means. Like when I wake up each morning, if I have terrible nightmares or boring dreams, as I have, they mean things, and I don't know exactly what they mean. So I will come back to psychoanalysis now, and I will come back to cinema after that. Before Freud, everyone thought that they knew that they had something hidden in dreams, that dreams are speaking to us, but what are they saying? So they were trying to find them in a stupid dictionary. And suddenly, Freud says "No. It's a language. It's words. It's images, but these images, which are so real, are actually words, and if you put them in the right order, you have a sentence, and there is a child inside you speaking." If you listen properly, you can hear the sentence which is in your body, even if you don't realize that it's your own voice, it's part of your own voice. You have another voice speaking, through your dreams. And it seems to me that is the same experience we have with images in films; images, really plain images, can be very expressionist. As soon as reality as such, as a tool of cinema, is screened, it starts to mean, to glow… and you say "Wow! Reality is actually incredible!" It seems to me that I go into a theater to remember that there is something which is a deep truth: that reality is fascinating… it's full of knowledge, full of different meanings. Not one meaning, but a bunch of meanings, which are just there. And that's what I'm doing when I'm directing a film. When you go to a session with a psychoanalyst, it's to get your life back, because in daily life, your experience is absolutely common and banal. During the session, most of the time it's boring, and suddenly a word appears, "Why did I pick that word?," and suddenly there are sparks, you know, that start to beat, to glow. You can re-appropriate your life through a session. That's why I go to analyst, that's why I'm making films, to re-appropriate my own life. That's why I can find another brotherhood between psychoanalysis and cinema.

Have you had the experience of being analyzed yourself?

I can say this because you are a foreigner. I would deny it if I was speaking with a French person. Yes. I've been through that kind of process, but late in my life. At one point in my life, before making films, I was already working in the film industry. My life reduced itself, all the doors seemed closed to me, you know. I wanted to make films and I was so on the border that I thought, "Why don't I go to see a shrink?" Because actually the suffering that I was experiencing was real, it's just real, so I can't be helped. I'm waiting to know if I will have the money for my film or not, and that's why I'm depressed. If I'm going to see a shrink, what will he say? "You just can pray that you will get the money and that's it." And one night, I had this strange dream, and it was not my voice in this dream, you know, and I realized that it was more complicated inside me than I thought. I realized that I was not the king of myself. And it was not me, but it was me. It was my dream, so I thought, "Oh, there are pains in my own body that I can't understand."

A kind of otherness talked in your dream...

Yes, someone else. I need to be in front of someone else so I can start to listen to other voices, where I am deaf to these voices on my own; I can't realize there is a little wounded kid in me that I am ignoring. I have been through this whole long process for a long time. And I was in such pain; I really couldn't live any longer. I was blocked on so many levels... So I met a psychoanalyst who helped me, then another one, and another one. It took me a while to find... I forgot everything about the books I had read. I didn't care. I just needed help. I had a very terrible relationship with one shrink, who helped me for a while and after that, the relationship didn't work any longer. Then a name was given to me, I was treated by a very well-known French psychoanalyst. She saved me. She gave me birth... and she died, which is a very strange experience.

While you were in analysis with her?

Yes. She was very old when I met her. She was not my first analyst. She was my first serious experience of psychoanalysis. I had three or four. But when I met her... it is something I've read about, this experience of losing your analyst, which is very strange... I think the experience of losing a patient must be very powerful, terrifying, but to lose your analyst... It's a gap, an absolute vertigo. It took me... today I can speak about that with you, in the past year and a half. For ten years I couldn't. It was such a grief, but if I compare this grief to the luck I had to meet this woman...

That was your last analysis?

No. After that I had another analyst, in order to recover from that grief, to mourn. I'm still not able to mourn that woman alone, the loss was such a big loss for me. Sorry to be so intimate, but I'm not able to deal with that loss alone. If I think about that, I'm desperate; but if I speak with someone else... Perhaps the psychoanalytic process for me finished with the loss of this woman, but I still need some help in order to recover what I want, to read again, to accept it and deal with it. So the main job has been done, but I just have some small worries here and there.

But before your first analysis, didn't you direct? Weren't you a director?

No, before my first analysis, as a young man I was so sick; I was unable to speak, unable to walk, unable to... I was a statue. I was not in good health and that was it. I was not able to express myself. It was... It was the first help that you can get.

First aid.

Yes, first aid! But it was not a psychoanalytic process. The psychoanalytic process started later, after my fourth film, you know. This woman knew something very powerful, when this relationship started. Today I'm more confident, I'm more alive, I am able to speak about it without crying. She just helped me to live, to love, to be, to have problems, to have solutions. She just helped me. I love psychoanalyst jokes, but I also love patients' jokes about the analyst, you know. I have a friend who has done different psychoanalyses his whole life. He started when he was thirteen; he is in his sixties. He's still going to see shrinks. And his jokes, when I met him... He's a line producer. The producer is the guy who finds the money, and the line producer is the man who spends the money *(laughter)*. That's my friend. And that's a joke that I love. Every time he was coming back from a session—he was going to three, four sessions a week—he said, "I feel as if I still haven't really started psychoanalysis." And I love these jokes. Because he was with the same analyst for fifteen years, and you have the feeling that you still haven't started anything, that you say these stupid things... And also this patient's joke... This feeling you can have when you are in your psychoanalyst's waiting room, when you see that your shrink has embellished the room, bought new paintings, new plants, new lamps... "I'm happy to see that all my money is here." You love that and you feel richer because someone else embellished... *(laughter)* It's a lovely joke and it's a feeling that we all experience. "We are making progress. Ok. We have a new arm-chair. Good!" This feeling is so funny.

What do you think about how psychoanalysis has been shown in movies?

I'm not a critic... Some of them are really good. In popular American comedies there are some wonderful scenes with psychoanalysts, one with the mob guy, I forget the title...

"Analyze this"?

"Analyze this" is a very good film. When you lack a sense of humor in a film, you know... What I don't like is when the character is going to see a shrink and the shrink is supposed to tell the absolute truth, or the patient is supposed to tell the absolute truth of his soul, I don't buy that. I don't think you tell the truth any more when you're at the shrink's place than when you are at a shop. It's a different kind of expressing yourself, but I don't like the idea that it would be sacred, or the absolute truth. The most psychoanalytic movies that I have seen are definitely

Bergman's movies, even if you very rarely have scenes with psychoanalysis, I think they are the films which are dealing most seriously with that.

What about fiction, the way reality becomes fiction and fiction becomes reality?

I don't know where fiction starts. I will start with the film I just did, that I'm finishing now, and the film I would like to write after that. I love psychoanalysis because it's against sociology, and sociology is my deep enemy. The idea of trapping a human being into a sociological determination... I think each one of us is more than that. We are more than sociological determinations. I know they do exist, but we are more than that. Fiction tells more truth than a documentary. Cinema is the perfect tool to re-appropriate my own life in a better way, to try to fix it in a better way. And I thought, now I have to try to find a story to be able to share that with an audience, with people who have their own worries, their own stories, their own personal stories... But to try to fix things in fiction that can't be fixed in real life. I think one of the reasons why I love to go and see films is that there are so many things that we cannot fix. But in fiction you can fix it.

If you had to compare, in a way, the work you do in your sessions with the work you do as a director, what do you think? Is the work you do in your own analysis closer to writing, or shooting, or editing?

I'm much more pathetic than that. I'm just trying to save my ass, period. So I'm not about to use the word "work" for myself, because I'm complaining, and ashamed of complaining, and stopping my complaining, and begging and not giving answers, because there's no answer that can be expected. So, I'm just pathetic, and I'm fine with that. Now, that said, if I want to compare, I would compare it to shooting. Because I arrive with cheap material, just like I arrive every morning on the set; I arrive and say, "Who wrote these fucking lines?" They are not funny enough, not strong enough, they are boring. Then the actors start to act, and (*he snaps his fingers*) something happens, and I can hear a meaning, something which was not written, which is not predictable, and suddenly I say "Ah, that's why he says that!" I can compare this to my session, when I arrive and say, "I'm waiting. I have nothing to say during the session, I'm waiting for the answer from the Festival de Cannes, the Festival de Venice, I'm devastated. I have a terrible relationship with my producer." So, nothing new. And suddenly, in a small corner, something of what I'm saying, something will happen in the relationship with the shrink, and there will be a spark of meaning.

And after that, is there a sort of "edition" when you edit your memories?

I talked to you about the experience of losing my psychoanalyst. I don't want at all to be cured. I don't want to edit it in order to have a better life and to be cured, because I loved her so much, I didn't want to ever finish my sessions, never! I want to be sick all my life, and to visit the shrink, and to stay in love with her all my life. Period. I don't want to be... I prefer to visit her rather than to be better and be independent at all, you know. I think it's so close to a love story. I love fictional love stories. So after that, you say "You are cured," it's too sad, you know. That's what I gain by saying I'm pathetic. I gain something; that way I will be able to see the shrink I am seeing my whole life.

Another link between psychoanalysis and cinema is something that can be heard about both disciplines: cinema will die, psychoanalysis will die.

I will answer with a joke that is not a joke. When cinema was invented... First of all—and this is also a link with psychoanalysis—poets, philosophers and psycho-analysts all started to write about films, as soon as you could see films. You always had intellectuals fascinated by films. So, at the birth of cinema, you could say it was a primitive art. Silent movies started to be more elaborate, and you started to have people saying, "Yeah, but cinema was much better when it was a primitive form of art. Today it's too elaborate, too *cliché*. It's not interesting any longer." And then you had the first film with sound, "The Jazz Singer," and people said, "Cinema is dead. Cinema was perfect when it was a silent art." After that, color arrived. And people said: "It's not an art any longer. It's finished. With color it's vulgar." TV arrived, and they said "Cinema is dead." You had this movement of deploring it ever since the birth of cinema. As soon it was born, people started to say, "Ah, we knew we had better days." And actually, it always found a way to survive. And today, cinema doesn't stop dying, you know. But it's funny. It's just a joke, you know, because the great Woody Allen films were astonishing, the great Bergman films were astonishing, and the silent movies are really good too, you know, but this movement of deploring it is an illusion.

It never stops dying. I love that sentence. Does it also apply to psychoanalysis?

I think it's a real worry. With cinema, it's just a joke, it's a popular art, so it's ok. But psychoanalysis deals with the conception of what a human being is. It's much deeper than that, and I'm pessimistic... There are some psychoanalysts or some patients and I can be part of them or not, but they do exist. It gives perspective to accept the full dimension of what a human being is, the full possibilities of what a human being is. And liberal ideology, to me, is to reduce a human being, to deprive human beings of their soul, of this ambiguity, of their sexuality.

Chapter 8

Georges Didi-Huberman, thought worker

The French essayist and art curator is the great image theorist of our times. Heir to the tradition forged by Walter Benjamin, Aby Warburg y Erwin Panofsky, at the same time, Didi-Huberman is an irreverent iconoclast and image connoisseur. Over the course of some thirty-odd books that range with ease from Auschwitz to the flamenco, from Pasolini to Bataille, from images' anachronism to the history of uprisings, he has restored images' capacity to return the gaze of those who gaze upon them. With a love for psychoanalysis, he recognizes the debt he owes to its theory, considering it his greatest influence.

The conversation between us begins in a Paris metro station after the opening of the *Soulèvements* (Uprisings) exhibition which he curated, held at the Jeu de Paume, and concludes in Buenos Aires, during one of the stops along the itinerary for this show, which—like the preceding one, *Atlas*—captures a snapshot of the state of the arts and the world.

In a tacit understanding, the conversation did without English as its *lingua franca*. Questions posed in Spanish with responses in French enhanced the potential for misunderstanding, and brought the dialogue closer to being an analytical conversation, giving rise to discoveries that can only be glimpsed thanks to the catalyst of error and of being "misheard."

At Paris, in the metro, I asked you if you were Jewish, and where your passion for images comes from, since they are proscribed in Judaism. Your answer to me was, in the wake of Walter Benjamin and Aby Warburg: "It's that I love sacrilege!."

The idea that Judaism is completely aniconic is a false one. There are very ancient synagogues with frescoes in Syria. Many of the Haggadah manuscripts are illuminated with illustrations. Images are an anthropological reality, not a collection of objects. You have them when you dream, when you create a literary image... The term image is very broad and operative on an anthropological level. Isn't the cloud that accompanies Moses in the Sinai an image? Clearly, in contemporary debates there is a Christian iconism and a Jewish and Protestant and Islamic aniconism, that is evident. This is a fight we have, look at today's Islamic aniconism: the Talibans blow up Bamiyan buddas, while the production of images such as photos of

DOI: 10.4324/9781032708591-8

political dignitaries propagates in a gigantic, monstrous way. Aniconism is commonly a pretext for destroying the images of the other. This idol-icon opposition exists in Christian history. Idols are the images pertaining to the other, and must be destroyed; the icon is that of Christ, and has not to be destroyed. This vindication of images in order to destroy images of the other—actually, a political question—is evident in Christianity, but it does exist in other religions too. All religions make images, we all make images. It is true that a generation of Jewish thinkers have excluded themselves from the religion—Benjamin, Panofski, Bloch, Karl Stein, Kafka.—and if they submerge themselves in images, it is undoubtedly in a spirit of profanation... They are my ideological grandparents, and I feel part of that.

On the other hand, since you are a psychoanalyst, I will tell you everything (laughs): my father was a painter, and throughout my life, my entire childhood, I lived in a polarity between my Sephardic father, who was in his studio all day long, making images, colors and forms (sometimes erotic) and my mother's Ashkenazi side, centered around the Shoah, and books...

Images and words... lovely tradition. And you emerge out of this mix.

Yes. At any rate, if you stop considering images sacrilege, if you consider them anthropologically necessary, you realize that the world of images and that of words are not separate. From there, since we are talking about psychoanalysis, is where my interest in the Freudian concept of "considerations of representability" arises. You may know this play on words: if you are afraid your wife could have tricked you (trompé, in French), you will dream of an elephant, because it has a trunk (trompe), that is the power of conversion between words and images. Bodies that make images, this is why I began with hysteria. Hysteria is that mysterious operation of the malleable transformation of something that pertains to the order of memory.

Charcot established that great theater of hysteria, and Freud was there, giving voice to what Charcot was reading in the field of the gaze, such as gestures. As if there was an epistemological schism between the fields of looking and listening...

Charcot, who is Christian, is interested in images; Freud, who is Jewish, is interested in listening. That division exists: Charcot wanted to see and Freud wanted to hear. Anthropologically, however, the division does not exist. In the most disorderly moment of a hysterical crisis, Charcot was not seeing anything other than a chaos of sorts: this pertains to the gaze. Freud recalls one of the crises he saw at La Salpêtrière hospital, and says that the chaos conceals the fact that the body involved is split in two: a masculine part, that of the violator, and a feminine part, the woman violated. One part of the body is in conflict with and fighting against the other. Freud notices this polarity within the gesture itself. You have to be very sharp to see in the midst of that maelstrom and perceive that line of symmetry! The unconscious specter dissimulates and takes on plastic figuration, in theatrical form. It's spectacular! Faced with an image, you discover polarities there, and you see that they are concealing an underlying unconscious specter. It is a lesson in methodology of the gaze. Charcot looking and Freud listening is the vulgar version, but there Freud gives us a better lesson on the gaze than anyone. And he is much better looking at a hysterical woman than at a Leonardo da Vinci.

But he also listened. At that time, Freud took a phrase that Charcot had pronounced off-hand: the sexual element is always at play in hysteria.

That is also looking: the hysterical women presented evidently sexual poses, you have to know how to look. I believe the opposition between image and word, gaze and listening, is a conformist, limited opposition.

Have you read Freud, finally, have you also undergone analysis?

I've never done analysis. One day I asked Pierre Fédida: "Is it a problem? I've never wanted to do psychoanalysis." He laughed and told me: "No, it's a very good thing, leave it at that" (laughs). It's also because writing is a self-analysis. When I write, even if I write about other things, I am writing a perpetual self-analysis, it's very important to me.

Is it possible, in some way, to look at what is heard and hear what is seen?

Both trade places with one another. We look with phrases and there are phrases that see. What I try to do—because what I love is writing, and not painting—is to make phrases that see.

You work with images in time, but there is something of a snapshot, something synchronous in the way of looking, while listening requires a certain diachrony. In this sense, might there be two different registers?

You are right when you say that listening is diachronous, but everything is diachronous. It isn't true that the gaze is outside time. In the gaze there are moments, instants, and also duration. I look at you and that lasts. Every photograph has a duration, a length of exposure. What we call a "snapshot" is the photographic invention of a very short exposure time, but even so, it is still time. For example, there are photographs of hysterical woman kicking the photographic apparatus where the foot is blurred due to a long exposure time. The notion of the absolute snapshot, with 0 time, is an abstraction. And the idea that we see all at once, in a single instant, is a typically modernist one, and false: the gaze is time. In front of an image, we are facing time, an image is time. Everything is time.

In this sense, reading images is akin to your way of conceiving of them: thinking in images...

It all depends on what you understand by reading... When I was young, I used to criticize the fact that images were considered to be text to be deciphered. Once you managed to decipher it, or to find the key to the enigma, it was finished. Later, reading Walter Benjamin's work, I saw a brilliant notion of legibility in it and I changed my mind. Images can be read, but in the sense Benjamin was talking about, "to read what has never been written."

Your concept of images is far from the commonplace—above all the psychoanalytical—that of them as being full, where nothing is lacking... In Lacan's work there is an era when registering the imaginary seems to pertain to a lesser category than that of the symbolic. You do not approach to them that way...

Is it because for me, the basis is psychoanalysis? My earliest reading in theory is Freud. I have been interested in art history since I was a little boy. One of the most important books in my life was Freud's book on Leonardo da Vinci, when I was an adolescent. It was also a way of discovering what was in confrontation with art history, and that—I remember very well—was linked to the discovery of sexuality. For example, that passage by Freud on fellatio... That was the first time in my life that I have heard of fellatio, in a book on theory (laughs). I wrote a book on Eisenstein, who says that the most important book in his life is that one by Freud. He tells that he read it on the streetcar while carrying a bottle of milk, and reading it, he missed his stop and then didn't notice that he had spilled the whole bottle of milk (laughs). When I studied philosophy, I wrote my thesis on Lacan. I began to read his work when I was 18, thanks to a fantastic philosophy professor in secondary school: I was a Lacanian, maybe too much; the problem with Lacan is that it is very difficult to let loose, to have a point of view: when it becomes dogmatic it is unbearable. When it is a toolbox, it is useful for reading other things... Lacan made me want to read a great number of things. My first book was about hysteria and it is very Freudian, and also Lacanian. Later on I spent a long time working with psychoanalysts.

Freud could, then, form part of that genealogy of sacrilege, along with Benjamin and Warburg.

Of course, his book on Moses, written and published when the Jewish people were in their greatest moment of danger, it's completely crazy!

To publish that critique of Jewish identity during a time when the Jews were in danger in Europe is an act of incredible intellectual courage. Hannah Arendt had that same courage. You call it sacrilege; yes, it is sacrilege to a certain extent.

Today, you are a kind of intellectual rock star, with enormous prestige, you attract a lot of people...

There is one sort of public, one that wants me to sign autographs or to take a picture with me, which is complicated for me... It's something that has to be dealt with. However, the memory of Benjamin stays with me: the aspect of him as a declassed man. He is a true master... Do you know that I was a declassed man for 35 years... I failed to achieve my qualification three times. My colleagues at the Academy didn't like my work, although I did gain recognition abroad, I was given many honors. Nevertheless, the idea of being a master of thought horrifies me. No one can look for someone else. Many artists say to me: "You, who know how to look, tell me: is what I am doing worthwhile?." I find that horrible!

Before, an art historian would look at and analyze works of art. Today, there are contemporary artists who make works inspired by your work.

Yes, that moves me. If I can inspire artists, that is an honor for me, but I want nothing to do with being a master! Those who come to me considering me to be a master do so with a slave's attitude, they are looking for a master. They call you "maestro," because they want a "master." They demand that philosophers be prophets. They ask me: "You, who have done an exhibition on uprisings, when will there be another uprising?." How on earth should I know? I prefer to be called a thought worker. Because that is my everyday life: I work with my hands on a large seamstress' table and I identify myself with an artisan: this is how I make my pieces, I cut them out, I am a laborer. Then, if my books help others to work, wonderful. But power makes me uncomfortable. In academic circles, the question of power is crucial... Foucault made that clear: knowledge is power. Knowledge should be separated from power. What I like is Nietzsche's "joyful knowledge." But there is a demand for power, and at times "pleasure" in power... I don't have it.

Psychoanalysts are also attributed with having knowledge, and this implies a power it isn't fitting to abuse. It doesn't always take place. Your position with regard to images, with regard to culture, supposes a position of distance that is quite similar to that of an analyst.

My way of working has ties with analysis. For example, rejecting sudden interpretation, rejecting coming to a conclusion: waiting, that is very closely tied to the psychoanalytic rule of interpretation. I learned that reading Freud. I feel it is necessary for me, precisely in order to not delimit the objects I study. It's what I aim to do, but I'm not sure whether or not I achieve it, it's always an attempt.

Many in France—Benjamin included—have worked with the idea of the fragment. There is something beautiful about the fragment, something that comes closer to what is human than any totality...

Yes, there is also the idea that truth is not whole in Lacan's work. So we will never say whole. A book is on a trajectory, in an adventure of thought. This is why I never change an old text, what improves it are the texts that come after.

There is an interesting idea in your work: to move away from the image as a veil and consider the image as a shred.

One concept exists that associates the image to a veil, to appearance, where the truth is behind it. On the other hand, there is the concept that the image is capable of ripping apart its own veil. That is what I believe. Giles Deleuze used to say that we do not live in a civilization of images, but in a civilization of clichés. And composing an image means tearing apart the cliché.

When you see a woman crying, a conformist Lacanian psychoanalyst will tell you that it responds to an ideological, imaginary scheme.

The disciples of Barthes will say the same thing, as will American art critics. What that means is that in a crying woman they immediately see a stereotype that is a veil, and the truth behind it must be sought. But there are certain images of crying women that rip apart the veil, that touch on what is real.

This is an important point in your work: images can touch on what is real instead of veiling it.

Only touch, like a word. The word "scream" doesn't scream. That doesn't mean that it shouldn't be used, sometimes it manages to touch on it. An image is modest. Something may touch on what is real. Not always.

It made quite an impression when I saw how you exhibited the photos taken by the Sonderkommandos in Auschwitz at the Jeu de Paume: small, hardly grandiloquent images torn out of reality...

I reproduced them because there are no originals for those photos, the film is the negative. The contact sheet is the only original in anyone's possession, the negatives are lost. And so, what I showed in the exhibition is the contact sheet, the direct positive taken from the negatives, which had never been shown in that way. These photos have always been enlarged to four meters, modifying the crop... I showed them exactly as they appear.

There is an image of Hiroshima where the radiation from the explosion functioned like a huge photographic apparatus, leaving the shadow of a person who was seated there printed on a wall... That image, on the one hand, and these small images of the Holocaust on the other, rupture the era. Do you believe that Auschwitz and Hiroshima are the events that define the contemporary era?

It's always dangerous to firmly fix things. Auschwitz is evidently an extreme case, but at the same time, there were hundreds of camps. It is an important name, but if it serves to conceal the rest, it doesn't function. Clearly, Auschwitz and Hiroshima are there, but if we talk about Hiroshima, why not Nagasaki? Summarizing is dangerous. The worst thing you can do with a name or an image is to fetishize it, set it in stone. It's dangerous and the same goes for words.

Your idea of the image as fetish is opposed to the image as symptom. When you talk about the image as a symptom, is it an approximation to a psychoanalytical symptom?

Yes, it is an approximation, but it is different. For psychoanalysis, a symptom is what the patient lays out in front, and the psychoanalyst has to go behind it. For me, what is laid out in front of an image is the representation, and you have to go behind it, because there is where the symptom is to be found. The psychoanalyst is in a particular situation: whoever goes to see the analyst, the first thing they show is their symptom. But when you look at an old painting, you don't see the symptom. The symptom is dissimulated, as in the case of a hysterical crisis, or in bisexuality, the unconscious specter is dissimulated. I have used the word "symptom" for a long time, I use it less nowadays.

When you utilize one word a lot it becomes magical. However, since the beginning, the notion of the symptom has always been important; it comes from the difference between Charcot and Freud. This is why the basis for my work in history, with hysteria as the starting point, is the new semiology that Freud invented, which has nothing to do with medical semiology. And in this regard I disagreed with Foucault; we had an argument one day: for Foucault, psychoanalysis was only the continuity of certain structures and conformity in medical discourse. He was not entirely wrong, there are many psychoanalysts who are like doctors. But the concept of the Freudian symptom is not a medical semiology concept, it's something different.

The ideas of montage and anachronism that are very present in your work also come close to psychoanalytical concepts. Free association is a kind of montage that is reconfigured all the time; and psychoanalysis' concept of temporality has a lot to do with the anachronistic, with the Freudian Nachträglichkeit (a posteriori).

Absolutely. The idea that I have regarding anachronism in images also comes directly from the Freudian notion of temporality: between memory, the present and desire. That sort of knot where you are in the present and suddenly a piece of the past emerges, or you have a desire; that is the Freudian analysis of subjectivity that moved me in the direction of the history of images.

If one looks at the contemporary era, with technology and hyperconnectivity... The psychoanalytic device is just a room with a couch and a chair, someone who talks and someone who listens, and it hasn't changed much in a hundred years. There is something of an anachronism there, and it winds up being powerful for that very reason.

Yes. At any rate, it wasn't psychoanalysis that invented the anachronism. It's already there on your bookshelf: if you put a book by Plato alongside one by Deleuze, you are right in the midst of an anachronism, that's how thought works. Everything marches along in that way: collisions and conjunctions between heterogeneous times. An image is just that: a collision, a confrontation, a conjunction between heterogeneous moments. There is never one time, there are always several, as in music. Time is neither a unitary nor homogeneous fact, but rather plural and heterogeneous.

What do we need images for?

I simply verify it anthropologically. I can't tell you the reason why, I don't know. I am an empiricist, I don't engage in ontology; I describe things in the most detailed manner possible. For me, the empirical dimension is very important, what is immanent rather than transcendent. We humans make images, gestures. Why do we make gestures? Observing how we make gestures and images is already enormous… The reason why is an extremely complex question. Why do human beings speak? Does it seem to you as if Freud explains that to us anywhere? No!

What Freud or Lacan work with is what we make of words. That is too big a question for me, I can't answer it. The question of why is almost theological.

And you are a man of sacrilege…

(Laughs) That's right.

What impression do you get at facing your own image? When you see yourself in a mirror or a photograph.

I don't like it at all. I can, eventually, listen to my voice. But I don't like seeing myself. The image I see of myself confronts me with aging, with death. So it's better to see more beautiful images, of others. It's a complicated question. One interesting response would be to tell you: every time I go to some new place, the mirror gives me back a completely different image of myself. No two mirrors are alike, the light directed at the mirror isn't the same anywhere. It's interesting to see how my image is different here or there. And it is always an unpleasant experience. But the interesting thing about it is that I notice that no mirror is the same as any other. One imagines a mirror to be neutral, but that is absolutely false. This says something about the image.

Luis González Palma has a series of photos of blind people. In literature, we have Saramago and his Ensayo sobre la ceguera (Blindness), Sabato and his Informe sobre ciegos (Report on the Blind, a long chapter from On Heroes ant Thombs), not to mention Borges… There is also the figure of Tiresias, a seer and at the same time a blind. When the eyes are closed, does one see?

Dreams are memories of images, they are images. The image passes through different states, including that of having the eyes closed. When you close your eyes, you see things. I don't know what a blind person's visual experience is like, but it's clear that when you close your eyes you see things: I close my eyes and I see what we call phosphene. For me, the image realm begins when you have your eyes closed, later it continues beyond that. Here we face the difference between looking and seeing: I see your computer in front of me, but looking is something different. We look at one another, the gaze is the result of what we are saying to each other, of the situation, and the gaze is functioning even when you close your eyes. Lacan says that in dreams, the function of the gaze is at its utmost power, it's magnificent. Which means that in order to look at a painting well, it should be seen while dreaming.

There is a difference between seeing and looking, like that which exists between hearing and listening... For you, is there anything that permits the gaze but not the ear? And at the same time, is there anything that enables listening but not looking?

Yes, listening and looking pertain to the same anthropology, but the more you listen, the less you look, as well as the inverse. When I look at a work that moves me, when I am in front of a painting, for example, it often happens that I am at a complete loss for words, not a single word comes to me. This doesn't mean that I am far away from words, but that new words have to be found in order to express that experience.

Chapter 9

Peter Eisenman, for whom one analyst is not enough

There can be no doubt that this New York architect likes to provoke. This is the only way to understand this secular Jew who was able to construct the Holocaust Memorial in Berlin as he brags about his friendship with Albert Speer, Jr., son of Hitler's architect and Arms Minister, or with Manuel Fraga, the last supporter of Franco, for whom he built the "Ciudad de la Cultura" in Santiago de Compostela.

Educated at Cambridge and a student of Gropius, this octogenarian and global architect has worked alongside Jacques Derrida and artists like Richard Serra, exploring architecture as an intellectual activity with no limits to the passion he puts into everything he does. Even when he undergoes analysis.

It should hardly seem strange, then, that he does go to analysis, ever since his first marriage, to the daughter of Jackson Pollock's psychoanalyst. And that he has even come to have two analysts… at the same time, for twenty years, in different cities. Today, his wife as well as his children, without exception, have gone through some type of analytical experience.

A smuggler who imports discourse from other territories in order to make them work from the standpoint of architecture, he considers that disciplinary models are insufficient when it comes to describing the world's complexity.

One autumn day, I spoke with this visceral, contradictory man, in English, at his studio in New York.

Did you find any inspiration from being in analysis?

My first wife's father was a famous psychoanalyst, psychoanalyzed by Jung himself in the late '30s. He was Jackson Pollock's analyst, the analyst who took Jackson Pollock from figurative work to his abstract style. So I grew up, during my first twenty years of my marriage, let's say, in a family where all we talked about was psychology. In 1976, I was put in charge of the American section for the Architecture Biennale in Venice. And I spent the whole summer doing that. And when I came back, the client for one of my best projects, a big house, said: "You are not interested in my house, you're interested in intellectual things." And he said, "We're done. You were supposed to finish drawings and you didn't do that, I'm firing you." I was really devastated. And I realized I couldn't continue. I couldn't be building

DOI: 10.4324/9781032708591-9

real sensation, feeling, digging into things psychologically and architecturally, if I continued like that. So I went into psychoanalysis. Two psychoanalyses, at the same time.

That's incredible.

I always felt that they were like foghorns in a foggy river. And I would go and hear this one, and I would move back. I was trying to stay in the center, between them. So they were really good. Because they were different types. So I've lived in Jungian typologies. From that point on, I think of people in that way. I think of my wife that way. She went into analysis. So in any case, what is interesting is whether or not I was aware, just looking back; my work changed from being in the air, and one of the big architecture critics said that I was like Icarus, who wanted to look into the sun and fell to Earth. And my work changed. I began working in the ground, in other words, in the unconscious. In both the individual and collective unconscious. And I started to do projects that meant digging into the ground. I did a project at Checkpoint Charlie in Berlin, a housing project; I did the Holocaust memorial in Berlin, which meant digging into the ground. I did excavation projects in Santiago de Compostela. So you can see it in the work, it's completely different. And that was the result. Suddenly I realized that I was doing a different work. And that came out of my psychoanalysis. And I've spent twenty years with two analysts. I've married a second time. My wife was really messed up, being the daughter of an analyst. The analysts are the sickest of the group, and they try to cure themselves through other people. Anyway, that's my theory. In any case, then, we got married in '91, and I was still doing analysis part-time. I was only with one then. And then I said, you've got to do this, because I can't live with somebody who is unanalyzed, and doesn't have a sense of who they are, analytically. And so she went into analysis for 8 years. She had a son, and I've had a son with her, and I have two other children. And they've all been in analysis.

Yes? With Jungian analysts all of them?

No, Freudian, whatever.

Lacanian too?

No. Nothing crazy. *Real* psychoanalysis. I still don't see the point of Deleuze, Lacan… Nobody has been able to tell me what was important about them for doing architecture. So that's the story. My whole world. I'm still teaching, I'm still writing, I'm still a thinking type. You don't change typologies, according to Jung, but you do open up to the unconscious, the dark side, and you try to develop contacts through intuition and thinking.

So, you began digging into the ground in your own analysis?

My own ground. I was trying to come back to earth. I lived in a thinking bubble.

But you have also said that your analysis ended your marriage and your academic life... Is that true?

My analysis ended my marriage. And it got me into building buildings, as opposed to being in academia. I started in academia, and I'm the oldest living architect in the world who teaches.

And as a Derridean, you have used many concepts and fields of knowledge, and imported them into thinking about architecture.

That's correct.

Do you also read psychoanalysis?

No, I read philosophy. I read fiction, history, I'm interested in films. I've worked with sculptors and painters in joint projects: Richard Serra, Michael Heizer. I've worked with Jacques Derrida. I'm very much interested in the culture of being, let's say.

And what do your students think about that?

They don't think. You suggest, "Hey guys, there's culture!" And if you can't read literature, and you can't see, and you can't look at art, and you can't look at films, you'll never do architecture.

I also think of psychoanalysis in this way.

You can think of anything that way, culturally. To me, you can't be a cultural professional unless you are literate in what's happening.

So for you it's very important to think about your discipline from abroad.

Correct. Also from within the discipline.

But there are many architects who think that it is necessary to think of it only from within the borders of the discipline.

There are many architects who don't think.

They draw without thinking. And do you think first, and then draw?

That's correct. And in both cases, whether you think and then draw, or you draw and don't think, it's all involved in a bit of narcissism, you've got to understand. A creative thing like architecture is very narcissistic. I mean, look, I go to the stadium that I built, the Super Bowl. That's narcissism, the fact of being in my stadium. It's like if you're a Catholic, doing a cathedral. If you are a secular sports fan, doing a stadium and then having 85,000 people there...Whaaaa.

You've designed your cathedral.

Yeah. I also designed a cathedral for the church of the year 2000 in Rome. I was second, I lost the competition. But I did a church, which was really interesting. Nothing like any church you've ever seen.

And for you, is architecture an art, a science? What kind of discipline is it?

Neither art nor science. It's a cultural discipline, that's it. It's not art. If you take the humanities as "Arts and Science," it's an art. But not an "Art."

Ok, but not a science.

For sure not.

And in your opinion, what is psychoanalysis? An art? A science? In your experience, as a user...

I'm not sure that it is a science. And I'm not sure it is an art. You could say it's another thing. I think architecture is neither art nor science. It combines them.

Something in between.

Yeah, maybe. I don't know. That's the dialectic, I want to say.

What dialectic is the one you like most?

You have to learn to see as an architect. Even though I think about the work and I'm not interested in imagery, you have to see in your mind as an architect. You have to conceptualize space. Stuff that isn't. I'm interested in that which is not present. In other words, I'm always doing work on absence. Absence and presence are the two major ways, for my teaching and for doing architecture.

You have said that just like Freud's thoughts on Rome, you worked in layers. Please tell me about this.

Absolutely. I've used Freudian ideas, I've never had a Freudian analysis.

So you've read Freud.

Yes. But I've read Marx and I'm not a Marxist.

I'm not saying that you are a Freudian. I'm interested in your way of thinking.

Yes, if you are a cultural person, you're going to read Freud. I've read Hegel and Kant in order to understand Derrida. I liked working with Jacques. He said, "Why do you need *me*? You are already doing what I do in architecture." No, there's no question: I *think* architecture. And I intuit. I have a sense of design, and I see. I know how to see. I was trained to see as an architect. And my students don't know what the hell I'm talking about. The first lesson I've learned from my mentor was on a hot afternoon in Italy in 1961; he said to me: "Do you see that building there? Go and look at it. Stand in the sun. I'm going to have a beer. You go stand in the sun until you can tell me something you cannot see." I thought, what is he talking about? And so I learned what it was that I could see that I could tell him I couldn't see.

Ok, there are things that we are not able to see.

Correct.

There are also things that we are not able to think.

Right. Here's the thing: architecture to me is not Modern versus Classical. It's abstraction versus phenomena. You have to deal with both, and how you deal with them is what makes architecture.

You have said "Psychoanalysis doesn't make you better, but it enables you to understand and accept."

And accept what is needed to be made better. This is pure Jung. I mean Jung says… Freud wants to cure, this is the way for curing. Jung says, no, this is a way of understanding, not curing anything.

Freud also wanted to understand, not to cure.

The difference is important. For example, people who are in architecture, most of my students, if you ask them, they want to cure the evils of the city. Architecture creates problems, it doesn't solve problems.

Questions, not answers.

Not answers at all.

That's a point in common with psychoanalysis.

Maybe. Since I don't know psychoanalysis…

You know more than you think.

I know less than *you* think.

You've also said that psychoanalysis obliged you to say more than you wanted to say.

Yes, absolutely! My analysis always was… The analyst would say… The first thing, so I got trained, was "Tell me what you don't want to tell me." And there was always something that I didn't want to tell him. So I would come in and the first thing I would say is "Here is what I don't want to tell you." Whaaaaa! I hate telling you, but yeah. And that was always the hardest, that first thing, because the rest was just playing with it, the rest was merely small talk. Yes. But the *meat* was right away.

Did you work with your analyst face-to-face, or on the couch?

One by phone. The other, face to face. No couch. At the same time.

Did they use to agree between the two, or not? Never?

That wasn't the point. I wasn't looking for a synthesis. I was looking for how to stay in the center. Not agreeing with either. Here's one, here's the other. I wanted to go here. If one said something that pushed me that way, I would move this way. If it was this way, I'd go back. It was very conscious on my part that I saw them as foghorns, warning me of the rocks. Don't come too close. So I wanted to stay away from both.

I have read something interesting about your work. For me, the concept of Zeit-geist is very important, and you have said that you didn't want to work inside our Zeitgeist, but...

We're all susceptible to the *Zeitgeist*, and what I discovered in my work was that the *Zeitgeist* was not neutral, and also that we couldn't use the *Zeitgeist* because it didn't have an aesthetic, didn't have a philosophy. But it was the first spirit of the time, in the history of culture, that was propulsive. The danger in that is that it doesn't take into account accidents, things that couldn't be predicted. I've discovered later, twenty years later, that the *Zeitgeist* was not a universal idea; it was actually a problematic idea, so since that time I've been trying to work against the current situation. And so I moved philosophically away from *Zeitgeist* because there's always a *Zeitgeist*. But it's predictive, it's compulsive, and it's always, usually, progressive. In other words, the *avant garde* is usually part of the *Zeitgeist*.

You like to work against the tide...

Against the *Geist*. Against the tide, yes, for sure.

Do you think that an architect—or you as an architect—must be an architect of a time, not of a place? Is time more important than place for you?

Time is more important.

You know that Adorno asked himself if poetry was possible after Auschwitz. Do you think that we can also think of Architecture after Auschwitz, or not?

Auschwitz has changed everything. If you were to go to my project in Berlin, the Holocaust memorial, it is really an amazing experience. It surprised *me*. It's not what I intended. It came out to be...

It's great to be surprised by your own work.

Absolutely. No question. I mean, I don't know how that happened. I didn't think it, to begin with.

And in what way has the Holocaust changed things in architecture, in your opinion?

It has changed thinking about architecture, let's say. It has change thinking. Period. Adorno didn't mean we'd better think about how we can make a new kind of poetry.

I was looking at your library, behind you, and you have Derrida on one side and Albert Speer on the other. Were you friends with Speer's son?

With Speer's son, yeah, very close. Speer's son said to me one evening in Berlin—we were drinking—: "Peter, let me ask you a question. When would you have left Germany? Would it have been January 30th, 1933, the day Hitler took power?" He said "No, you wouldn't have left then." He said "Kristallnacht, November 9th, 1938?" He said "No, you wouldn't have left then." "September 1st, 1939?" He said no. So I said: "Albert, when would I have left?" Listen to this, he said, "You never would have left because you thought you had friends like me." In other words, I thought I would be saved by Albert, and...

And it wouldn't have happened...

It wouldn't have happened. That was amazing. What a thing! You never would have left because you thought you had friends like me. He said: "Peter, I was Hitler's only godson. I used to sit on Hitler's knee with my father when I was four years old, and he would pat me and play with me." I was thinking of having Albert be my son's godfather, so that my son could say "my great-godfather was Adolf Hitler."

You like to provoke.

Yeah, that's a... why not?

In your opinion, should architects be like stars, or should they hide behind their work, like an analyst perhaps should?

Every discipline has heroes. Architecture is one of the few disciplines that doesn't like its heroes. There are heroes in literature, in politics, in painting, in sculpture, in music, there are heroes all over. Why not having heroes in architecture? It doesn't depend on anything, they're no different than the heroes, you know, in music. The hero complex is dead right now, in the *MeToo* movement. White males can no longer be heroes. They have to be evil. It's not a good time for white males.

We finish the interview with a provocation. I like that.

Chapter 10

Andrea Fraser, the artist who commits the body

The conversation with this artist, who leads the movement of institutional critique and questions art world budgets from inside that same world's legitimacy, lasted longer than any other.

As it happens, this artist, a full-time professor living in California who utilizes psychoanalysis in a highly productive manner to conceptualize her practice, has had the desire to become a psychoanalyst herself. And she has quite a lot to say.

With her irreverent and provocative interventions, parodying cliches, the jargon, and the power of the elites who hold sway over contemporary art, she has managed to earn a place within it.

We had lunch in New York one Saturday during the final days of summer. The slight woman waiting for me at the door of the restaurant did not seem to be the same person who had filmed herself having sex with a collector in order to problematize—among other things—the relationship between artists and collectors. Or the one who had embraced, half-naked, a column of the Guggenheim built by Frank Gehry in Bilbao in order to question the place that museums have acquired in contemporary times. Or who, through the acuity of her words and her body, had been capable of parodying therapists and patients or the different figures to be found in the exclusive world of contemporary art.

I would like to ask you about "Untitled." You decided not to show it, and that appeared to be a good strategy: people wanted to know. I imagine that when it happened, it caused something like a revolution.

It was an interesting process because I had the idea, and I told people about the idea, and then a few months later I shot the videotape. Quite a few people in New York at that point, who knew about the work but hadn't seen it—it hadn't been shown—were talking about it. There were heated conversations, arguments about the piece, but no one would talk to me about it.

Nobody wanted to talk at first, and then everyone wanted to talk about the piece...

Well, people who knew me wouldn't talk to me about it socially, but people in the media, members of the press, writers, wanted to talk to me about the piece...

DOI: 10.4324/9781032708591-10

And your mother?

I grew up in a countercultural family. My mother was in the women's movements in the late '60s, and came out as a lesbian in the early '70s. Then she got a PhD in psychology and developed a practice as a psychodynamic psychotherapist. When I was growing up, she was very connected to a certain perspective within feminism that was quite opposed to pornography. "Untitled" left me with some concern about how my mother would respond. I remember her saying "What are you going to do after this?" Such a great response! But then there was a really awful article about it in the New York Times Magazine. There was some aggression in this piece, and when that came out, my mother's reaction to it changed and she became very protective.

You know the psychoanalyst's job has been identified with prostitution in some way, to hire some listening space.

I remember reading a reference to a comment made by Freud, and I could never find it again. Of course I can go back to "Untitled," the fantasy of the psychoanalytic prostitute, because in fact, "Untitled" came quite directly out of my experience of being in analysis. What I talk about is how "Untitled" developed; I contextualize it as developing out of the evolution of a model I worked on, or art making as a kind of service, the activity as a service provision rather than as a model of art making goods, production. Other than producing works in a studio that could circulate in the market as commodities, I work with organizations, institutions and sometimes with individuals as well, on a fee-for-service model. In "Untitled" I've kind of flipped that model. On the one hand, I took it to an extreme of what is sometimes called by prostitution, the oldest profession, which is a service profession, but instead of it being a fee for a service, what I was producing was a cultural commodity that is the videotape, and that was being sold. So, while ostensibly it looked like a fee-for-service situation, I was bringing the cultural commodity back in. So, even though the metaphor was one of prostitution, what I was doing was... I was a pornographer, not a prostitute.

It was during analysis, in the sessions, that the idea appeared?

I don't know if it appeared in the sessions, but I was certainly grappling with an erotic transference in my analysis, and I was very aware at the time (I haven't talked about this publicly or in any other interviews) that the idea of doing "Untitled" was bound up with the fantasy of having sexual relations with my analyst, or my analyst crossing that boundary of abstinence and of providing sexual services. So I joked about it with him, saying something like "Oh! If 'Untitled' is ever written up in a psychoanalytic journal, it should say 'Andrea Fraser takes acting out to a whole new level.'" I recognize it as a kind of acting out. It's funny, the difference between acting out and sublimation. My psychoanalyst made the best joke about "Untitled." I was talking about how, when it started to be reported in the press—from my perspective a kind of fake art scandal, I don't think it was much of a scandal, it was certain people in the media wanting to produce a scandal to sell—there is a lot of nudity and sex in art and there has been for a very long time, but one of the things that might appear to have made "Untitled" more scandalous than some other performance artworks that involve sex is that, because of the conceptual nature of the piece, it didn't appear to require any specifically artistic competence. So his joke was "Well, at least no one will say my five-year-old could do it."

But you have managed to build a special object... There's a tradition of artists producing special kinds of objects, mysterious objects, to make people pay millions for them. And you managed to give a certain mystery to that piece: you don't show it apart from exhibitions, the name is "Untitled" there is something interesting that happened in that piece.

Right. There's a number of different aspects of the work... it's a complex work because on the one hand, it's important that it exists as a commodity, as a videotape that is an edition.

Were all of the copies sold?

No, I sold three. I decided to stop. I've been very conflicted about participating in the art market in relation to exchange around artworks... I've worked with galleries and I didn't work with galleries, and I did services only with institutions, and I worked with galleries again, so "Untitled" was part of this. When I went back to working with galleries, in the art market, at the point I made that move I felt I was betraying something that I have tried to stand for, and that is also where the concept for "Untitled" came from. I was selling myself. There are individuals who wanted to buy it, and I haven't sold it to individuals. It's not that I won't, it's that I'm not selling, only to institutions.

And are there individuals who wanted to buy it? Like voyeurs? Like a commodity?

It's very hard to speculate at this point because most major collectors now work with consultants who tell them what's interesting for them to look at, and what's interesting artistically, economically, so I don't think they are interested... I think it reflects the advice of the consultants they work with. Also, the way it is installed, the installation specifications for the video are that it can only be shown on a monitor, not so big, and it has to be shown in an otherwise empty room. The room has to be of a certain size, that is fully lit, it doesn't have to be overlit, and without seating. And the installation specifications were conceived to create a lot of space around the piece, a sense of both distance and proximity as you view the video, but also to expose the viewer in the room, to leave the viewer feeling exposed in the act of watching the video, and also to situate the video in the architectural space of a museum, where it's shown.

Was the sound separate?

The video has no sound, it's silent. It's a silent argument, so I did not use the sound.

But it's exhibited with sound...

Subsequently, I made a separate installation, a separate work with the sound that was recorded with the collector, but I edited the sounds that he made. I edited him out.

What difference did you find between the auditive and the visual dimensions? Because they are two different...

... completely different kinds of work, in a way. The video is sixty minutes long and it's unedited. And the exposure of the video has as much to do with the fact that it's not edited, that everything that was recorded was shown, as it does with the bodies that are exposed or revealed. The audio is densely edited. It's only ten minutes long and it was edited from more than an hour of audio, but it feels much more exposing to me, it feels more revealing. I'm a performer, I perform. I'm not particularly trained, but I've had quite a bit of experience at this point, by the time I did "Untitled," as a performer. If there's a camera in the room, I know where my body is in relationship to that camera. It's kind of second nature, a second skin, that one develops as a performer. So there are ways in which, in the image, I did not feel particularly exposed. In the audio, I do.

Did the idea for "Projection" came to you from your analysis?

No... later. My analysis in New York ended in 2006, when I moved to Los Angeles, and in my first couple of years in Los Angeles I did feel some need for additional analysis, but I didn't want to start another analysis. And then I met an analyst in Los Angeles at a lecture, and we started talking. He somehow became aware of "Untitled" and he told me about a form of psychodynamic psychotherapy that is always videotaped. When I heard about this, I also started... the idea of a kind of intensive, short-term form of treatment, the promise of dramatic change, the fantasy of quick results. I thought, "I would like to have these videotapes. I might be able to do something with these videotapes."

Did you ask for them?

Yes, before. When I arranged it, prior to the first session, I talked to the psychiatrist and his practice is to give the patients a release to sign, to acknowledge that the sessions would be recorded, and then the patients have the option of agreeing for the sessions only to be recorded and viewed by the therapist, or also giving permission for the purpose of presenting the material in professional contexts. I did not give permission, but I also asked. That's not what usually happens; usually the patients don't get the videotapes. And I was really surprised when I was researching this approach, that there didn't seem to be any theorization of the role of the camera in the therapy, which shocked me, because the setup of the room was face-to-face. There's a chair, there's the psychiatrist, me, the patient, an array of microphones, they are very present, there is a camera above the chair, and the video has a split screen. I was very aware of the camera in the room. At some point in the therapy, I talked to the psychiatrist about the method itself, and about how it was conceptualized, to work out the theory of the therapeutic action underlying the method, and it sounded a lot to me like a very classic concept of therapeutic action going back to the analyst as a kind of superego, and with the therapist, in this case, to be taken on as an auxiliary superego. I think it's conceptualized as being applicable fairly broadly, but with the thinking that most of the patients who would be coming to this kind of therapist would be suffering from a kind of attachment trauma that produces depression, anxiety or self-destructive behavior, and that the analyst, from the position of this auxiliary superego, will be able to get to the root of that attachment trauma by going straight for defenses. It's quite aggressive, activating and releasing a kind of primal rage. It seemed to me that the function of the camera in that setting was central, as kind of the gaze of the superego, that the camera was taking part.

But you have done reading from different psychoanalytical schools. Psychoanalysis has a strong influence in your work, from a theoretical point of view.

Absolutely.

And from an experiential point of view?

I think a lot of artists who engage with psychoanalysis are working in traditions that might be associated with surrealism. One sort of sees their work and you know they are working with methods of free association, with dream material, with often also sexual imagery, and so on and so forth. Psychoanalysis is recognizable in their work as content. That's not the case in my work. There are some pieces—mostly "Untitled" and "Projection"—where one might recognize content which could be associated with psychoanalysis, but psychoanalysis informs my work much more as a method, a way of thinking about artistic practice and how artistic practice might be effective in making an intervention and engaging with… in the relationship between the artist and the spectator, the artist and the institution, the institutional frame, in reflecting on the processes and the development of my work. So, in that regard, my engagement with psychoanalysis never appeared in a way that is, well, divorced from my engagement with the social and institutional frame of art, and I think that's very different from applied psychoanalysis. So in this sense, there is an application of psychoanalytic theory, but the application—using the word *application* is something I don't like— of my experience of analysis really started in the early 2000's, because I didn't really have an experience of analysis before. As I said, "Untitled" emerged directly from my analysis and then some subsequent works in writing.

Your work as working through your analytical process?

Yes.

Many artists are not capable of speaking about their work, and it seems as if in yours, theorization goes in parallel with the work, before, during and after the work.

Yeah... my work is an ongoing investigation of what the conditions and possibilities of a critical art practice are; now, I would probably say analytic practice more than critical practice. In that sense, the works are kind of case studies, experimental situations in which I test out... no so much testing out a theory of what critical art practice is, but also to use the practice itself as a kind of research in the development of a theory, of a method. At the same time, I came out of an era of art making and a kind of art education that was very theoretically focused, and I think it was a process for me to develop out of that theoretical focus —although it may look as if I haven't developed out of it all that much— towards an appreciation, an investment in the experiential dimension of engaging with artworks, and that's also where the influence of psychoanalysis, my experience of psychoanalysis, of psychoanalytic group relations, I think, has really had an impact on coming to understand art. It's out of my experience with psychoanalysis that I came to understand and appreciate much more this sort of experiential dimension of engaging with art and seeing the kind of intellectual process of decoding, or of discursive analysis, or the analysis as a kind of social task, as a process that is activated by the experiential.

You know many artists are afraid that if they undergo analysis, they will lose something, their source of creativity. You don't think that way...

I don't feel like I've lost anything in analysis, which might indicate that my analysis was very incomplete, but I didn't feel like that in the process; perhaps in group relations in many ways. It's not that I think group relations had more of an impact on me than psychoanalysis; I don't think I would have been able to do group relations without having done psychoanalysis. But in some respects I'm more aware of changes, in a diminishing of anxiety and defenses, changes in the patterns of relating as a consequence of my experience with group relations.

Did group relations, in your opinion, have more of an influence on you?

Yes. What I'm referring to when I say group relations is what is sometimes called the Tavistock Method; it's self-defined not as therapy, but as a research method for learning about group organizations, leadership and authority, usually in an organizational framework, not only, but specifically about the unconscious processes and dynamics of groups.

With your institutional critique, you are like a foreigner in the art field!

I don't know... It's a kind of typical way of thinking about artists, functioning at the borders, at the boundaries or edges of society. I'm really an insider. I have a lot of access. I have a lot of privilege in the art field. I have a lot of recognition at this point, but I've also tried to maintain a distance. Being engaged in other fields like group relations, psychoanalysis or academic fields is part of maintaining that distance, which does allow me to preserve the capacity to develop perspectives that people who are only inside are not able to develop.

Do you think of analysis in terms of performance?

It's not that I think of analysis as performance, it's that I think of performance as enactment. Thinking about my experience of enactment in psychoanalysis in the early 2000s, it started to have an impact on how I thought about performance; both performance art as a sort of specific and conceptually composed form of art, but also how one might think about a whole range of phenomena, including other kinds of art that are performance, as enactment, in terms of enactment. I'm trying to think how it goes for me, from psychoanalysis to performance... but I think you are kind of more interested in the other direction...

From performance to psychoanalysis.

Yeah, you know, there is one sort of boundary, on the border, of all the ways in which I want to find parallels and homologies between psychoanalysis and art, and the frame and the context, and in terms of practice, in terms of process, in terms of relational dynamics and so on and so forth. The one boundary that I find and come up against over and over again is between what I think of as the acute self-consciousness that defines contemporary art making and the unconscious process that, you know, hopefully is emerging in psychoanalysis. Of course, this is not to say that the unconscious process and materials don't emerge in art—of course they do—but the relationship to it is vastly, radically different. And that's where it becomes challenging to think about the intersection, for me, between those two arenas of activity. Because for me, what defines performance is more than anything else that it is an artistic practice, is that acute self-consciousness, because if enact-ment is just what we live...

Without consciousness...

Without consciousness, every day, all the time. Psychoanalysis frames enactment in a particular way that allows for its analysis, but in its unconscious dimension. Performance frames enactment in a completely different way that allows for its cri-tique in a certain sense, but usually in ways that completely exclude this unconscious direction. And, in fact, its condition as performance is that self-consciousness, and is that framing. It's how we separate the everyday kind of flow of phenomena of enactment as something that is consciously crafted and composed and conceptual-ized as performance. That's the frame that makes it performance, which, then, at the same time specifically excludes what's unconscious. To me that's fascinating. I think that artists always aspire to transgress the very thing that defines what they do, so performance art has perhaps always aspired to connect to the unconscious, to the spontaneous, to the chance procedure. But it never does. All it does is to pull more of the unconscious into... more of the arbitrary, or the accidental into the sphere of composition in some sense. It only goes in the other direction, so it's really not possible because of what defines it as a practice, but that doesn't mean that it's not there all the time—the unconscious—of course, it's there. It's just excluded from what defines performance in some sense as performance, so this is the thing that I'm trying to work on in the teaching I do.

Do you teach to art students?

Yes. What became very important for me in teaching is to try to get at what remains unconscious in our engagement with art with students, both in what we do as artists—I say "we" but I'm really focusing on my students—what remains unconscious for students in what they are doing, but then nevertheless is central to how their work is experienced and received, and what remains unconscious in our engagement with art.

Do you think something must remain unconscious?

Yes! My ambition with teaching is not that everything should be conscious, but that students are able to recognize and appreciate, to accept the unconscious dimension of what they do. And a lot of that in the first instance has to do with diminishing anxiety, and defenses; that, and shame and not knowing and not being in control of the work. There are a lot of art students who train that way. One of the things I often give students to read is Winnicott's essay on "Communicating and not communicating," which I love because I find that conflict, that struggle, in many artists' work; in my own work I recognize it. I think it's one of the best pieces of psychoanalytic writing about art. I think it really captures one of the defining elements of contemporary art and my experience of being an artist.

In your opinion, what is an artist?

Artists hate that question. I don't have an answer for it. The artist is a myth. That's what I believe. An artist is a myth, which is also to say that an artist is a fantasy, a really compelling myth.

Chapter 11

Luis González Palma, deliciously anachronistic

One of Latin America's most outstanding photographers, Guatemalan Luis González Palma is also a man of the world and someone who seems to come from a different time.

Having been instrumental in the introduction of contemporary art in his country, and after periods of living in Paris and New York, he settled in Cabana, a town in the mountains surrounding Córdoba de la Nueva Andalucía in Argentina.

There, this artist from a different, deliciously anachronistic time reads, draws, and meditates, elaborating work that moves away from the Central American profile and figuration that gained him recognition worldwide, in order to investigate the possibilities for abstraction that photography has to offer, with no small degree of risk involved.

There in his mountain refuge, I encountered an artist who not only plays with and models the gaze—the wound that can only be healed by way of images—but grows increasingly more sophisticated, who also cooks like a professional and practices the art of friendship as few know how to do.

Not many people know that in addition, for years he has been a devout participant in the practice of analysis. Whether it is because he is conscious of the fact that no escapes childhood unscathed, or because he finds it to be a fertile laboratory for thought, there he is, week after week. In spite of this, he has decided to never lay down on the mythic couch, in order not to forego the domain of the gaze.

Here are just a few fragments of the infinite conversation we have continued over the years.

You conceive of images beyond the register of the imagination, you also include their symbolic weight, their real root system...

What is real is our own death and the death of all forms of representation, our fictions and realities. That is why every image has symbolic weight, concealing its mystery from us, interrogating us in silence and leaving us stranded in the face of our limited interpretations. We need to think of the image, to think of ourselves

DOI: 10.4324/9781032708591-11

by way of the image. We see from the standpoint of our experience, and in that intimate act, we configure our relationship with the world. The sensitive information an image transmits is outside of its space of representation, it is in our realm of imagery. On that basis, we feel it and find ourselves affected by it. This is how we learn to see what is all around us. We need images to give us meaning, to accompany us, to recognize ourselves, with something that fills our existential void in an illusory manner. Life is always searching for the same thing: to see death with open eyes.

What other modes of the sensory realm does looking bring into play? Is what is being looked at heard, smelled, touched, tasted?

There is a particular music, silences and rhythms, there are terms in common: intensities, thicknesses, densities, echoes, chromatic values... There is a sort of visual ear or a sonic eye. In the quiver that you feel in front of an image, something happens to your body, it is perceived in the abdomen, just like sound. You caress with the gaze, you claw at the world with your eyes, trying to recover some part of the vertigo that living implies. We want to devour the world's visual dimension with the entire body, we need to see with our hands, look with our tongues, taste colors, smell textures... The gaze is fundamental in elaborating our subjectivity. We need all of our senses to construct our visual image of the world, in order to create fictions that will serve as our support, based on the images that delight or frighten us.

We tend to think of the gaze in a horizontal manner, as if to establish or to highlight some parity. At the same time, other ways of looking exist: micro and macroscopic, telescopic, oblique, low angle or high angle...

For me, there is a silent energy that separates space and time, that divides and unites at the same time, that moves through a void in order to alight on a surface, returning with unheard of force deep into our eyes, like an echo of our own desires. It is the encounter with and farewell to our secrets and projections. To look is to encounter something that is not seen. It means the elaboration of a continuous mourning, because as we contemplate the world, something of us is lost. Our gaze finds us to be fragile, thirsting for meaning. To see is to allow death to live inside us, it is to translate the fleeting into memory.

Has your way of looking changed over the years?

Looking is always amazement. I continue to depend on looking in the same way I did as a child. In spite of years of psychoanalysis, in the face of the other, the fragility of my gaze is the same it was during childhood. How I relate with those fictions or forms of representation called reality today is a different matter. I cannot approach them the same way that I used to when I began to take photos. Everything flows, changes; I am a different person, the world is a different one.

Is the country one lives their childhood in the one that leaves its mark?

It is for me. I once read somewhere: "No one escapes childhood unscathed," and I repeat the phrase, which isn't mine.

Now it is. The phrase belongs to the person who says it.

The country where you spend childhood gives you wings and restricts you; you contend with that for the rest of your life, it marks your need to invent a parallel world. The world is not sufficient. You have to invent something in addition.

Is it possible that the world you invent for yourself isn't sufficient, either?

You always fail. The work of an artist is to fail better, it will never be sufficient. But generating a world to accompany you will always be necessary. No image is innocent. One knows and does not know what it conceals.

You often talk about desire, and at the same time, about being free from desire, in relation to a Buddhist influence. There is a contradiction, or at least a tension, there...

There is the desire to represent a world visually, a world to accompany me and give me meaning. But in order to capture that world, I need to put aside my own desire and simply open myself to the possibilities that life has to offer to me. To be open to that encounter, rather than to actively pursue it.

That gives the impression that you are attempting to dispossess yourself of that— very Western—will of sorts for dominion, for searching and even for creating. Although you do renounce desire of this kind, you do not erase it on a different level, without which you wouldn't be an artist, you would be a hermit...

Without that desire ideas would not be in motion. You create images because you feel alone. They are ways of feeling accompanied. So, then, the need to generate images emerges from solitude itself, out of my own incomprehension. When one allows a certain degree of aperture, ideas come. The desire to create is there, but what sometimes happens is that when the desire to have an idea is there, the idea doesn't come. It's a strange thing.

Psychoanalysis works with this premise: if you give yourself over to a kind of listening without attempting to capture anything, the analyst's unconscious registers previously unknown articulations. If someone gives themselves over to speaking by saying whatever comes to mind—it is very difficult to reach that state—discoveries appear that would never have appeared otherwise.

That is exactly what I want to talk about. The desire to be surprised by something that pops into my head. If the idea that is born does not surprise me, it makes no sense to keep going. I know it's going to fail. If it doesn't fail, and winds up being a masterpiece, there's no need for me to do anything else. Luckily, we fail; it's the motor to keep on insisting.

Over the course of your career, a clear path can be traced that goes from figuration to abstraction. As if you were backing away from Catholicism into Judaism or Islam, where images were proscribed. It's as if you were "de-imaging" your work...

It is a desire to reach a point of nothingness as plenitude, that would contain enriching visual modalities. There is a church in Chichicastenango, in Guatemala, that I used to go to on certain occasions. They celebrate Christian mass there, but also indigenous pagan cult services where they get drunk, shout out to God and bring candles and flowers. And the main altar, upon which an indefinite number of candles have been placed during the church's five hundred years of existence, is completely smoked. You can't see anything. All black, like some sort of giant Malevich, where the people come to pray to it. No one has ever cleaned it. Cleaning it would be sacrilege. So that black is full symbolically. It presupposes time, depth. As if we could give shape to time.

Tarkovsky used to talk about "sculpting time" ...

There, time as sculpture is very evident. Entering that church and seeing how people pray to that nothingness, to that black, fascinates me. It's one of my life's fundamental images, and moving toward it has always been latent in me. I had to run a course through the figurative in order to finally come closer to it.

But it continues to be an image that is prayed to, even though it is an abstract image.

An image bears a certain sacredness. In my case, the images I look for have to bear indescribable, extra-artistic aspects. It may be that what you pray to in that black wall is yourself. I seek to capture an image in which to see not only that smoke reflected, but the gazes that inhabit it. And what that mass, black enough to be a mirror, is doing is materializing the gaze.

Do images have memory, then?

Yes. As Georges Didi-Huberman says from the standpoint of philosophy, images are complex. What we see is not the image, it's something else, there is an experience.

Didi-Huberman speaks about images as a theologian, you speak as a believer... You speak from a certain faith in images, and while he studies them, you invent them.

I need to inhabit them.

You once said that "the gaze is a wound and the image is the scar." Does the image you invent suture a wound?

That's it. There are works that affect me deeply. Louise Bourgeois would make sculptures with sewn cloth. For me, it is the representation that comes closest to what I think about human beings. It x-rays a life experience, since her work is a consequence of what she lived, it is tied to her childhood, her solitude, when you cannot do anything with the few words you have. You have to live more time in order to take up once again the threads you left tangled up, to give them a less precarious meaning.

Is seeing less seeing more?

Why is there such an obsession with being seen by the other? Your work is a part of you, the offering you give to the world. But one always wants someone to see it, for your gaze to be made public. And if it isn't, it hurts. It's like being sent back to the frustration or incapacity that you have as a child, facing a world of adults in which you're unable to do anything. You make your work to emerge from the paralysis that you bring with you from childhood, and you expel it into the world so that someone else will see themselves reflected in it.

Is everything in childhood?

A large part is, undoubtedly. I don't remember my childhood.

In your analysis, has anything appeared to dissipate that forgetfulness a little?

No. The truth is that the person who remembers my childhood, and hers, is my sister. And that recollection has cost her dearly.

Is it better to forget?

No, it's better to make art.

But in some situations, it's as if it's either art or insanity...

In some cases, yes. But creating distances in order to avoid continuing to be a victim of your childhood. Because there, you are a passive subject. One is spoken for, cared for, manipulated by someone else. And art takes its vengeance. That passive subject from childhood takes the floor to speak, and does whatever it pleases with that childhood.

A novel.

That would be very good.

But one where you write the script yourself. There is also a family novel in the case of a neurotic. We all tell ourselves a novel of our lives, but the script for that novel was written by someone else. And when we think we are telling our own story, we are actually telling a story where we occupy a place that someone else assigned to us. Art reappropriates the story: I am going to tell it my way.

I very much like when Rauschenberg buys an original drawing by De Kooning and then erases it. That's an interesting thing to do, with something that has weight for you, your father's voice, for example, to transform it into something else. You make it your own, at that moment it no longer signifies anything, and at the same time, it signifies quite a lot. The simple gesture of erasing is powerful. As if I were to buy a painting by Bacon and paint over it, or pour turpentine on it and dissolve it. It's a gesture…

Like when Ai Weiwei breaks the urns.

Of course. In that gesture of destruction, one makes a great gesture of creation. You take a life experience and smash it to pieces in order to make something else out of those pieces.

That's a good definition of analysis, except that there, it happens privately.

Ballard used to say that every morning when he woke up, he put his feet on the floor and a grenade would explode, pulverizing everything. He would spend the rest of the day gathering up the pieces. I feel I can identify with that, but I don't know if I am him, or one of the pieces, or the grenade, or the room. When a work moves you it's because you are in the work. Even if you don't know in what part. That may be one of the reasons why you see a work, and you continue to see it, finding more and more in it.

Is it better not to know so much, or not to know completely?

You're never going to know. I see images as living things, never static, many accompany you, they get old, they change as needs do.

Which ones accompany you?

Ah… Now, what can I tell you? Well, my great influence is the baroque…

From the baroque to abstraction. The baroque is the negation of the void. What is not there is alluded to via excess, a defense mode for alluding to what is lacking.

Yes, it can be so excessive that there is nothing. You're in New York, in Times Square, and there are so many images that you don't see anything. The excess takes you right back to nothingness. The sum of all the colors takes you to white. The thing about an image that captures you is never in the image, but in the way you look at it. The image is just a detonator.

It isn't one who is looking, but rather the image that looks at us, isn't that so?

There is reciprocity; I see an image as an organism, as an experience. You see something and you endow it with potential. It's when your works are born in spite of you that they are necessary.

As if you were a medium, not an artifice...

Exactly, the image is simply given to you.

In this sense, being an artist isn't a choice. Whether or not they are conscious of it, an artist lets themselves be carried along by something that goes beyond their will.

It's an inevitable experience.

How does an artist see psychoanalysis? Susan Sontag would say that it was an unrecognized form of art, linking it to performance...

There is something of performance in setting out to talk, to surprise yourself with what you say, there is where you really reflect. It's an unexpected encounter. You encounter something about yourself that you didn't expect, and that helps you to reflect on what it is that you feel about life, because in some way it's something you have hidden away. That idea of psychoanalysis, free association, is difficult; it consists of taking the ideas that come to you and expelling them.

To take and to expel.

Right. It's the opposite of meditation, which means leaving the mind empty to allow thoughts to pass through. In analysis, you have a different attitude, you have to expel the ideas that worry you. In my case, however, I go very much programmed ahead of time. That is, for me, free association... isn't all that free. I don't allow it because I'm paying a good amount of money, so to rave on about my ideas and think about the cat, about my father, about a trip or some dream don't contribute anything to me. I have to focus.

But that's strange. You say that things happen in the space of analysis like they do in art, the possibility emerges that something surprising may happen. But that in some way, you don't allow surprising occurrences to appear...

Yes, they do appear.

They appear in spite of your will to rein in the situation.

Right. I need to be looking my psychoanalyst in the eye. I don't function well talking into a void, lying down. For me the couch makes no sense, I feel absolutely lost. I need to see and be seen. I construct myself beginning with how I see and how I am seen. Language is something different. I also analyze the psychoanalyst, his gestures, his posture, sometimes I feel that he is bored, sometimes he is attentive. And very often I see the void, because seeing the void is a seeing without seeing.

You need to experience a situation where the gaze is present, looking at the analyst; but at some determined moment, you need to divert your gaze...

Yes, often I need to move away from that axis of the gaze in order to concentrate on some idea that I'm concerned with. I wouldn't be able to elaborate the idea in depth, which is what I want, if I am looking at a face. Effectively, something of the emotion of the couch is there, of gazing into a void, but while seated.

In some way, then, you meet up with the void.

In order to think, yes. I believe it has something to do with meditation: to see without seeing. To see a space without consciousness of what I am seeing, letting ideas flow. And I am often surprised by something I say. And obviously, the analyst has a lot to do with it, in how he elaborates what I say and how the conversation continues.

Have any discoveries in connection with your art work, or that lead you to produce work, appeared in that space?

No, they are two different things. I talk about my work and I believe that I have understood certain aspects of it based on my analysis: the search for the gaze, the determination to portray someone who is seeing me, seeing the camera, seeing the viewer, to turn me into something like a mirror, the awareness of having a gaze that sustains me, to generate images that sustain me, for example, are thoughts that have emerged on account of analysis.

Analysis has served to understand, not to invent...

No. Inspiration comes outside, walking in the mountains, behind the wheel... In psychoanalysis I try to understand. I see a film and the critique from the standpoint of analysis is richer, deeper and more complex than an art critique. Reading art magazines has left me bored. On the other hand, I read a psychoanalysis magazine and say Wow! Phenomenal ideas.

What turns out to be interesting is a foreign gaze...

Absolutely. Sometimes, seeing exhibitions and magazines, I say "we are only masturbating." Making works and more works... Where does it all wind up, what are we doing? There are extraordinary artists who manage to get away from that, but it's disappointing to feel I'm part of a community like this, creating works to see who can make the biggest hit, instead of digging deep into yourself to make a work that opens up a world for you. And psychoanalysis permits just that. I have tried, in some way, to be the psychoanalyst of my own work.

How?

I have attempted to understand it based on the little I know about psychoanalysis, but like my wife says: "You've spent twenty-five years in psychoanalysis, it hasn't been worth shit for you!" (laughs). What do I say? Well, it may have served for when I am giving a workshop and I say: "Aha! You give your project a name that has nothing to do with what it is about, why is that? I think that you are talking about mourning the death of your mother." And the person starts to cry. And that isn't a session of psychoanalysis. I can see the same thing in someone who presents their work to me.

In some way, could it be that someone who has spent years talking in a psychoanalytic context at some point begins to function with a psychoanalytic ear?

I am more interested in listening than in seeing.

What is the difference between listening and seeing?

If your attention is on the image, certain things go unnoticed, certain intonation, certain words. You have to be able to talk about your own work. Before, images spoke for themselves, you didn't have to say anything. I don't believe in that: you should sustain the image you generate in words.

Listening recovers some things that escape from an image.

Yes. It's that an image also whispers.

You use an auditory verb, with a visual noun...

Right. It's a cenesthesia of sorts. A language that isn't altogether verbal but isn't altogether visual, either. There is something of an image that you feel and perceive that comes from the order of music. You have to listen to what the image shows, to what the image hides.

And does that thing that an image hides appear in an auditory register? Is what is being looked at heard?

Yes, that's it. When I pay attention to someone who is speaking about their work, I am paying attention to what the image conceals.

Is it as though images involve a dimension of deception, and by listening—on the basis of an account of that image—something truthful appears, something that would otherwise remain hidden?

Yes, an image veils what it is that constitutes it. Every image conceals something.

Is it that an image conceals words, and by listening, you restore to it the words it leaves outside?

An image detonates a visual experience, but a verbal one as well. I would not be able to understand an image without words. Otherwise, I would be close to an image that approaches the sacred, the unspeakable. An image that leaves you mute or blind. When I say that an image whispers, what I am trying to say is that it is like a poem, but a poem's profoundness is not in its sound, nor in its words. We are in the space of poetry when we exceed language, when it ceases to be what it is.

Might there be something that sustains language, yet exceeds it at the same time?

Of course. It is there that I feel we are in poetic space.

Can a session of analysis be a poetic space?

It provides you with all the possibilities. It could generate a kind of poem in common. A crucial moment can arrive when both find their eyes are watering, an encounter. Like art, I feel that it fulfills the same function in some way. If art is a form of salvation, I also see psychoanalysis as a form, I don't know if of salvation, but yes, of being able to contend with yourself.

And do you see it as an art, as a science?

As an experience that comes closer to art. Had I recorded my sessions, I would be able to read a strange novel there, without rhyme or reason, a kind of diary, an autobiography that would surprise me.

There is a legend that says that many artists don't undergo analysis because they are convinced that their creativity comes from their neurosis, and if they were to be cured, they would lose the thing that feeds their work...

One begins analysis for the same reason that one desires to be an artist: being unable to deal with the world. The issues that artists are concerned with are not many, and they are always the same ones: love, death, suffering, pleasure, desire.

The same issues that appear time and again in analysis...

In all mythologies, as different as the ways they are elaborated may be, the fundamental concerns are the same: heartbreak, solitude; from the earliest poetry up to what is written today. Art recycles. Anish Kapoor thinks that the work of art is the creation of personal mythologies. Our works are a mythology that we invent, with other mythologies as the starting point.

Your work is tremendously poetic, visual poetry...

Poetry appears when language crumbles. An image has to be more than an image, to transcend itself, to evoke something that language doesn't manage to transmit.

Does an image have a greater potency to evoke than a word?

Yes, there are images that evoke something more... Language would become tangled.

The gaze sustains, but the analytic situation is conceived on the basis of taking away that support... On what, then, would it be suitable to sustain one's self?

Gazes are inaudible voices that come into play there in an oblique manner. By not exchanging glances, both the person analyzed and the analyst direct their gazes into the void, there is a floating gaze, lost in space. To see without looking helps you to concentrate on emotions, and generates trust in that the analysis will be upheld in words, in silences, in the intonation or the emphasis of your story. Taking away the gaze to a certain degree undoubtedly enables more careful listening and narration, it sharpens the subtlety of the listening and intensifies the emotional wandering. As someone in analysis, I think that you should go along substituting images with silences and words, giving voice to your images.

What place does psychoanalysis have in your work?

You choose to be an artist because you feel uncomfortable facing the world. Art is a powerful form of contending with this nonconformity and giving it a different meaning. You begin therapy for the same reasons, in order to confront some dis-content, with some degree of discomfort regarding yourself and life. Both my work and the psychoanalytical experience emerge from despair, they are close siblings. In both spaces, I have tried to contend with my ghosts, with the fears that torment me. We create because we are not happy, and in that condition we elaborate images that are dictated from an unconscious that has given meaning to our way of look-ing. The psychoanalytic experience opens fissures in our overwhelming forgetful-ness, sheds light on that corner of the room that has remained in darkness. My work is a reflection on the human condition, on what it is to know that one is living in an ominous world, alone and adrift, immersed in a universe that is completely indifferent to us.

Chapter 12

Eric Kandel, the neuroscientist who loved psychoanalysis

I met with Eric Kandel in the office that Columbia University assigned to him after he was awarded the Nobel Prize, a space that—although surrounded by libraries and laboratories—might well be an office pertaining to the Director of some huge multinational.

Can someone simultaneously be an authentic New Yorker and a European, born in Vienna at a time when Freud might still be spotted in one of its cafés? Can someone be a humanist, a lover of art and literature, a restless historian of their own time, and a conscientious investigator of the physiological basis of memory, all at the same time? Can someone be a highly reputed neuroscientist while at the same time defending psychoanalysis as the most sophisticated way of comprehending the human mind?

The man I interviewed in New York can quite evidently accommodate all of these apparent contradictions, and he has found a way, in close to a century of existence, of leaving his fertile mark on this era.

Let's start by talking about cities. There are three different cities that are very important for you that are also very important for me. Let's start with Vienna, your place of origin. What happened in Vienna during various decades is wonderful, like what happened in Cordoba, Spain, during a period of time, or in Florence during the Renaissance. You know that Vienna was the core for many things. Why was that, in your opinion?

Well, it was the capital of the Austro-Hungarian Empire. So a lot of people, Jews for example, who were living in Poland in the ghettos when Franz Josef declared all people as being equal in 1870, many of these young Jewish people moved from their little towns to Vienna. So Vienna's population grew immensely and the Jewish population also grew proportionately. And that brought together many interesting people from all over the Austro-Hungarian Empire.

This meant that many discoveries that happened there were not made by the Viennese, but by foreigners...

Well, that isn't true. They were encouraged... But Vienna grew tremendously, so foreigners came and they contributed also. But a number of very gifted people were already there.

DOI: 10.4324/9781032708591-12

Do you think that Vienna was like a melting pot of different cultures and different languages?

Yes, yes. But it had its own distinctive culture. Certainly its music was very strong. Haydn, Mozart, Beethoven, they all lived in Vienna, so the musical culture was very powerful.

And there's a strong mark on your work, from Vienna.

Yes, I have been influenced by my life in Vienna... Having been born in Vienna. Yes... not all of it positive, there is some negative...

I can imagine. Because Vienna, and Austria in general, didn't do the work that Germany did, to work through the Holocaust...

No, they did not. They pretended that the country was innocent.

They pretended, yes.

I don't have the picture here, but one of the early things I did when I got back to Vienna was to get them to change the name of the Lueger University of Vienna, which sits on part of the *Ringstraße* (Vienna Ring Road) that is called *Dr.-Karl-Lueger-Ring*. And Lueger was a fantastically anti-Semitic mayor of Vienna. And to think that the university is sitting on this part of the road is unacceptable. So they changed it after all to the university name. But I put a lot of pressure on them to do that.

Do you agree that some discoveries, for instance, the discovery of the Unconscious by Freud, or some philosophical works, or some artistic works that took place in Vienna in those years could not have happened unless...

It's probably true. There was wonderful intellectual activity in Vienna at that time. It was extremely conducive to creative outbursts in music, and art and literature, yeah.

And the paradox is that the country that expelled your family received you as a true Austrian-born scientist when you got the Nobel Prize.

Yes. And now they've been very nice. If you look behind you, what they gave me the last time I was there, about a year ago, is a special award from the Medical School: an honorary doctorate of Medicine. And I've got all kinds of awards from the Austrians... I have most of them at home, but... Heinz Fischer, the president of Austria until recently, became a friend of mine.

He's no longer the president, but for twelve years he was the president. And he and I were quite good friends. It was a nice period, I was very comfortable.

He is a president, I imagine to be completely different from Kurt Waldheim, for instance, who was also president and also a former SS official.

Yes, completely different.

In your opinion, what was the reaction of the Viennese people to these new discoveries? Freud's discoveries, Schiller, Klimt...

I was too young to really appreciate this personally. But historically, it's well described; they had the same reaction to Freud as other people did. Some were enthusiastic, most were skeptical. He had a large school; Freud had a good following in Vienna until Hitler came.

And in a way, you were nearly contemporary with those analysts who fled from Europe, from Vienna, in a sort of diaspora, because of Nazism. You were born a bit later, but not that many years.

No, I was very friendly with the next generation. Kris, Lowenstein, I knew them all. I was very friendly with Ernst Kris. I dated his daughter for a couple of years. We're very good friends, we're still very good friends. And I knew Anna Kris, the daughter, Marianna Kris, the mother, and Ernst Kris, the father. So Ernst Kris and Marianna Kris were very good analysts.

Ernst Kris was very famous for a lot of important theoretical work. He also was an artist earlier, a very famous one. So he combined art and psychiatry...

That was the point where you came in contact with psychoanalysis for the first time?

My interest in psychoanalysis is through them. They got me interested in psychoanalysis.

Love came first, in your initial contact with psychoanalysis, because you were in love with Kris's daughter.

Yes, yes...

And are you still fond of psychoanalysis?

Yes, very fond.

Why?

Because I think it has a lot to offer as a conceptual framework, and it has a lot to offer therapeutically... it has many weaknesses. It has not devoted itself to showing that it really works, it hasn't done many outcome studies. I mean, there are many exceptions, but it has not been systematic in proving that it's really effective.

So take Psychoanalysis in contrast to Aaron Beck. He developed a therapy which is different from psychoanalysis, but immediately did outcome studies and showed under what circumstances it works, and under what circumstances it doesn't work. A much more scientific approach. Psychoanalysis by and large has not done that.

And what about psychoanalysis nowadays in the US?

It's disappearing.

Disappearing? Here? As a clinical experience or as a theory?

Both, to some degree... It's very sad, very sad.

Because I have read in your works that you still think that psychoanalysis offers a most comprehensive...

It's wonderful. I like psychoanalysis a great deal, but I'm unique. Not many people feel that way...

You're unique...

I'm not unique, but the analysts certainly do feel that. There are very few people in analysis in the United States. A lot of people are in psychotherapy, but analysis per se is in serious decline.

But analytical therapies? Not four or five times a week, but there are still a lot, aren't there?

Once or twice a week is a lot.

Once or twice... but with a psychoanalytical approach?

Yes. Or variants thereof, but it's not as popular as it was 30 or 40 years ago.

Even in New York, which is one of the capitals...

Even in New York! When I was in medical school, every single one of my friends was in analysis. I went to medical school here and I was in analysis here. I was in analysis in Boston and here.

So you were in two different analyses.

Yes. My most important analysis was in Boston.

For many years?

While I was a resident. I think it was four years, three and a half years.

And was it a good experience?

Excellent... I really benefited from it.

Because at the end of that analysis you decided to become a scientist, not an analyst.

No, I knew that beforehand. No, I think somewhere along the line I decided I would not have any practice at all, because you can't really do good psychotherapy if you see patients only one day a week. And science really requires an intensive effort. So I decided I enjoyed research so much that I would devote myself to it. My colleagues were disappointed; they thought I should do some therapy…

Your psychoanalytic colleagues?

Yes, very disappointed. They thought maybe I should specialize. I said, what should I specialize in? Well, hypnosis. That isn't interesting for someone who likes psychoanalysis. So I decided to drop it. For a while I did supervision of residents. One day a week. And you can be very helpful doing that. And I did this at Harvard, where it worked really well, but then later on when I came to NYU, the residency program at that time was not very good. So the supervision wasn't very satisfying, so after a year or two, I stopped.

But did you suffer a lot by quitting clinical work, or not?

No. I like research much more.

I can imagine, or I assume, when I read your books… that you had very good analysis. Because the end of the analysis enabled you to become who you wanted to be.

A better human being.

Not only a better human being. Who you wanted to be, a scientist. Not an analyst, not to identify yourself with an analyst…

Right.

But to become a different person.

Yeah.

Let's go back to Vienna and the place of Nazism and the role of science in connection to Nazism. I'm very interested in knowing what you think about that.

Nothing. There was no connection between science and Nazis.

I'm sure that true science has nothing to do with that, but the Nazis, you know that Rudolf Hess, the last Auschwitz commander, said that in his opinion, in his crazy opinion, Nazism was applied biology…

Pure shit! I can also say I'm the biggest man that ever lived. What does it mean? Nonsense.

Ok. Do you think that psychoanalysis could have been invented by another person, who was not coming from a Jewish tradition?

Sure.

Or do you think that the fact that Freud was a Jew was very important in his discovery?

He thought so. He once gave a talk at the B'nai B'rith or somewhere in which he pointed out how proud he was of being a Jew. And I think there is something the Jewish culture has of self-examination which is very important. But listen, I mean, very important ideas have come from other people. Hartman was not Jewish and made fantastic contributions in psychoanalysis.

And... can you imagine a Nobel Prize given to Freud, or not? Would it have been impossible?

I think his contemporaries found it difficult, whether to consider him a scientist or an artist... a literary giant. And he certainly got literary awards. He was not, in his time, an empirical scientist. He didn't show that it worked. So it lacked scientific evidence, that was a weakness of his. But you know, it was a major contribution.

You know that the only prize he was given was the Goethe award.

Literature. Right.

Can you read in German? Were you able to read Freud in German?

I read him in English but I can read in German. He wrote very beautifully.

Did the Nobel Prize change your own life?

Oh sure. My God, yes.

In what ways?

Well, people treat you differently.

Yes.

Every book that I publish—I don't ask for this—automatically puts that in. Every book, every English book says "winner of the Nobel prize."

But intimately, what has changed in you?

It's a major recognition. So people respond differently to you. They invite you to things that they might not invite you to otherwise. The university is very proud of you. It treats me... there are two Nobel laureates in Brain Science at Columbia, and they treat us very well. I mean, look at this office.

This is great. It's very nice. And you didn't have it before the Nobel.

No. I had a nice office but it wasn't quite as nice as this one.

Ok. You know... I will tell you something personal. My father studied in Stockholm, at the Karolinska Institute, where you received your prize. And he had been studying there to be a neuro-radiologist, but I received many psychoanalytical books from him. He thought during many years about being an analyst himself. But he decided to do something else and went into... He married my mother in Stockholm and I was conceived there, and he decided not to become an analyst. And I decided to become an analyst myself, reading his books. When I read your memories, your book, I thought a lot about that, because I felt that there was a hidden tradition, a marginal one, in your case... but you're still fond of psychoanalysis.

Very fond.

And in my case, I received that from my father, who wasn't an analyst. I laughed when I read that, because I have read, wait a moment, I need to quote you. You wrote that your "beginnings as someone who wanted to become an analyst wasn't a detour or a deviation, but the bedrock from which all the things you were able to build later was built." Can you explain this and talk about it?

Well, I mean, my experience in Vienna and my interest in psychoanalysis influenced all my later decisions. I went into Brain Sciences really as a continuation of trying to understand the mind. The next step after you understand it in psychological terms, is that you understand it in biological terms. And biology is a natural continuation of psychoanalysis. That's the next step. The biological underpinnings of the Ego, the Id, and Superego.

Freud wanted that in some way.

Yes, he was way ahead of his time. He said someday, biology is going to come along and all of my stuff is going to be wiped out. He said that.

And do you think there will be something like a pill to treat neurosis?

It has nothing to do with a pill. It has to do with understanding.

Yes. And in the therapeutic field?

The therapy doesn't have to change. But he didn't have a biological understanding of where the Ego, the Id, and the Superego are. But now we would have an understanding of how they interact with each other.

And what do you think about the research that's still being done inside of the psychoanalytical community? Do you know what research some Psychoanalytical Societies are doing now?

I know about some, but...

What do you think?

Not enough, number one, and they're not that strong.

And where does your inspiration come from? From the scientific field, or from art, or from everyday life? Where does it come from?

There is no single source. It comes from many different places. Different people are inspired by different things.

In your case?

Discovery.

Because you are a strange model of a scientist, who is very committed to humanistic...

Ah, but many people are...

Yeah, many but not all... you love art...

No! Well, you can do science in many different ways. And I've brought an interest in art to my scientific endeavors. I'm now exploring the biological response of people to works of art.

In this book.

It's a beginning.

There are others?

We're working on the next step now.

Ok, ok. In your opinion, Erik, is psychoanalysis an art or a science?

In between.

In between.

It's an art trying to become a science.

It's an art trying to become a science. Let's talk a bit more about that, I find it interesting.

They have not done outcome studies. They haven't done studies on why it works, with whom does it work. They haven't explored the mechanisms of psychoanalysis very much, the analysts. They were not trained as scientists.

And do you know about contemporary traditions in psychoanalysis?

A little bit. In Europe it's much more serious, psychoanalysis, it's more experimental, more rigorous than it is in the United States. Much stronger, yeah.

Ok. And What do you think about the future of psychoanalysis?

Uncertain.

Why?

How many people are going to psychoanalysis now compared to fifty years ago?

In my country, many people.

Yes, in South America, yes.

In Eastern Europe, many people.

Ok, I can only speak about the United States.

Yes, I understand. You know well what happens here. And you see no future.

You could not become the chairman of a Department of Psychiatry in the 1960s unless you were an analyst. Now, if you're a psychoanalyst, you cannot be the chairman of a department. It's too narrow, too restricted. Biological psychiatry, that's what you have to be in.

And in a way, that impoverishes psychiatry, I imagine, to forbid psychoanalysts.

It doesn't help it any… yes, it narrows it. Yeah. It's not good.

What do you think about the Freud's ancient project of psychology for a neurologist?

He said, this is nonsense. And the diagrams are ridiculous. It was an honest attempt to develop a biological understanding, but he said we're nowhere near there, we don't understand it. Someday, he said, we'll have a biological understanding of it and many of my ideas will be wrong. He was right.

And in terms of a biological understanding of the unconscious, for instance, at what stage are we now?

At the beginning.

At the very beginning.

Not the very, but you know…

You're a pioneer.

Yes. People are not studying it, you see… if you go to any New York psychoanalytical Institute, how much effort are they putting into research?

Not very much?

That's it.

You know that psychoanalysis has, historically, had two different ways to begin a conversation, to enter into a field, or into a country. There have been two ways: through science or through art. In some countries or at some times, like in Paris, it has entered through art's gates. In other countries, like the US, it has entered through science, through the medical profession, mainly. Do you agree with that? What do you think?

In some cases, art is emphasized more than others, but it has to enter through medical gates, I mean... Maybe not, maybe you're right. People can treat it just as a theory without having any clinical application. You may be right...

Which field is more open to new discoveries? Art or science?

Well, it's much easier to make discoveries in science than in art. But many people, myself included, are becoming interested in having a more empirical approach to art. How does the viewer respond to a work of art, what is the difference between the viewer's response to abstract art versus figurative art? I'm trying to work on that.

That's your work nowadays.

Yeah.

But there's this... you want to link the world of science and the world of art.

Yes.

To bridge these two worlds.

Yes, yes...

I've been looking around here, at Columbia. There are two main buildings. This building and an art building.

Next door. And we have an artist in residence here. We always select an artist and he spends one year, comes periodically, and interacts with the scientists. Jeff Koons.

Jeff Koons was here, Wow!

Just finished.

Wow. During a year he worked here.

Yes.

Do you enjoy Koons' work?

I like it a great deal. We're very good friends.

Wow.

[Shows video about himself]

I will look at it carefully. It's very nice. A very nice experience. I imagine you en-joyed it a lot.

Good. Yeah, I had a good time. All right…

Do you know Anish Kapoor's work?

Yes. I know of it but I don't know him personally.

It's very interesting to think about in terms of your research. I will meet him too, in London. Do you think that artists see things first compared to normal people or even scientists? Do artists go in the avant-garde in relation to the others?

It varies so much. Not only does it vary in any given generation, but from one gen-eration to the next. They have different attitudes toward art. So there's a great deal of variability. They certainly look at their own art differently than the beholder, right? They're creating the art.

Do you also collect?

Oh, yes, I have a very nice collection at home. I have some Beckman, Nolde, and the Israeli artists, I have a beautiful collection of work. I have very nice stuff at home.

Do you enjoy collecting?

Oh, very much. And we spent a fair amount of money on art. I mean, not hundreds of thousands, but we spend thousands of dollars on some works of art…

And what place does art have in your life?

It's very important. On weekends we used to go to one museum at least.

Do you work with reductionism in art as well as in science?

Well, in art less so, but in science, yes. I take a reductionist approach, yes…

Can you tell me more about that?

Well, I think that I began, of course, by applying it to science, which is historical; it didn't begin with me, it began hundreds of years ago. To take a complex aspect of art, learning memory, and studying it as a very simple example. A simple reflex that can be modified.

In the Aplysia...

Yes… see how that works, and then use that as a way to begin to build up to more complex things. It's been useful in most areas of science, and I've shown that it was useful in the biology of learning and memory as well. And in art, I also take somewhat of a reductionist approach. Abstract art in comparison to figurative art, and now we're carrying out an experiment with a colleague downstairs; we're imaging people, like yourself, looking at three different works of art by the same artist. Figurative, transitional, abstract.

Three different stages of the same artist.

Yes. So how do you respond to a work of abstract art, compared to a work of figurative art?

What did you discover? There are many artists who have evolved from figurative art to abstraction.

Sure.

Ok. In science, reductionism is a very important tool, I imagine. Is there something that gets lost in this way of working?

Of course. When you simplify, you lose something. You gain the power that you have better control, but you have to realize that you're using a reductionist approach.

How can we recover what is lost?

One thing at a time.

The mind fits with that model of working.

Sure.

You have trust in the future.

Yeah, yeah.

And does reductionism have to do with minimalism, the smaller the better, in some way?

Yes. There is some overlap, yes.

Could you connect that with psychoanalysis in any way?

Reductionism is… in psychoanalysis, it's the opposite of reductionism.

Why do you think so?

It speaks about the richness of the mind.

Yes, but something interesting happens. When you are in analysis for many years, and you have talked about many things with many words, at the end of an analysis, not that many things remain.

Good point. There are central themes that you return to time and time again because they're so central to you.

When I was reading about reductionism in your work, I thought a lot about reductionism in the analyst's interpretation, because we so often use many words, and perhaps make small points.

Excellent. Good.

Are we done?

I think so, no?

Chapter 13

Sudhir Kakar, a guru between two worlds

This conversation with Sudhir Kakar—dressed in kurta, vest, and pants—begins in a boisterous coffee shop at the Ambedkar University in South Delhi, and it concludes by way of a written exchange, better suited to the questions I present to him. The oral and the textual merge together much as East and West do in this Indian psychoanalyst, writer, and intellectual, one of the world's most influential personalities according to publications such as *Le Nouvel Observateur* or *Die Zeit*; he is an interpreter of Indian mentality, as accustomed to giving conferences in Europe or the United States as he is to conversing with a guru's wisdom with the Dalai Lama or Hollywood stars.

Recently departed, his presence and his words have now become a unique testimony. Sudhir—with whom I was able to meet in Vienna or in Rome, in Tehran or New Delhi in order to continue our conversation—leaves us this register of his thinking, always a counterpoint to the West, and at the same time, always illuminating. Between the lines, our conversation also testifies to the endearing presence of this warm man, who, removed from the frenzy of civilization, seemed to levitate with each step, with an ability to listen that is rarely found.

You are at the same time a novelist and a psychoanalyst who writes essays... How do you decide whether to write a novel or an essay?

I like doing both, for the different satisfactions each offers. Non-fiction is written in a discursive mode. Its pleasures lie in the effort to think clearly, in building arguments, critically engaging with other scholars and disciplining one's own ideas through scholarship. Fiction is written in a connotative mode. Imagination takes precedence over knowledge and the discoveries made on the way are often surprising and greatly satisfying in the creative "rush" they offer. The decision to write one or the other depends on the demand my psyche is making on me at that particular time.

I've got the feeling, here, listening to you, that you are a sort of guru... Is it a correct impression?

I also got the feeling! *(laughs)* How does one get knowledge? The Western idea is very much critical thinking... here the idea is to completely surrender to the guru,

DOI: 10.4324/9781032708591-13

that you will absorb more from the guru, surrendering, than with critical thought. But after you have absorbed… you must kill him after—not from the beginning—with critical thought.

But at the end, the disciple must kill the guru, or the psychoanalyst… or the father…

Or what he stands for… That which you are no longer needing, because you have the guru inside.

The word "guru" doesn't have prestige in the West, like in India, where it is a more complex issue… Can we think of the psychoanalyst as a type of "guru" practice?

Gurus are not uniquely Indian, although India seems to be their natural habitat. Their appeal is to everyone who shares the romantic vision of reality. In contrast to the tragic vision, which sees life as full of incomprehensible afflictions, where many wishes are fated to remain unfulfilled, and which comes to an end with the death of the body. In the romantic vision, life is not tragic, but a romantic quest. The quest can extend over many births, with the goal and possibility of apprehending another, "higher" level of reality beyond the shared, verifiable, empirical reality of our world, our bodies, and our emotions. The guru holds the promise of access to this "higher" reality, full of radical transformations of life and consciousness. Another reason for the attraction of the guru lies in the fact that, except for the psychopaths, most human beings are deeply moral in the sense that there is an unconscious longing for an ideal self that is free of all-too-human distortions of lust, anger, envy, narcissism and so on that afflict our empirical selves as we experience it in our daily life. The guru then incorporates this ideal self. Establishing a relationship to the guru through two great constructs of human imagination, idealization and identification, is establishing a relationship with an ideal, moral self. For those influenced by modern ideologies of egalitarianism originating in the West, the susceptibility of a follower to the charisma of a guru will appear as the reflection of an enfeebled self, of a psychic helplessness that needs to be reversed by an idealization and identification with a guru who kindles hope through his own possession of an unshakeable self-confidence, encompassing compassion and a certainty in his convictions. For such a modern person, the follower's surrender to the guru is a sign of infantile regression, the surrender of adult agency. The traditional Indian take on surrender is radically different and much more positive. One guru writes of the follower's experience: "When you surrender to the guru, you become like a valley, a vacuum, an abyss, a bottomless pit. You acquire depth, not height. This surrender can be felt in many ways. The guru begins to manifest in you; his energy begins to flow into you. The guru's energy is continuously flowing, but in order to receive it, you have to become a womb, a receptacle." Another extols the merits of surrender thus: "There are only two ways to live: one is with constant conflict, and the other is with surrender. Conflict leads to anguish and suffering… But when someone surrenders with understanding and equanimity, his house, body and heart become full. His former feeling of emptiness and lack disappears." The Western experience with demonic charismatic leaders of religious cults or nations (Hitler, Stalin) will naturally have difficulty with the traditional Indian extolling of surrender, and with idealization and identification as motors of psychic transformation. Both, I think though, would agree that the attraction of a guru is a phenomenon that lies at the very beginning of human life and interaction. Yet the "guru fantasy," namely the existence of someone, somewhere, who will heal the wounds suffered in early relationships and remove the blights on the soul so that it shines anew in its pristine state, is common across many cultures. Irrespective of their conscious subscription to the ideology of egalitarianism and a more contractual doctor-patient relationship, many Western patients approach analysis and the analyst with a full-blown "guru fantasy" which, however, is more hidden and less accessible to consciousness than is the case in India, Iran or other Asian countries.

You have been a sort of interpreter of the "Indian mind" for the West. Do you think that this work can be done by a Westerner, too?

Certainly. One only has to be aware that psychoanalytical knowledge of a culture, of the "mind" of its people, is not equivalent to its anthropological knowledge, although there may be some overlap between the two. Psychoanalytic knowledge is primarily the knowledge of the culture's *imagination*, of its fantasy as encoded in its symbolic products, its myths and folktales, its popular art, music, literature and cinema. A Western analyst who is willing to immerse himself in the culture's imagination for a long period, speak its language and encounter its people in the clinical setting can certainly do this work.

What has the West done and what does it continue to do with Eastern traditions, and vice versa?

I believe that an increase in the mutual exchanges between psychoanalysis and Eastern meditative healing traditions holds the best chance for a rejuvenation of both traditions. In the West, the psychoanalytic reception to Eastern traditions has been limited to a few psychoanalysts who have been interested in learning and reconciling Buddhist philosophy and practices of ameliorating suffering with their own tradition of psychological inquiry. In the East, the interest of spiritual "masters" in learning from psychoanalysis has been even more limited. I believe this can, and should change for the benefit of both. To give just a few examples: In psychoanalysis, empathy is a core requirement for the attending analyst, the chief tool for gathering data for understanding the patient. Tolerance and compassion are the precursors to empathy, and we can fruitfully look to Buddhist and other spiritual traditions for pointers in their cultivation. Indeed, it is odd that aspiring psychoanalysts have often only heard about—but have no personal experience in—one of the profession's chief requirements: listening to the client with free-floating, evenly hovering attention, which each analyst picks up more or less informally and unsupervised on their own. Such an experience, which is missing from psychoanalytic training programs, could be easily provided through a short four-to-five-day meditation workshop, such as that of *vipassana*. As the analyst C. Clement, reflecting on her own experience has observed, the analyst who has experienced this mode of meditation is likely to listen to her patient differently. She is likely to be more attuned to subtle, emerging twinges of fear, sadness, or helplessness. Such an analyst is also able to hold these feelings longer and more deeply without reaching for the reassuring effort to organize and interpret. This brings me to a much more difficult issue. Can the Buddhist and psychoanalytic methods of transforming emotions be reconciled? Here my answer is a qualified "No." In psychoanalytic therapy one seeks access to the client's unconscious through methods such as free association, that is, saying whatever comes to the mind, paying attention to the client's slips of the tongue, hesitations, dreams, fantasies, and to what is going on unconsciously between the client and the therapist. Language and words play an important, though not an exclusive, role in psychoanalytic therapy. From the Buddhist perspective and its emphasis on *direct* experience, language and words *distract* us from direct experience. They create distance from the immediacy of experience in order to do the cognitive work necessary for communication to the therapist. This disdain for language is also shared by Hindu spiritual traditions. As the 16th century Indian saint Dadu puts it: "The guru speaks first to the mind, then with the glance of the eye. If the disciple fails to understand, he instructs him at last by mouth." "He that understands a spoken word is a common man. He that interprets a gesture is an initiate. He that reads the thought of the mind unsearchable, unfathomable is a God." Here psychoanalysis diverges from Eastern traditions, but it can heed Buddhist warnings on the limitations of language and become much more sensitive to the nuances of silence and other non-verbal communication in the therapeutic setting. In my opinion, psychoanalysis cannot and should not reject the medium of language and words that has brought it such rich dividends of insight into the workings of the human mind. It can also wonder whether the exclusive Buddhist focus on *direct experience* stems from an idealization of its meditative practices. But then many psychoanalysts look upon and are proud of their tradition as a hermeneutics of suspicion, and believe that many Buddhists operate in a hermeneutics of idealization. Where psychoanalysis can contribute to Buddhist practice is perhaps by making it aware of the unconscious dynamics of the student-master relationship. That is, of having the student become conscious of his changing, transference reaction towards the teacher and the spiritual teacher's unconscious counter-transference reactions towards the student. It can make the spiritual master aware of the psychological danger posed by the massive idealization of his students, a danger that increases with one's prominence as a teacher. Negative transferences, negative feelings, and malignant projections are easier to handle, since they cause severe psychic discomfort, compelling us to reject them by discriminating inside between what belongs to us and what other students are projecting onto us. This painful motivation for repelling the invasion of the self by others does not exist when such projections are very narcissistically gratifying, as they are invariably in the case of adoring students. It is difficult not to at least smell the incense smoke being burnt at your altar by many proclaiming your greatness.

In the end, psychoanalysis will doubt that transformation of emotions or their complete elimination as a goal of spiritual practice is not a forever achievement, even in the case of enlightened masters. It remains constantly under threat from the darker forces of the psyche. One is never not human.

Your training analysis was in German... What is left when you are analyzed in a language other than your mother tongue? What do you gain?

When I look back at my training analysis in German, I can only say that my intense need to be "understood" by the analyst, a need I shared with every patient, gave birth to an unconscious force that made me underplay those cultural parts of my self which I believed would be too foreign to my German analyst's experience. In the transference-love, what I sought was closeness to the analyst, including the sharing of *his* culturally shaped interests, attitudes and beliefs. This intense need to be close and to be understood, paradoxically by removing parts of *my* cultural self from the analytic arena of understanding, was epitomized by the fact that I soon started writing short stories and dreaming in German, the language of my analyst, something I have not done before or after my analysis. Later, years after the analysis was over, I also realized that there is a degree of emotional poverty when the analysis is conducted in a language other than the mother tongue, wherein much of one's native culture is encoded. One's mother tongue, the language of one's childhood, is intimately linked with emotionally colored sensory-motor experiences. Psychoanalysis in a language that is not the patient's own is often in danger of leading to "operational thinking," that is, verbal expressions lacking associational links with feelings, symbols and memories. However grammatically correct and rich in its vocabulary, the alien language suffers from emotional poverty, certainly as far as early memories are concerned. The emotional shortcomings of a language acquired later—German in my case—has been dramatically demonstrated by an experiment in which subjects are asked the following question: a train is approaching at high speed. If you can push one individual on the track, stopping the train, it will save the lives of six others standing a little distance down the track. Will you push that individual in front of the train? Asked and answered in the mother tongue, most people show signs of an emotional dilemma and would not push the person to his death. The same question in the acquired language evokes much greater calculated rationality, and the readiness to push one person in order to save the lives of six.

Foucault, who didn't like psychoanalysis, thought that it was a sort of spiritual transformation. What is the place of "the spiritual" in psychoanalysis?

Foucault is right if we reimagine psychoanalysis, not only as a medical treatment but also as a spiritual enterprise, a transforming quest for self-knowledge that extends the range of our compassion and empathy. A successful analysis would then be one that leads to self-understanding and the growth of a wisdom that enriches our life with meaning and motivates us to act beyond our narrow interests. It will not be content with reaching the Freudian ideal of the autonomous individual, but will view it as a stepping stone to the caring individual. Psychoanalysis will then be seen, as I prefer to do, as a modern meditative practice, a two-person (analyst and analysand) "rational" meditation, taking its special place among other introspective methods that stem from the spiritual traditions of the world.

What will be, in your opinion, the future of psychoanalysis?

I believe classical psychoanalysis has a limited future as a method of treatment, although psychotherapies informed by psychoanalysis will continue to attract a person who not only seeks symptom relief, but also their "meaning." Its future will be for all those who seek a deep introspection, especially biographical, into the makings of their psyches.

Psychoanalysis since its foundation has highlighted history. Do you think that now-adays we must pay the same attention to geography?

I believe that in the future, the more important contributions to psychoanalysis that could rejuvenate its current stagnant theoretical/conceptual state, could come from Asia. The *geography* of psychoanalysis will become as important as its *history*. The Asian contributions to psychoanalysis will, first, relativize what are today often regarded as universals. Second, in my reimagining of a future psychoanalysis as a meditative discipline, the Asian contributions will provide impulses from the meditation practices and concepts from the rich spiritual traditions of their societies, without psychoanalysis losing its uniqueness as a quest for psychic truth.

Please tell us something about the kern complex, but in the Asian context: Ganesha, Ajax, etc...

Freud considered the myth of Oedipus as a hegemonic narrative of all cultures at all times, although enough evidence is now available to suggest that its dominance may be limited to some Western cultures at certain periods of their history. In other words, the Oedipus complex, in one variation or another, may well be universal, but it is not equally hegemonic across cultures. The version we have from psychoanalysis and the signal importance paid to this version is singularly Western, not quite as ubiquitous in the imaginations of other peoples. In most folktales around the world, for instance, it is matricide and not parricide that is central to the story and its imaginative power. In India, the hegemonic narrative is that of Devi, the Mother-Goddess in her many forms, and what I have called "Maternal Enthrallment" of the pre-oedipal and oedipal periods. By maternal enthrallment I mean: the wish to get away from the mother together with the dread of separation, the wish to destroy the engulfing mother who also ensures the child's survival, and additionally in the male child, incestuous desire coexisting with the terror inspired by an overwhelming female sexuality. Coming to the triangulation of the oedipal period, for the boy, the father is less a rival than an ally in the encounter with an overpowering maternal-feminine; the son's need for an "oedipal alliance," that is, for the father's firm support, solidarity and emotional availability at a stage of life where the dangers of maternal enthrallment were at their peak, outweigh the oedipal conflict. In the Ganesha complex, the myths have the son sacrifice to the father his own right to sexual activity and generational ascendancy. The son does so in order to deflect the father's envy and his primal fear of annihilation at the father's hands while keeping the bond of love between father and son intact. The Ganesha myth also inverts the psychoanalytically postulated causality between the fantasies of parricide and filicide. It is charged with the fear of filicide rather than the oedipal guilt of parricide. In another of its variations as the Ajase complex, Okonogi has postulated it as the dominant narrative of the male self in Japan. And, in Iran, it is also characteristic of the major Iranian myth of father-son relations, that of Rustam and Sohrab.

Do you find that psychoanalysis, which is so sensitive to personal differences, is less sensitive with cultural ones? What might a "culturally sensitive analyst" be?

He/she recognizes that human beings share universals, but these are much fewer than what many, if not most, analysts believe. The culturally sensitive analyst recognizes that many psychoanalytic propositions on what constitutes psychological maturity, gender-appropriate behaviors, "positive" or "negative" resolutions of developmental conflicts and complexes, that often appear in the garb of universal truths, are actually the incorporation of Western middle-class experience and values into psychoanalytic theory. To give one example: The differentiation of human beings into male and female genders is universal but it is our cultural heritage that further elaborates what it means to be, look, think and behave like a woman or a man. This becomes clearer if one thinks of Greek or Roman sculptures which have greatly influenced Western gender representations. Here, male gods are represented by hard, muscled bodies and chests without any fat. One only needs to compare Greek and Roman statuary with sculpted representations of Hindu gods, or the Buddha, where the bodies are softer, suppler and in their hint of breasts, nearer to the female form. The visually lesser differentiation between male and female representations in Indian Hindu culture is reinforced by an important, widespread form of religiosity, of Vaishnavism, which not only provides a sanction for man's feminine strivings, but raises these to the level of a religious-spiritual quest. It is a culture where a culture-hero like Gandhi can publicly proclaim that he had mentally become a woman, and that there is as much reason for a man to wish that he was born a woman as for women to do likewise, and take for granted that he will strike a responsive chord in his audience. Between a minimum of sexual differentiation that is required to function heterosexually with a modicum of pleasure, and a maximum which cuts off any sense of empathy and emotional contact with the other sex, which is then experienced as a different species altogether, there is a whole range of positions, each occupied by a culture which insists on calling it the only one that is mature and healthy. But I would also add that as someone aspiring to be a culturally sensitive analyst, I am not a cultural relativist but a minimal universalist. Even as I question much of psychoanalytic superstructure, I continue to stand on its foundations and subscribe to its basic assumptions: the importance of the unconscious part of the mind in our thought and actions, the vital significance of early childhood experiences for later life, the importance of Eros in human motivation, the dynamic interplay, including conflict, between the conscious and unconscious parts of the mind, and the vital import of transference and countertransference in the therapist and patient relationship. All the rest is up for grabs and just as we have begun to talk of modernity in the plural, of different modernities, perhaps we will soon be talking of Japanese, French, Chinese, Argentinian and Indian psychoanalyses. Perhaps we need to look at universals not as what is shared but as what we should have in common, not as what **is** but as what is desirable.

What are the links between religion and psychoanalysis?

Since Freud's stern dismissal of religious rituals and belief in God as remnants of infantile mental life, psychoanalysts have prided themselves on their a-religiosity. But we must remember that though Freud dismissed religious beliefs and rituals, he was more circumspect, if not respectful towards the third and, to me, the most important aspect of religion: religious feeling. Although calling the pinnacle of religious feeling, the *unio mystica*, a regression to the primary narcissism of the infant in an "oceanic feeling," at other places Freud regretted having ignored the "rarer and more profound type of religious emotion experienced by mystics and saints." My point is that we need to realize that this so-called religious emotion is not limited to saints and mystics, but is a fundamental need in human beings. It is actually not religious at all and most of us have experienced this emotion in perceptible moments of elation in the presence of nature, the thrill in front of a work of art or hearing a piece of music, ineffable intimacy with a loved one after the sexual embrace when the bodies have separated and are lying together side by side, but are not yet two in their responses. There are many other such moments, minor epiphanies, which escape our conscious awareness since we expect the mystical experience to be the province of mystics and saints, and thus an exception rather than a rule in human life. The siren call of religion lies in the promise and delivery of these moments: in rituals relating to rites of passage, worship at home or at temple, mosque or church, festivals and pilgrimages, mystical practices and so on. It is the religious moments that overcome what the Irish poet William Yeats in his poem *Meru* called the "desolation of reality." They are flashes, that in the words of the English poet John Keats "light up the narrow, mundane world of daily existence, a world which has always been inadequate to our experience and unequal to bear the burden of our hopes." These flashes of light are like musical moments and phrases that suddenly and inexplicably move you without your knowing why. Freud, famously, was immune to these. Religious experience and emotion is more akin to music than to art and literature. I believe we psychoanalysts need to identify with Freud's strengths rather than be constrained by his limitations, whether in relation to music or religious experience. I also wonder whether this deafness to the music of religious experiences (in Christianity, perhaps in the Protestant churches more than in the Catholic ones) is another reason for the crisis in the liberal order in so many countries of the world? It would be a folly to dismiss the religious impulse that is found not only in traditional religions, but in all ideologies and movements that promise the individual the experience of transcending her individual boundaries, the experience of being part of something greater than one's individual existence. Besides the reality and pleasure principles, there is also what I have called a unity-seeking principle, impelled by Eros in its widest sense, which we ignore at our peril of seeking a fuller understanding of the human psyche.

What are the differences, in general terms, between the mind in the East and in the West?

Very generally, there are two versions on the nature of the person and of human experience that are mixed in different proportions in Asian and Western minds. One version, dominating the mind of a modern Western person is also the basic storyline of psychoanalysis, with its roots in the Enlightenment. This version holds that human satisfactions and goals are fundamentally personal and individual. Each of us lives in his or her own subjective world, pursuing personal pleasures and private fantasies, constructing a lifeline which, when his time is over, will vanish. The essential function of society is to preserve the possibility of that personal fulfillment. Society cannot provide anything positive; it cannot add anything essential to individual fulfillment. What it can do is to prevent something negative, the interference with individual satisfactions. The other storyline of the mind, common to many Asian civilizations, is a counter-view which exalts the community *vis-à-vis* the individual. This view stresses that belonging to a community is a fundamental need of a person and asserts that only if a person truly belongs to such a community, naturally and unself-consciously, can she/he enter the living stream and lead a full, creative spontaneous life. Both visions have their dark side. If the shadow side of individualism is an unregenerate pursuit of selfishness and unbridled greed, then the dark side of communitarianism is its exclusivity, intolerance and potential for violence. We need to realize that both visions persist in the psyche, even if one is more dominant at a particular historical time. For instance, in the West, communitarian vision of life has not become outdated, regressive, pathological and so on. In its malevolent form, we encounter it today in the resurgence of nationalist communitarianism in most European countries and racial communitarianism in the United States. In contrast to the modern West, the Eastern view (though I am primarily talking of the Indian view, with which I am most familiar) of the self is not that of a bounded, unique individuality. The Indian person is not a self-contained center of awareness interacting with other, similar such individuals as in the Greek and post-enlightenment European civilizations. Instead, in the dominant image of the culture, the self is *constituted* of relationships. An Indian is not a monad but derives his personal nature interpersonally. All affects, needs and motives are relational and his distresses are disorders of relationships, not only with his human, but also with his natural and cosmic orders. Corresponding to the cultural image of the body in constant exchange with the environment while ceaselessly changing inside, the Indian person, too, thus tends to experience himself as more of a changing being whose personal psychological nature is not constituted of a stable, but a more fluid "sense of identity" that is constantly formed and reformed by his interactions with the environment. The Indian person's boundaries—between self and others, between body and mind—also tend to be less clearly demarcated. As a corollary, it follows that a large part of individual happiness or suffering in the Indian mind would be viewed as the individual's share of the happiness or suffering of his family or community, his salient group in a particular context. In individuals, of course, the individual and relational way of perceiving the self and the world will be mixed in different proportions, though one would expect one or the other to dominate in a particular culture. Let me add that I am not advancing any simplified dichotomy between a Western cultural image of an individual, autonomous self and a relational, transpersonal self of Indian culture. Both visions of human experience are present in all the major cultures, though a particular culture may, over a length of time, highlight and emphasize one at the expense of the other.

You have patients from different countries… What possibilities and limitations do you find in working as an analyst from a different cultural context?

How should a psychoanalyst approach the issue of the cultural difference of his client in his practice? The ideal situation would be that this difference exists only minimally, in the sense that the analyst has obtained a psychoanalytic knowledge of the patient's culture through a long immersion in its daily life and its myths, its folklore and literature, its language and its music, an absorption not through the bones, as in case of his patient, but through the head and the heart. Anything less than this maximalist position has the danger of the analyst succumbing to the lure of cultural stereotyping in dealing with the particularities of the patient's experience. In cross-cultural therapeutic dyads, little knowledge is indeed a dangerous thing, collapsing important differences, assuming sameness when only similarities exist. What the analyst needs is not a detailed knowledge of the patient's culture but a serious questioning and awareness of the assumptions underlying his own, the culture he was born into and the culture in which he has been professionally socialized as a psychoanalyst. In other words, what I am suggesting is that in absence of the possibility of obtaining a deep psychoanalytic knowledge of his patient's culture, the analyst needs to strive for a state of affairs where the patient's feelings of estrangement because of his cultural differences from the analyst are minimized and the patient does not, or only minimally, cuts off the cultural part of the self from the therapeutic situation. This is possible only if the analyst begins to value his own Unknowing, to convey a cultural openness which comes from becoming aware of his culture's fundamental propositions about human nature, human experience, the fulfilled human life, and then to acknowledge their relativity by seeing them as cultural products, embedded in a particular place and time.

He needs to become sensitive to the hidden existence of what Heinz Kohut called the "health and maturity moralities" of his particular analytical school. Given that ethnocentrism, the tendency to view alien cultures in terms of our own, and unresolved cultural chauvinism, are the patrimony of all human beings, including that of psychoanalysts, the acquisition of cultural openness is not an easy task. Cultural biases can lurk in the most unlikely places.

Do you think that middle-class Western patients' minds shape psychoanalytical theories?

Yes, overwhelmingly so. Most of our knowledge on how human beings feel, think, act, is derived from a small subset of the human population which the psychologist Joseph Heinrich calls WEIRD, the acronym standing for Western, Educated, Industrialized, Rich and Democratic. Psychologists, sociologists, psychotherapists and philosophers are as WEIRD as the subjects of their studies, ministrations or speculations. It is this small group of statistical outliers, overwhelmingly Western, urban and middle-class that provides us with both the producers and subjects of our contemporary psychoanalytic knowledge, which we have then blithely proceeded to generalize to the rest of humankind. Shared by analyst and patient alike, pervading the analytic space in which the two are functioning, fundamental ideas about human relationships, family, marriage, male and female and so on which are essentially Western in origin often remain unexamined and are regarded as universally valid. As has been said, if a fish was a scientist, the last discovery it would make would be of water.

You are on both sides, even with your clothes... it's difficult to find someone who combines a Western education in an Eastern mind. What about the future of psychoanalysis, seen from your point of view in the East?

I think that psychoanalysis in the West or in the East will have to leave the medical model completely. Its future is a very modern meditation, of two people together, a joint meditation. Problems disappear by doing meditation, but that's not the most important part. Healing neurosis as a byproduct of the meditation, but a meditation with words also, different from a mystic one.

Chapter 14

Anish Kapoor, the amateur foreigner

When he received me in a sitting room in London's triangular block, where his sculptures come alive, I had already walked around the exterior of the place. I had seen the small army of collaborators dressed in white coveralls and masks, who looked like they worked in a painting factory rather than the studio of one of the world's most brilliant sculptors. And I had also seen a Mercedes Benz SUV enter, with one of the headlights broken and a screen for children facing the back seat, driven by the alchemist of sorts who had imagined this place.

I waited for him in an office with pale oak floors and white walls covered with books, miniatures of his works, and sketches for future exhibitions, with London's cloud-covered sky beyond the large windows. Anish, thin, with his hair much shorter and less dense than it usually appears in images of him, is simply and smartly dressed except for one detail: he wears red leather sneakers, spattered with paint. Only his shoes reveal that I am sitting in front of an artist in his studio, and not a retired professor or an architect or a star designer. As always, God is in the details.

The appointment that he had proposed—I later realized—was set to last 45 minutes. It isn't much if I compare it to the four hours that other interviews had occupied, or the two hours that they tend to last on average. Afterward, I comprehended that he had allotted me the same amount of time as a session of analysis. On my part, I was willing to make it worthwhile. And Anish, with the English of a British gentleman and the stamp of a foreigner, offered me an alibi, the *bocatto di cardenale* that every analyst awaits, a slip.

This may be why we took more time than had been scheduled. We spoke until a call came from his wife, with whom the artist has recently had a son, and he spoke with infinite sweetness before bidding me farewell with a hug.

Have you ever been interviewed by an analyst... outside the consulting room, I mean?

I can tell you that Julia Kristeva and I did quite a long thing together. We were in long association, over many, many years. And then, of course, I've had this very long conversation with psychoanalysis myself of, God knows, thirty... forty years or something. Yes, I did thirty years of psychoanalysis.

DOI: 10.4324/9781032708591-14

With different analysts?

With different analysts, yes. Really good for the most part. One was a very, very difficult period, with an analyst with whom I did not connect. I stuck with it for too long. Other than that, on the whole, I feel somehow that psychoanalytic process and the process that we go through as artists in the studio are very closely related. I take it that what one is doing in a psychoanalytic exploration is looking to the parts of one's self that one either does not know, or does not know so well. And of course, associated with it has to be the myth-making parts of one's self. The stories one tells oneself as if they are real that may not be. We all do this in different ways. And of course, the process is that the real world—you lie there on the couch—the real world has its real effects. And one throws them in the air, cries with them, does whatever one has to do with them. But before long, they're in the room as an event. Variously named by various analysts, but they're there as an event. And that's what the work is. The work is then to work with this event. It's exactly what an artist does. What have I got to say as an artist? I've no interest. *In itself*, it's of no interest. What I know, what I think about the world... Ah, that's all commentary, that's not what art is. And it is, therefore, this quest for something that I don't know, I can't name, I can't quite give a vision to, and it's that struggle... to deposit something. With young artists, people who come and work at the studio, I find myself saying to them all the time, "Don't think, just do it." And then there's this beautiful phrase that says, "first idea, best idea." Go with it! It doesn't really matter what the idea is. The work of being an artist is obviously *after* that first stage. How does it become a work? It's a problem. The question then is, how do you solve it? Can you solve it? Can you leave it unsolved? Is it enough to deposit the matter and not necessarily solve the problem? I think that can have huge emotional content. And one often does ask, where does it come from? And to go on to one more part of that, in a world full of objects—you know, I'm a sculptor principally—why make another object? One does have to ask oneself, why bother? My answer to that is that in a world full of objects, there are very few that maintain mystery... psychic mystery, physical mystery... It's very hard to name themes that are truly mysterious. However, in a psychic world, there are lots of mysterious things. So how can we not translate them? That's one question. And is it that, in the attempt to make an object, it's sufficient to somehow come to the mysterious object, the object that has the same questions that we would ask psychically? Meaning that I don't know the answer. I think there's profound truth in that. Some way, there, there's something deeply meaningful, however. Mysterious. Because it must go to the core of our being.

And are you still in analysis?

No. It took me two years to feel that I could stop analysis, with a lot of pain, a lot of difficulty. But last summer, I decided that the right thing to do was to end it. So it's the end!

Did the consulting room work as a sort of laboratory for your artistic work, or do your analytical process and your working process follow different paths?

I put it to myself in different terms. I was born in India. My father was in the navy, and we as a family moved from house to house. So home was a weird contingent thing; we didn't have one house where the family grew up.

You're used to being a foreigner.

Yes. And my mother is Jewish. So we've followed that. Exactly right, an outsider in some way. I still find that very painful and very difficult.

To be an outsider?

Yeah, but I'm an outsider, I know it. You know, I came to the UK in the early seventies. And even though I hold a British passport, I've never actually been able to accept that I'm British. I'm a foreigner. I'm an Indian who lives here, or a Jewish Indian who lives here, whatever you like. So this struggle for home has been a really kind of complicated, complex, personal quest. The consulting room is, in a way, a psychic home, at one level. Quite literally, the couch is, if you like—do I dare? Yeah, I dare—*momma*, at one level, *what do I need*. I really don't feel my experience is that foreign from a lot of people's experience. That there is, if you like, a constructed dynamic in the consulting room that happens… that plays directly with the inner psychic space. In a way, it is a mirror—I know this is one of your interests—but, of course, it is the mirror image, or comes to be. It isn't that it is, it *comes* to *be* the mirror image of the deep, or one of the kinds of deeper process that is going on there. So I'll give you a full example. My brother and I left India in nineteen seventy. I was like sixteen and a half years old, way too early to leave home, at least for *me, and* for my brother, who is eighteen months younger than me. So we went to Israel. Anyway, I had a terrible crisis. We had family in Israel, my aunt, who was always a bit shamanistic. My mother came to visit after too many months, and it was a difficult time, I was really going through hell. She came to visit and my aunt, in her shamanistic way, said, "No, what you have to do is… you have to go to India, bring some earth from India, and you have to put it under Anish's bed." So, my mother went to India, went back, came back the next time, brought this earth…

Mother earth.

Yes, and put it under my bed. So deep ritual matter, you know. In my work since then, I have discovered that there are two real ritual matters: one is earth, the other is blood. Those are the real ritual matters, the rest… We'll talk about that later maybe. So in a very kind of literal sense, the earth was under the bed in my psychoanalyst's room. It's a very powerful sense of why… After all, why is one an artist, what is there to do, if not to enact some primal ritual matter? And this ritual is deeply mysterious. Why does it have to be like that? And actually, weirdly, it's as if it's alchemical, I guess. It's as if something happens to matter. So I once had a conversation with a physicist, Jacob Burb, who works with nanoparticles, tiny particles. I said to him, in the process—because what we know about tiny particles is that they can't be observed objectively, that they respond to the eye of the viewer, that the particle can be in two places at one time, depending on how you look at them—I said to this guy, is the particle different in art than it is in ordinary life?

It depends on the viewers...

At one level, yes, but if we're talking about physics, about the particle itself, is it different? Meaning, has it gone through some transformation in its process when it is art different than when it is not art? In the end, perhaps it's all fiction, and fiction reveals greater truth than does so-called reality. But the point is that it's a fiction that seems to work, and that is the weight of it, really.

So in a way you work building fictions, effective fictions.

Effective is important. Yes. Effective fictions. I'll take that. The question there is, is my fiction your fiction? What I mean is that a fiction may come out of my psychic life, my undiscovered or half-discovered, half-known psychic life. Does it speak to *your* fictional psychic life? And what we seem to say is that almost irrespective of culture—I don't want to go into a union kind of take on this—but we seem to share psychic fictions of so many kinds. And that is something that at one level is joyous, of course; it gives us a sense of identity or can, with our fellow women and men. That's perhaps partly why artists do what they do.

I agree. You know that I don't like applied psychoanalysis, the work that psychoanalysts used to do with artists or artists' work. But I found that what you do with your work is beautifully applied psychoanalysis, because you manage to figure things which are very difficult for us to explain or to build in a way, like the object, the non-object, the mysterious object. All of the things that you manage to make carry something... it's very difficult to represent an object, and you manage to do something with that.

I don't know what to say to this, other than it is, of course, what I'm after. And one has to be in this endeavor... fearless. Fearless means what? Fearless simply means don't stop yourself. If you have to go there, just as one does, if you like, in psychoanalysis, after a while. It takes quite a long time, I believe you can't do it in the short term. But after a while, who cares? Say whatever, let it happen, let it be free, open it. Let it go wherever it goes. It doesn't really matter. Can one do that as an artist? You know, if it's to be sexual, let it be deeply sexual. Don't be afraid of it. If it's to be terrifying, then let it be truly terrifying. That's very, very hard to do. I've got a lovely story about that. In nineteen thirty-four, Picasso did a show at the Museum in Zurich. Of course the art world, the small art world that there was in those days, thought it was wonderful. But then Carl Gustav Jung did a review of the show, and he wrote about it, and you know, we may agree or disagree with him, but he's not a fool. He wrote about it, and what he said was, "marvelous, interesting, but Picasso is a schizophrenic and it's very hard for us to read this other than in terms of a malady." John Richardson, a great art historian, then makes a commentary in which he says: "Jung doesn't understand the aesthetic language and sees it all as horrific and terrible, and schizophrenic. In fact, if we think of Picasso as a shaman, then we see that Picasso is performing a shamanistic act in order to fight evil with evil, because there's no other way." So powerful! And I think this is the key question. Does one have the guts, the fearlessness to let it be a shamanistic act? Not anyone can be a shaman.

So, nowadays, true artists are the shamans?

I don't know, we always have been. Marcel Duchamp once said: "the artist is a mediumistic being who draws things from the cosmos and puts them in front of us, but that is not enough. It is only the viewer who comes and completes the circle." That's why John Richardson is so brilliant, because he recognizes that the process needs this completion, that evil can only be fought with evil. That when you look at those grotesque images, it's not enough.

Perhaps all of us are foreigners in a way. The unconscious makes us foreigners in a way. But being a shaman as an artist condemns you to be a foreigner, indeed more of a foreigner than others, could that be? A professional foreigner?

Oh, maybe an *amateur* foreigner, because one does not want to be a professional! But I understand. I have to say yes. One doesn't want to somehow either romanticize or exoticize this so-called foreign status. But one does have to recognize that it's actually probably true. But the problems today are quite severe and they are political, sadly. In today's art world everything is for fucking sale and everything is buyable now, like this (snaps his fingers). And that brings with it huge problems. How, then, can one maintain the sanctity of—forgive me for using this word all the time—of the shamanistic process? And it is sanctity that's required for it. It's a public act in a way, but it has to come from that deeply melancholic reflection.

Why?

Let's just think about this for a minute. What do I know? What does the shaman do, in some mythic place? Well, he or she performs an act of possession. I think there's no way that that is joyous. That is deeply melancholic. I suppose it's falling into oneself, falling, truly, into a space of unknowing. How else can it work? And any unknowing is tragic. Can one be joyous and unknowing? Only if one can maintain innocence… Can one maintain innocence as you get older? Very hard. Look, it's all fiction. That's the point of it really.

What do you think or how do you feel about the fact that the objects you invent are sold for a lot of money?

These are the problems. This is what I was trying to say. The only way one can deal with that is to accept that it's all fiction. All of it.

Money is also fiction.

Exactly. If money is fiction, too, then it's really the only way to deal with it. Money and art have always sat next to each other like this. So we are not to be embarrassed about it, on one level. Of course capitalism is really problematic, because it is anti-utopian—fundamentally—which means that those little bits of utopia that we think we can catch in buying an art work and so on, it's as if what they do is... to commodify, that's the problem, they commodify fiction. And from the artist's perspective, the only way to deal with it is to think that money is another *perfection*... eh... fiction! Money is another fiction!

A perfect fiction!

I'll take the slip! And so, when you see a Picasso on the wall that's worth fifty million or a hundred and fifty million dollars, whatever the number is, in a way, what you are looking at is the commodity, the money, the fiction of the price *and*, hopefully, the discomfort of the work. That's why I think Picasso is great, they are worth a lot of money and they remain uncomfortable. They never stop saying fuck you, in other words.

Also the work produces some discomfort in the owner, in the viewer.

In the viewer. That's what I'm talking about. I'm saying that even though it is worth a lot of money, it produces discomfort. And *that*, I think, is a bridging of this problem of money. Not all work does that. Some works just go in the opposite direction.

Which ones?

Fictionally, *La Mona Lisa* does not make you uncomfortable. Its discomfort is its mystery. What is the mystery? Is there a smile? Why is she smiling? Is that a smile or not a smile? We don't know. Mystery is the other way of overcoming the fiction of money.

Anish, do you remember the distinction that Freud made after Leonardo, distinguishing the arts per via di porre, per via di levare?

No, I've never read it. Go on, tell me what Freud said.

Freud said that Leonardo said there are two types of visual arts. Per via di porre *are arts that add something, like painting; and* per via di levare *are arts, like sculpture, which carve out and make something appear. You are a sculptor, but a special kind of sculptor. What do you think about this distinction? I want to know about the way you think about your work.*

Yeah, of course. The additive and the reductive, as processes. I have read this before, actually. So one might think about this in two different ways. One might say that there are two sorts of objects: mind-born objects, and body-born objects, and that they are different things. Personally, I'm interested in the confusion. Let me try to explain. I make quite a lot of things that are very geometric, that are almost—you could say—completely mind-born... Geometry, after all, is a tangible, knowable science. That's the problem. The truth is, however, that when a geometric object becomes so pure and clear, and it's taken to its essential geometric conclusions, the weird thing about it is that it's deeply mysterious. So it's apparently a mind-born object, but when you take it to that end degree, and push it, something happens to it, it becomes mysterious. It causes a kind of problem with your body. That's why it's mysterious. Of course, I'm thinking of a certain kind of mirrored objects that I've made over the years. So, if you like, mind-body confusion, understanding-not understanding confusion, is one way of thinking about this problem of the visceral. Where does the object live? In making objects today, as always, you can add material or take material away. I don't feel that's the problem any longer. That's not really the problem.

What is the problem nowadays... the contemporary one?

It's very hard to talk about this, really. As I've tried to say up to now, the problem is not what I know how to do. The problem is what I don't know how to do. Therefore, if I'm working, let's say—and I do work—in a piece of stone, do I need to know what I'm going to do before I start working a piece of stone? The answer is... well, *some* of the answer is that I sense that I know a little bit, but really I'm going to let it happen and I'm going to keep working at it, keep going with it, until something can form itself. Now, that's very hard to do with a piece of stone, because it requires pre-knowledge. It almost says "see me." So somehow, one has to kind of balance *see me-don't see me*. That's probably true of all materials. Stone just makes it very obvious. I expect that that's what Leonardo was talking about, really: the object that's revealed from within, opened up, taken out. But is that—you know, post Freud—is that really where we want to go? I feel we need to kind of confront one's self, and therefore the viewer, with the completely unexpected. And what is that? And you can't do it all the time. Sometimes, occasionally, there's the "ah, what?" Where does that come from?

Only very few times do you discover something. Sort of like epiphanies...

Precisely. So one just has to be open to them. You don't sit and plan, ok this is the work I'm going to make. It's the practice that reveals. Just as in psychoanalysis, it's the practice that reveals.

Without the practice, this long practice, you don't have these tiny moments.

Precisely. These moments of insight. Yes. So in that sense, a shaman is not a part-time practitioner. A shaman is a shaman always, every day, every minute. That's hard, but it's also, I would say, it's exactly like being a psychoanalyst. You know… you can't switch off. I don't see us as being that different from each other.

One more thing that you talked about… blood and earth. I know that red and black are very important to you. Please tell me something about that…

There's a wonderful anthropologist called Chris Knight, and he wrote a book called *Blood Relations* in which he proposes the idea that culture originates with women, not with men. I try to take it one step further, and I'll tell you how. So the idea is that women menstruate, and they have an act of blood. But when women are together, they menstruate together, all women. So when you live in a small tribe or in a small group menstruation happens together, and it comes to be a social act of bonding amongst women. And he extends that, through all kinds of evidence, to say that the bond, of course, has to be with the earth, because the earth also bleeds in the form of red ochre, and that women might have covered their bodies in red ochre as an act of solidarity, and that the first act of culture must have been musical dance that comes out of this act of solidarity. So it's deeply political, it's kind of Marxist political, I feel that's very strong, but it also psychically feels right. Of course, what that does is leave the men out. It seems to me that what that does is to speak of blood as a kind of primal ritual matter. It has to say that what it does is to gather together. Where does this blood come from? Where does it go? It's a natural extension that all of the objects of blood are horizontal, but this is the speculation that I put on it, that all of the objects of blood are horizontal. That, if you like, the goddess of the earth bleeds and the women of the earth bleed to give red ochre. So there are all these acts of horizontality. It's only later in culture that we turn horizontal to vertical, and god becomes blue. All gods, they're all blue. They become blue and vertical and they live in the sky and they never die, and they have no blood. And it's a very curious kind of turning, of the horizontal into the vertical, and a kind of—I'm going to say—an alienation of the god-self. Because the god-self, when she was in the ground, was somehow palpable, there. In the sky, we lost ourselves in some male vision of a never-ending, never-dying, alien, foreign, outside being. So sky, in that sense, is not ritual matter. Blue is not ritual, red is, and black is of the earth. But it has a whole translation that's very clear. I'm putting these things together theoretically, after the fact, so it's not how I… I am Indian, and one of the great things in Indian culture is, and it's kind of unspoken, but it's the idea of the auto-generated, the self-born, the self-made. Nobody made it, it's just there, it was always there. Psychically, of course, that is speaking of the self-evident fact. The fact that… it's there. What's the question? It almost always comes from the earth. This idea of the preexisting psychic condition is utterly fascinating to me. Everything is fiction, as we know. So, what comes before all objects of the world that are art is the objects that were there which are not made, the auto-generated, the pre-existing. Psychically, of course, or let's say the other way around, in material world terms, it's much harder to understand as an idea, because it's full of subtlety. The fact that somehow, whether it's the mother goddess or whether it's Venus or Gilgamesh, it's revealing the endless journey into the night. It does speak of pre-existing conditions that I feel are magical and superpowerful.

My last question... Is there an image from your origin that runs through all your work?

Yes, there is one. It's a cave. But it's not the Elephant, and not even from my origin. It's an image by Mantegna, the great renaissance artist. It's an image of Christ, it's called *Christ's Descent into Limbo*. Christ is standing at the mouth of a cave, and from this cave there's all this kind of darkness emerging, and he has a stick in his hand, and he is about to descend into limbo. Of course, limbo is the classic image of the unconscious, Dante's kind of in-between state. It's something I've come back to again and again and again... this idea of the hero with a stick, meaning even the hero needs a guide, the hero can't go alone into the darkness. Even Christ can't go alone into the darkness. So this thing of the fragile human being who nonetheless can be... who can make this descent. The idea of the dark, unknown-known, or the unknowable known.

Chapter 15

Julia Kristeva, the foreigner

That is how Roland Barthes referred to the young, beautiful, and intelligent young woman who had arrived in Paris just before May of 1968. She was coming from behind the iron curtain, something which—adding even more *glamour* to her legendary figure—recently garnered her an accusation of having been a spy.

However, she is actually a brilliant intellectual, semiologist, author of some twenty books, and a psychoanalyst, one of the only two interviewees in this series of conversations who is a practitioner of the profession, in addition to having undergone analysis. On the other hand, she is a mild-mannered feminist and a great thinker regarding alterity.

She is also a person who cultivates matrimony as one of the fine arts. She has been married to cult writer Philippe Sollers since she first arrived in France, and she received me at her home facing the Jardin de Luxembourg in early Spring, where we conversed primarily in French about femininity, foreignness, maternity, and poetics, among many other things.

Why do you say that you "travel yourself"?

As you may have noticed, there is an error in the title to my book, because in French, you do not say "I travel myself." You say "I rebel myself," "I liberate myself"; but you say "I travel." I comment on this explicit defect to demonstrate that it is a voyage with myself into my inner self. And why? In the first place, to advise the reader that I am a foreigner and that I employ French as a foreign language, so that he or she is able to look for the foreignness within themselves. The second point, why do "I travel myself"? I was born at a time when the world was boiling over: on June 24th, 1941; on June 22nd, Nazi Germany had attacked the Soviet Union. I spent my childhood in Bulgaria, a country occupied by those Germans who then became Communist; a region of the world where traveling was not possible. Traveling was absolute freedom. My father, who was a believer, taught me that one had to learn foreign languages. He would say: "You have to leave this intestine of Hell." That is what he called Bulgaria, asserting that it was in the Bible. But I think he invented it. He would affirm: "You have to leave Hell and there is only one solution: to learn foreign languages." So first it was Russian, and then French

DOI: 10.4324/9781032708591-15

and English. In my head, I already traveled myself. I went along constructing myself with many spaces, languages and cultures. Then, I received a scholarship from the French government to do my thesis in Paris.

Did Roland Barthes used to call you "the foreigner"?

Yes, he would call me "the foreigner." He received me in his seminar and I began to do thesis work. At the same time, I came to know of Tel Quel, the magazine run by Philippe Sollers; in addition, I used to write back and forth with a young woman (because young people pay attention to foreigners) who introduced me to Aragon, who said to me: "A thesis on the birth of the novel needs to be done." With my thesis and my translations of Bakhtin, my contribution was post-structuralist, because it meant traveling between many structures and seeing the text and the context, the structure and the history. I was already in France while carrying out this work, as part of my universitary period, contributing with something new. I felt that the only way to keep a culture alive was in that aperture and that foreignness.

As a foreigner, how did you wind up in a discipline like psychoanalysis? Although it is, in some way, a discipline of foreigners, in addition to being foreign as a discipline.

In Bulgaria, psychoanalysis was not discussed because it was a decadent, bourgeois science... My father had a book on psychoanalysis, by Freud, in Cyrillic. But he would never show it, I didn't even know that we had it. We used to have an enormous reading room, and he had put it on the last shelf, alongside Dostoyevsky, who was prohibited... So when I reached France, I know that Freud existed, but I hadn't studied psychoanalysis and had absolutely no idea what it was about. It was Philippe who sent me to Lacan's seminar: I didn't understand a thing. We had to travel with him to China. We were the first Western delegation to travel to the country, the group Tel Quel, in 1974, and Lacan was supposed to accompany us, but in the end he didn't, due to some issue with the person he was going to go with and...

His "secretary"...

His secretary, let's say. His companion had offended him, she had been with another man, and Lacan felt very humiliated, and so we witnessed the turbulence between Lacan and that girlfriend, the result of which was that he didn't go to China. So it is understandable why I didn't undergo analysis with Lacan: because I saw him in that situation, which was very humiliating for him, and I didn't want to do his analysis, I wanted to do mine. I was very disappointed by what I saw in China. When I came back, I gave up Chinese and politics, because I was asking myself where all the hope of May '68 was, in a culture with a different history, with calligraphy, Chinese writing, the implication of the body, women's role in Taoism, etc. And I said to myself that however long I may live I wouldn't be able to do anything to change the world. And at the same time, I was fascinated. I felt fascination for the relationship between Chinese mothers and their children. I told myself: "I have to turn myself into a mother and dedicate myself to individuals, to people. And the only thing there is is psychoanalysis."

After that trip, you decided to become an analyst...

Exactly. And when I returned from that trip I went to see Lacan and I said: "We know each other too well, you can't be my analyst—I didn't mention that he had disappointed me—who do you recommend?" And he spoke to me about the man who was with his lover. My response then was: "I'm not going to enter into that harem." And I told Ivan Fonagy, a linguist in exile from the East, about the story with Lacan and he said: "You should go to the classical Freudians," and he referred me to a German woman who went on to become my analyst.

What did undergoing analysis mean in those days? What was your life like with that experience, with analysis as an experience?

This is what happened... I saw the limits of politics as an answer to human malaise. I have the impression that the whole mutation that we are living through today, with Internet and globalization, makes something that has still remained sensitive after '68 explode. We live in a world generated by what Hannah Arendt calls secularization, where ties with religious tradition are cut off. Neither God nor master. We have created a humanist and secularized democracy. And this system, which was formidable for me, because it is much better than totalitarianism, ceased to be the solution. We don't know which political action must be taken. But it has seemed to me, both reading Freud and on the couch, that an individual's malaise can be accompanied, improved or transformed, and psychoanalysis has shown itself to me as the only possible commitment. First, in order to live in this world and to help others, but also and above all, for my own self. That's what I said when the analyst I consulted asked me: "Why do you undergo analysis?" I answered that, in the first place, in order to leave abstract language. I spoke French very well when I arrived, but writing in it... I would write in concepts, in theories, and I wanted to get away from that abstraction and come closer to drives, the unconscious and psychic alchemy. And she asked me: "How are you with regard to your...?" because I had spoken to her about my father, and the matter of getting out of the intestine, and she asked: "And your mother?." I said that I had the impression that my relationship with my mother had been like a balloon touching marble: bouncing away. That I strongly yearned to be reunited with my mother and to become a mother. Psychoanalytical practice has allowed me to come to terms with my desire for maternity. I wasn't like those little girls who play with dolls and want to be mothers, I was very good at math, I was learning French and English, I was an erudite woman, and with psychoanalysis, I had that transformation as well. And then David was born in 1975, and I wrote books that bear the mark of psychoanalysis.

It's while you were in analysis that you've discovered that you wanted to be a mother and also to become an analyst.

Exactly. I wanted to write, and also to become a mother and an analyst, to make that analytical experience a profession, to have a commitment that was neither political nor religious, and not to simply dedicate myself to writing. I wanted to have a different kind of writing, but I didn't see myself alone with my book and in the library. I wanted to have a human relationship.

In your opinion, what is the value of analytical experience?

It's very individual. I think that now, in this globalized world, we are reaching another paradox. Everything is increasingly global, generalized and common. People think in clichés, everyone dresses the same way, the same brands for everybody. This on the one hand. And on the other, every person is engrossed in themselves: there is that singularity that can give rise to narcissism, but I also see it from a very positive point of view. Human creativity is singular, and that is the goal of the analysis: to give each person their singularity. That's why I cannot give a global response to what the value of psychoanalysis is today. I believe that it is centered on each person's singularity, it awakens it and stimulates it, so that each one has some way to resist banalization. Psychoanalysis offers the possibility of making people emerge from banality, granting them their singularity. Each session is a poetics and each person is a poem. There is no experience that can be compared to another, and that is what I attempt to do. Evidently, there are a lot of clichés and banal things, but until the thing that is incomparable in each person is found, no analysis is being done.

You have said that literature and psychoanalysis are the same thing...

They are quite similar to one another. At the moment when I begin an analysis, I do the work of listening to the singularity of each story, every free association; each person tells their own novel and on the couch, every person becomes a writer. We very well know that when analysands are unable to put together an account, it is because they are defending themselves, and when they manage to reconstruct their family history, the analysis is more fertile. Narrative ability is important for the evolution of analysis, but there are also differences. Psychoanalytical ethics are not attuned to a beautiful narrative. Psychoanalysis is an exercise in singularity and it is solitary. There, too, there is a difference. Not only do we have an ethical stance that permits us to keep our distance from the narrative, we also remain in solitude.

Do you tend to think of psychoanalysis more as a science, or more as an art?

Neither one nor the other. It is a unique experience because it has something of art, precisely the story, the ability to narrate, to utilize language in different registers. When I listen to a patient, the communication doesn't pass through the subject, verb, predicate and the story alone, but also through all the pre-verbal signs— codified emotions—intonations, rhythm, which refer to...

To music...

Exactly. Lacan speaks about a broken tongue. The tongue breaks like a piece of bread. The broken tongue. The scars of language in the embrace, in the tongue that trembles, in lapsus, in inventing a word or making a gesture on the couch in analysis, all this is of a semiotic order, not a symbolic one, and it refers, precisely, to meaning and not to signification. In psychoanalysis, all these dimensions in language are heard. Upon hearing them, then, one is submerged in a musicality of language that is an art of some kind, if you like, but at the same time, the dimension that Freud denominated science is there, which requires exactitude; although as I see it, he has created a human science. It is an ethics that is suspended, put between parenthesis, that glides above every science, and is not guided by a concern for curing; no one is going to be cured. Freud has said three things to give us points of reference: "Where 'it' was, 'I' should come about": there is a malaise, I want to cure someone of that malaise, but I want to allow them to make their voyage to the sources, and then we will swim together in order to leave. Accordingly, that is where we will intervene, in the transference. I will swim with the patient, I will return with him, we will leave together. That is the interdependence ethics. And two other principles: the pleasure principle and the reality principle. In pleasure, there is no need to give way, what is needed is to search for it. One is here for their happiness. The analyst attempts to comprehend the most archaic, the most forgotten and the most repressed sources, those most dissociated from pleasure and desire, in order to restore them. They have the right. Lacan said: "Not to give way in desire," but that is an invitation to perversion. On the other hand, the reality principle returns the other to the rules and their own manner of acting in response to prohibitions: to recompose them, reject them, but never to deny them. This whole system is extremely complex, but there we can contribute the human spirit, in a world that Freud described as being extremely anguished in his final texts. Society will become increasingly more acculturated and increasingly restrictive, we can see that already. The belief is that with globalization, everything is allowed, but everything is allowed in the sense of Dostoevsky, that is, murder, violence. This permission is also extremely limiting. Society must not be counted on in order to grant freedom. Society is there to develop the technology, which may or may not help, but in a certain magnitude, it leads to robotization, to a sort of transhumanism. These are things that we cannot avoid. Psychoanalysis is there to permit the speaking animal to renew themselves and to conserve their singularity, which is their freedom, contained within this system which will be increasingly restrictive due to being increasingly technical.

What do you foresee for the future of psychoanalysis?

It is on a complicated path, because there are many difficulties: psychoanalysis is rejected by public authorities, ignorance and disregard. It is no longer fashionable, it isn't a good era for psychoanalysis. At the same time, I see that people are lost, they don't believe in anything or anyone. For now, the analytical pact is the only answer we give in response to the need to believe. I think the objective of analysis is the possibility to create connections. So, then, if we have that ability to create connections, with psychoanalysis we also have the ability to undo them, and to conserve freedom.

I would like to ask you something else. What did Lacan do when you decided to take your own path rather than the one he had indicated? What happened then?

I criticized Lacan, but he was fascinated by what I had done, he had invited me to present my work in his seminar. I've considered going, but I was distressed, I was a young mother, and I told him: "I can't go." He invited me to lunch. At that time there was already tension within his school, which would subsequently be dissolved. And he said to me: "Look, you aren't meant for schools."

A foreigner!

Exactly! Make your own way! There is something to that. I believe that we are ephemeral, but I think that psychoanalysis is true. Of all the discourses that exist today, the only one that speaks about the transformability of the psychic apparatus, about the survival of the individual, of the person, is psychoanalysis.

Is it easier for a woman to be a foreigner?

Your destiny is to be a foreigner. But you shouldn't live with it as if it were a curse, but as an opportunity, because it provides the maturity of having gone through stages like these, saving them for yourself, and at the same time, to be able to make the most of them. When, with the help of psychoanalysis, you manage to overcome those stages, if you manage to navigate through all that, you reach a maturity that you men do not have.

Does a sort of affinity exist between the feminine position and the analytical position?

Exactly. In the final years, Freud accentuated women's bisexuality and looked for the feminine in the man in order to rehabilitate it. In a debate with Marie Bonaparte, he said: "But what does a woman want?." Freud inscribes the feminine within the larger ethical questions of the future of civilization. Is Mr. Freud's symptom that he was asking what was feminine in himself? Is it that it is women that he doesn't manage to analyze? What is it that they want? Or is it a wager, in order to discover an answer to civilization's malaise in the feminine side?

A wager?

As if it were about seeing (about to be discovered), perhaps, his daughter Anna's homosexuality. It isn't known whether or not Anna Freud had truly lesbian relations, but at any rate, on a psychic level, women fascinated her. Could it be that this is also what he was asking himself? He was constructing, and transforming, his idea of sexuality, which he now considered bisexual, and perhaps he was thinking about how he might give free rein to desire that is complex and transformational at the same time, as happens in women. But when he tells himself that women are transformative, I say it, and some people may say: "You want to say that women adapt." No, that isn't what I want to say, but instead that they appear to adapt, but don't believe in it, they continue to be foreigners.

They don't adapt...

Right. They look to go one step further, they think that everything is an illusion, but they will take one more step, and this implies the greatest of commitments. An enormous number of women exist who, by virtue of wanting to believe in someone, of wanting to reach the phallus, the father, become sanctimonious. But at the same time, there are the great rebels, the great mystics, the great revolutionaries. Women are very sensitive to the death drive that fuels humanity.

Are you an optimist?

I am an energetic pessimist. I believe that the death drive forms part of Eros. I read a lot as a child, I wanted to be an astronomer. I continue to read now. Among the large theories is that of the cosmos, that of the Big Crunch; everything is going to be destroyed, everything advances further and further toward expansion. It is Eros that dominates.

Chapter 16

Hanif Kureishi, the indigenous Londoner

I spent a long time trying to get in touch with Kureishi. When at long last, after countless obstacles and setbacks and having been subjected to an interrogation worthy of some greater cause, I obtained his approval, I traveled to London immediately. I was already there and had not yet received the coordinates of where we would meet, as if it were a rendezvous between spies, but that same day, a couple of hours beforehand, an address in West London appeared in my e-mail.

As soon as I arrived at the three-story Victorian house where the British writer of Pakistani origin received me, I knew that I was going to feel comfortable during the encounter. We spoke there for a couple of hours in English, drinking tea under the watchful eyes of a photograph of Kafka. He said that part of his professional trade was giving interviews—even though I knew that they left him exhausted, because always being asked the same questions he was obliged to give the same answers—and that he had at least one a week. However, that if he had accepted my request this time, it was because I was a psychoanalyst.

The same reason why others had rejected my proposal was, in Kureishi's case, the reason for accepting it. Anyone who has experienced the delicious novels and essays by this olive-complexioned, compact, and muscular writer knows that he has close contact with psychoanalysis. This is true to the extent that even today, he gets on his bike and rides to see his psychoanalyst twice a week, and he maintains that it is, as he says, the best conversation in his life.

Are you still in analysis?

Yeah.

Do you enjoy it?

That's why I go. I've seen my analyst last night. Yeah, twice a week I go. Twice a week, for twenty-three years. I've only just started…

With the same analyst?

Yes, I was thinking the other day, well, I am paying to listen to him speak. When he speaks, he is a very interesting man. I enjoy talking to him. I can talk to him

DOI: 10.4324/9781032708591-16

about my dreams, my mother… but I can also talk to him about Kafka, about Dostoievsky, I can think about that. So it's the best conversation in my life. That's why I go. I can't say that I am particularly crazy and need to be fixed.

When someone reads you, Hanif, there's a permeability to the unconscious. I have the sensation, when I read your work, that you are in analysis…

Shall I start at the beginning? I will say that at university, I read philosophy and I was always interested in the history of ideas. One of my lecturers was a professor who had been in analysis with Melanie Klein, and he began to talk to us about Freud, about the unconscious. And I began to use, very early on in my writing, a method of free association which I call *free writing,* which you might say is a Freudian equivalent of free association. And I use that in the morning when I sit down to do my daily pages. So you write down your dreams, you write down your associations, you write down something your mother said when you were 4 years old, blah blah blah. And I found that the best way to create material for writing was to use this method of writing from the unconscious. And I found that much of it was rubbish, but inside, there were pretty good ideas here and there, which I would catch, and then use them in my stories, novels, essays… When I used this method of free association by writing, I found that I said things that I didn't know that I was going to say. Later on, when I did psychoanalysis, I saw that this was a beautiful idea. So I would like to think that the best ideas that have occurred to me, have occurred to me automatically or without coercion… and as you know, the idea of free writing, as in free association, is to suspend the super ego. Stuff occurs to you freely, which you can then explore. So I've always used this in my writing, I've always been interested in the unconscious because of dreams and later on, ten years later—well, many years ago when I began my psychoanalysis—I saw the unconscious from a different point of view, through the reflection in the analyst. But I saw early on as a writer that the best stuff comes when you're not looking. So that's my story, and when I am writing, I start early in the morning. I sit down fresh and I have no inhibitions; I have no super ego. I try to write as spontaneously as I can. Later on, when you are writing a novel or a movie or whatever, you craft it, you shape it, but the initial impulse is from the unconscious.

So there are close links, in your opinion, between psychoanalysis and literature…

Well, as you know if you read Freud's work, it's full of references to Sophocles, to Shakespeare and to Ibsen; Lacan was a very close friend of the surrealists, and was very interested in Joyce. Psychoanalysis to me has always been closer to literature and philosophy than it has been to science. If you study psychoanalysis and literature, they illuminate one another. If you wanted a look at what men and women were really like, you would look at the history of the culture. Poetry, literature, painting, music, you would see what men and women were like. You wouldn't find that in the scientific treatises or psychology. So, there's a big overlap between psychoanalysis and literature.

In what way did you become an analysand, how did you first arrive to the couch?

Well, as you know, psychoanalysis was very fashionable in the '60s. Now, say you have a symptom; there are a thousand analysts, the union analysts, the chanting analysts, there's an aroma therapist, if you look in the phone book, there are thousands of therapists. I have friends who are analysts, who live in Paris, and they just don't have any patients, because analysis doesn't promise you happiness. Analysis doesn't promise you anything. If you go to any other therapist they say yeah, in six months you'll be happy. Analysis offers you nothing, really, except to sit in a room and talk. So I am worried about psychoanalysis, I worry about the future of psychoanalysis, as a practice. Don't you?

In Latin America, psychoanalysis is still very important, even though it's not a fashionable thing. People love to take pills, or undergo cognitive treatments rather than psychoanalysis.

Same in London. Anybody in London who goes to a doctor and says, "I've been feeling a bit depressed," he'll give you pills. I love drugs, but I only like illegal drugs, the only ones that are good for you. Anything prescribed by the State, you might as well forget about it. But I worry about psychoanalysis, because I love psychoanalysis and I think that it's a beautiful idea that you can sit in a room with a person for twenty years, just talking, what a great idea that is! But I can see that it doesn't offer anything. Though I can say that it has saved my life.

Is that true?

Many times, in many ways, yeah.

Can you talk to me about that, or is it too private?

Well, I can talk about it in general terms, by which I mean that one of the things that psychoanalysis might stop you from doing is being so self-destructive. And Freud, I think, said at one point or another, that all of psychoanalysis has to do really with mitigating the effects of the super ego, or, let's say, the death instinct or the possibility that we will hurt ourselves. So it has saved me from that, which is a lot. And also I would say that it has enabled me to learn to speak, because there are many writers, actually, who don't like to speak because they like to write. So they find their inspiration or their creativity in their private spaces, in their room, writing, and there they can speak the truth.

And what about you?

I've had to learn how to speak. If you come from a background like mine—I grew up in the 1950s, before the breaking of taboos—where there's much you didn't say, that you weren't allowed to say, and speaking was very controlled in the suburbs, there was a lot of stuff they didn't want to hear. So you have to learn, if you are an ordinary neurotic like me, how to speak.

Has psychoanalysis helped you to learn how to speak?

You teach yourself by hearing.

Hearing yourself speaking.

And hearing yourself not speaking; you hear where the limit is, you hear where the boundary is: everything that you might think, that you cannot say.

And what about that? How much can we speak or even write about what is impossible to say? Because you have quoted Wittgenstein in some essays...

I was fascinated by Wittgenstein, and that's how I got interested in Lacan, because of the concern with language, and he wrote about the idea of a private language, which interested me very much. Because it's impossible—a private language—but there's another private language, which has to do with inhibition, has to do with the limit on speaking.

And do you work on the boundaries of speech?

I don't know. I'm aware, though, when I'm writing, of that which you are afraid to say and that which you can't say and those things that you are nervous about saying and often have the most meaning, most often have the most force, or are most electric, yeah.

What place does psychoanalysis have in your work and in your life, nowadays?

It's very central to me; the work of Freud, and the work of Lacan, but mostly Freud. Freud has had a huge influence on cinema, and you still see it when you think about sexuality, think about childhood, when you think about leaders, whatever, so for me it's become impossible to think about the world without thinking through Freud, using Freudian ideas. It's central to me. Psychoanalysis isn't fashionable, as you said, but it's everywhere. It's in the culture. If you speak about architecture or about sexuality, you can see that language is absolutely full of psychoanalytic ideas... often in a way that is stupid, and misunderstood, but it's there.

Susan Sontag has said that the psychoanalytic session has an aesthetic form, and could be a sort of installation or performance. No one has paid attention to the aesthetic features of a psychoanalytic session. What do you think about that?

It's certainly a performance, you might say.

A performance by two people.

It's a show. There's no other idea in the world like the idea of the psychoanalytic session, is there? This Freudian idea that two people would sit in a room, man or woman, or two men that will sit in a room for twenty-three years, just talking, maybe twice, three times, whatever a week... that they would just talk, and they would talk about the most stupid things. In fact, the stupidity was the essence of the work, you might say. That's an extraordinary idea. You can see why it's not fashionable! Because it's such a bizarre idea, it's a beautiful idea, though. And it seems, as I get older, more and more of a beautiful idea. That you would pay to sit in a room and talk rubbish for years; it seems fantastic to me. It's an absurdity. Psychoanalysis is not a talking cure, it really is a listening cure, it's a being heard cure, you might say. When you feel that you are heard it's very healing or relieving.

You have said that nowadays nobody listens.

No, everybody is distracted, nobody wants to hear. I see that with the students. They come around to see me, they sit there, sometimes they just talk, then they just fuck off and leave and you think, these people have no ability to listen, no desire to listen. There's no space, there's no dream, they can't just sit. I say sometimes, why don't you just sit there and we can look out the window? We can sit here for half an hour, and they can't bear to do it. It's very difficult to do. The ability to bear silence is very important, though, I have learned. I go into the room of my psychoanalyst, it's totally quiet, there's no noise, there's no radio, nothing. We just sit there in silence, and the silence is beautiful and the silence is the medium, it really works. And in the silence you have ideas, too. I mean, this isn't meditation; in meditation, the idea is to get rid of your thoughts. Now in psychoanalysis, or the silence of two people together, like you and I, you have good thoughts, interesting thoughts, creative thoughts.

In what way do you think that your own analysis has determined your way of storytelling?

That's a very good question. I hope it made my writing less logical. I hope it made my writing stranger.

Stranger even to you.

I hope so. Psychoanalysis enabled me to think more freely, non-defensively. Psychoanalysis teaches you that you have the thoughts or the feelings you have, so it enabled me to think more freely. When I was young, I was very inhibited, nervous about people, nervous about speaking, nervous about my own thoughts. My thoughts felt dangerous to me. In psychoanalysis, you learn to say everything, and when you've said it, you realize that it causes no harm, in fact it's rather interesting. It enabled me to think, say and write things that I thought were shameful, but were really quite interesting. To think more freely, to have more ideas, so that your psyche becomes, let's say, more of a democracy. There's more stuff in the democratic republic of your psyche.

"The democratic republic of your psyche," I like that.

To have more thoughts, and to be aware of what you are repressing, or closing off, in so far as you can. I was always interested in dreams, fascinated by dreams, and I worked for many years with my analyst on dreams. For a long time, the dream stuff was really of interest to me.

It's the title of one of your essays...

Dreaming and Scheming. For years we did that, and I found it profoundly illuminating to think and talk about dreams, and as you know, the language of dreams. I found it very freeing. I mean, I'm not psychotic. Which is a shame, for an artist.

Not being psychotic is a shame? Do you think that only psychotics can be good artists?

Mostly yeah, don't you think?

No, I don't agree. Psychotics suffer a lot...

I know, I don't mind... haha! But I imagine in my fantasy that there's a freedom in psychosis that there isn't in somebody who has been inhibited...

I don't think so. There is a lot of suffering in psychotics, not freedom.

But psychotics have a lot of theories, don't they? And I find the theories quite creative.

Yes, it's true. In a way, perhaps Joyce was very close to psychosis.

Lacan thought that about Joyce, yes.

When you talk on the couch, do you think you are alike a character?

When I talk on the couch, I don't have a self. You abandon the security of the self.

But imagine for a while that you can watch yourself and hear yourself speaking on the couch...

When I'm speaking on the couch, as you know, it's not a normal conversation, obviously, so I'm not trying to say to the analyst, "How are you? How are you feeling?"

It's sort of a crazy conversation.

Yeah, so in that sense, he is not a person, because we don't follow the normal conversation rules: "How are you feeling today? How is your cold?," blah, blah, blah. And I am not myself, either, so I wouldn't say that I was a character. I'm just a machine that makes words.

You have shown yourself a lot in your novels and essays, but even though you're talking about you in a way which enables the reader to feel that you are talking about yourself, I imagine that your true intimacy is also fiction.

Yes, it's artificial, I have created it, and I'm doing it, it's a fiction, it's a performance. A book is—what did Philip Roth say?—that we are sit down. You know the stand-up comedians? We sit down as comics, so we are providing stories, as you say, about ourselves, about a fictional self, to entertain the reader. In psychoanalysis,

I´m not trying to entertain my analyst at all. I'm not even trying to entertain myself, I'm just speaking, so I would say that there's no character, there's no self, if you are open to being analyzed. It's much more random, if you are lucky.

You make a very precise use of some psychoanalytical concepts. Do you usually read, not only Freud, but also Winnicott, Lacan or Bion?

I've read all that, but I try never to use technical language. I'm writing for ordinary people who have heard of Freud, or read Freud but are not psychoanalysts. And most psychoanalytic writing is very bad, and difficult to read. Lacan is impossible to read, Freud is a great writer. So I would use psychoanalytic concepts, but I would use ordinary language. But then again, my analyst uses ordinary language as well.

What do you think about failure and success?

Well, you might say, if you are a Freudian, that failure is something that you make, or failure is something that is very important to you, and my father failed, you might say, as a child in his relationships with his parents, which was very bad. And he failed during his whole life as a writer; he was humiliated by the publishing world, because they didn't love his books. And he spent his life, I guess, as a man who was humiliated. I spent some of my life being humiliated, but now I have a very long analysis, so I sort of got over it. Now you might say that what you call success and failure, neither of them are issues for me anymore.

You don't believe in success...

I don't think about it either. I would think about happiness, or the ability to love somebody or to be loved, or my ability to bring up my children, or my ability to be a friend.

You know that's a way in which Freud defined mental health: the ability to love and the ability to work. You can do both things.

Just about *(knocks on wood, tapping the table).*

In my country, the wood can't have legs...

Oh, really? I didn't know that! It works anyway. In a way, you might say that you've become... you can transcend the idea of failure and success. I write, and some people like my books and other people don't like my books, but I write them, and I have my family, so I don't think about that.

Do you think that writing a book, for instance, could replace an analysis? Could it occupy the same place as an analysis?

Well, Lacan said, didn't he? that it was Freud´s original sin, to have analyzed himself. And he analyzed himself, you might say, through his letters with Fliess mostly, and anybody else would say it's impossible to analyze yourself. It's like seeing the back of your head, it's impossible; you can't see your own unconscious. So I don't believe that a book is an analysis.

I don't know if you have read the letters written by Freud to Oskar Pfister, the priest...

No, I haven't, are they interesting?

In one of them, Freud said that Pfister was a good man; he was a priest and he was also an analyst, and Freud said that to be a good analyst you can't behave like a "good person." An analyst must behave like a bad guy, like an artist—he said—who spends all the family's money to buy the materials to paint. He must behave like a malefactor, and when I read some of your works, I find real guts in the way that you speak about your life so openly, like with a sort of bluntness. I know because I have read you have paid a cost for that... It doesn't come free to write about the family, for instance.

It's a price worth paying. There's always a price. What do you think about the price of silence? The price of silence is high, it's more expensive than speaking, there's always a price, as you say. Psychoanalysis would explain to you that there is no safe place, there's no place of safety. If you are silent, it's dangerous, if you speak it's dangerous, it's always dangerous.

Do you find analysis a dangerous activity, in a way?

When I lay on the couch and I start to speak, I find it dangerous; what I'm saying I've never said before. Even yesterday, when I went to see my analyst, and I got on my bicycle and went down there to see him, I was very nervous. I said to him, "I've been seeing you for fucking twenty-three years, lying here, and I'm still nervous"; he said, "That's good, that means it's working."

Hanif, in which of your books do you find yourself most clearly you?

Probably the early ones. Particularly *The Buddha*, because when I read about my parents, if I open *The Buddha* and look at it, it's like watching a movie. Suddenly you see your parents, there's your mom, "Hey mom!," and there's your dad. Because when I wrote that book, my parents were still alive and now, thirty years later, I can see them; there they are, this is what they said, this is what they did. I was more naïve when I wrote this book, you might say; I just wrote it down, what I saw, what I remembered, what they said. So it's a glimpse. A book is like a dream from a long time ago, and everything is clear suddenly. You know when you have a dream, you don't understand it, but when years later you look back at the dream, it's completely clear. A book is like that, so I can see. But I wouldn't read it; if I open it and see a few pages and there they are, there's my dad. Amazing!

Do you agree with the division between fiction and non-fiction?

Not really. To me it's all writing, it's just writing. For me all writing, making a movie or writing even journalism, it's all writing to me. I like to write close to life. My books are about meaninglessness, about unhappiness, about sexual failure, about disaster, as well as being about desire and happiness and families. I want to write about black, dark things, in an interesting way, for a big audience.

Do you think that the writer and the psychoanalyst could share the place of the foreigner in some way?

You might say that psychoanalysis would promote the idea that everybody is a foreigner, because they are strangers to their own unconscious, and they are also strangers to the unconscious of other people, so this idea of the foreigner is very central. Freud was a foreigner too, being a Jew in Vienna at that time.

But a writer—and I think that also an analyst—is never too integrated to their society, like other professionals are...

I don't want to be integrated. I like not being integrated. When I was a child, I wanted to be integrated, but now that I am an adult, it seems to me that not being integrated is a very beautiful idea.

What is the sense of foreignness, living in London nowadays?

I feel a foreigner in London because I speak English! Everybody is speaking Spanish, Italian, Farsi and Arabic. Nobody speaks English in London. I have said that I'm the only person now who speaks English, I'm the indigenous Londoner.

Chapter 17

Daniel Libeskind, nomadic architect

The fact that we met in New York is merely circumstantial. Because the meeting involved a nomadic architect, someone who has lived for long periods of time in eight cities, in synch with the pace of his projects. He has left his mark on every one of them, veritable milestones that go beyond constructing urban icons. Libeskind is an architect who has managed to establish his footprint in each place, carving out a space where the catastrophes that makeup who we come into plain view. It never ceases to amaze me that someone who is able to conceive works so connected to one place and destined to last can be a wanderer by nature.

We converse in English in his studio in Manhattan, an entire floor that survived 9/11, just meters away from Ground Zero. He imagined a masterplan for this site that rehabilitates the area that was destroyed, while at the same time leaving memory and the cavities produced by the terrorist attack in place.

I am received by a slight man dressed entirely in black with contrasting brown Texan boots, accompanied by his wife and partner, Nina, in the midst of the hubbub of a small industry, both of them intrigued by the fact that a psychoanalyst has come to interview him. We talk with his home library in the background, and it is as if Libeskind's thoughts flow from there like fresh water emerges from a subterranean spring. There, architecture is not an isolated cenote, but part of a liquid network where literature and philosophy, history and geography, geometry and religion all connect to form part of a single discourse.

I'm very interested in architecture. To be sincere, I don't know whether or not you have any relationship with psychoanalysis, but I love your work. Did you have any relationship with psychoanalysis?

Not a personal one, but I'm a student of philosophy, of Lacan, or Brecht or Freud. I've read many of their works. One of the founders of phenomenology together with Freud, open the first clinic in Berlin in 1909 or something, so I know a little bit, intellectually, about the birth of this field, the history of psychoanalysis, the history of psychology… sure.

DOI: 10.4324/9781032708591-17

And do you think it has had any influence on your work?

Not in a direct way, no. But I do consider that architecture in general… forms the subconscious, you know, people's lives are encompassed by cities, by architecture, but on a subconscious level. Actually, for me, Freud was right when he compared the mind to Rome. He said, you know, the human brain is like Rome because of…

The layers…

And on the surface you see some fragment, but really, the story is in deep layers of erasures and of catastrophes and…, you know, crisis. So, that's true in architecture as well, in terms of just the way architecture is conceived. Think about it. It's a trauma to be in architecture because you have to dig the earth without machinery. Even for a small building, you know, even building a grave, you have to dig… and then you don't see the foundations, the foundations are hidden. So we take cities and buildings I really would say, in a kind of subconscious way. That's why I think people are able to put up with reality, because if they were to see where they live, and what it really looks like, what the space is about, they might truly be astonished, you know, and rebel. But, anyway, I've worked on a number of projects that deal with trauma, the Holocaust, and so on, and my idea was very simple: you cannot hide trauma. And that's also true in an architectural, urbanistic way. Not to make it appear not to have been there, but to make it very visible, and make it part of the experience of orientation.

I'm sure you know this, but Günter Grass has written about "Writing after Auschwitz." Can we speak about a sort of "architecture after Auschwitz"?

Ah! Look, something that Adorno said, that after it you can't…

No poetry is possible…

No poetry, no architecture, no art… But it's not true. One needs to rethink, you know, to relive, the experience in order to produce something that is valid. I didn't study the Holocaust in books. It was part of my experience. Because my parents were survivors, and I grew up under anti-Semitism, and under communist totalitarianism. Anyway, what you do in anything, affects everything you do. It's catastrophes that transform us. They transform existence. And when you look at the world today and see the catastrophes and, you know, what do you attribute it to? I don't attribute it to the last election, or the last fifty years or whatever. It's attributed to the murder of millions of Jews, and millions of others, as well, as a result. Those people are here. That's… that's… why the world has changed, in a Heideggerian way, it's really just the murder of spiritual carriers, of culture, of tradition… So, yes, it's everywhere, it's very close to me, not just for those projects, but every project. When I built the house in Connecticut, you know, a beautiful green site, idyllic, my first thought was: who lived there? Native American people. What happened to those native people? So, that was the form of the building, it's a house, an intimate people house but it's affected by the thought of what happened and of course, what happened in our experience. The *Shoah* is something that is not about to be changed, it's not something you can relativize, and it really does depict, to me, the change of the world, change of art, change of … and I think it isn't possible to build a building in India today, a school house or a vernacular housing project in China, you know, without those buildings being affected by the *Shoah*.

In what way?

You know, they wouldn't know if we were building them. They may have never thought about the *Shoah* but the result is they are transmitting that event in their architectural building, for sure.

It's impossible to avoid

It's impossible to avoid. It's… it's a ghost, a phantom that has presence in everybody's lives because it's there.

It lies in the unconscious of humanity.

Yes, and it's true. I think that event, and probably also the dropping of the atomic bomb on Hiroshima and Nagasaki, these two events are definitely there all the time, not like, you know, the elephant in the room but in a very existential way, and people may have never even heard of the events *(silence)*.

An architecture without memory is impossible, in a way.

Of course, because architecture is… you know, we would have orientation architecture. The window, the door, the street, the tree, the open field, is really a system of memory that sums up who we are. It's a reflection of our directions in life. So, true architecture is not just built for habitation. It's not only an issue of… of shelter. It's a major orientation in the world, or major orientation in existence. Memory is, I think, definitely—for me—the ground of architecture, it's not an additional element to think about.

And can we talk about a sort of unconscious of the city?

Yes! The city is the great unconscious. We talk about traffic, we talk about pollution, we talk about higher buildings, transportation, but not the actual… what happens in a city. The structure of the city determines our lives. The window, what you are looking at, determines who you are, the shape of the window you have… the wall you are looking at, the other office in this case, over there. So, it's the great unconscious and I'm always perplexed that even great philosophers and scientists are oblivious to where they are. So ideas travel far and wide, but when you look at the life of a philosopher or scientist, it is very conventionally based on this unconscious, and not just the table, and the pen and the chair. And that's the mystery because we don't choose where we are born, we don't choose who our parents are, we don't choose any of it. It's just kind of happening to us and we think that we'll find our home somewhere, but we know that the home is no place to go because in a final existence, you know, there is nowhere to escape to. So we live in between, in this kind of gap of uncertainty that is not often brought into consciousness and if it is brought to consciousness, it's usually in a catastrophe, it's usually in a dysfunction, in a collapse, in a storm where that field is revealed for the first time.

Do you think—in architecture, in your work—with catastrophe as a horizon line in some way?

I think so, yes. I think the world in many ways is in a catastrophic state, as it was then, and not just the obvious. There are catastrophes that constitute our orientation in space.

And what can we say about catastrophe? Because we can use a lot of words, perhaps say many words, or we can place a void, as you did in Berlin. That's one way of dealing with a catastrophe, a special way.

Well, to bring it forward, as I said, not to hide it. To create a space that is, let's say, immune to our desires, a space that is completely separate from usability, from function. In the Museum, in the Jewish Museum, when I put the word *Leere*, in German, *emptiness*, it's a word that usually means there is nothing above or below, but I used the word void, which means that it's a space that really has no part of the system I used, which is not architecture. It's a kind of para-architectural system because I used music to construct the building, you know; I completed an opera by Arnold Schönberg. Yes, you know Schönberg was working an opera, Moses and Aaron, in Berlin. When he was exiled from Berlin, he didn't complete it, so there are two acts and the third act remains empty. He left Berlin. It's discontinued. At the end of this opera there is a voice of Moses, it's an *aporia*, it's calling to God and that's the end. Silence. Nothing follows in this conversation. I always thought I could complete the opera in the building by way of the acoustics of the footsteps of visitors across the void, as a kind of an answer. In the third act, what does Moses hear from God? He heard that echoing of the shoes across the void, and it's very structural in my plan. It's not a metaphor. I actually used the music of Schönberg, the proportions, the numerology in Schönberg.

There are many ideas converted into architecture, materialized as architecture...

That's right. architecture is not supposed to take things and materialize them from outside architecture. So, for example, the fact that in that building there is no atrium. It's the only museum, to my knowledge, that doesn't have a public space that resonates and redeems the experience of the visitor, sort of "Ah... I understand." It's just entering into a black... a black aisle when you walk up the main stairs.

It is, I mean, an uncomfortable experience to visit that museum. That's what you wanted...

Of course, of course. I mean, it has a story but the story is layered with complexity and different... different colors.

You spoke about Schönberg, and you can produce music. In your architecture, you included the sound I mentioned in a way. Not only the visual, which is more common.

Definitely. Well... Because our orientation is to the ear, not to the eye. Sense of balance. It's in the inner ear, not in the eye. The eyes come secondary to our sense of orientation and space. So I always think of the acoustics.

So... at first, a sound. There is always a sound. When you design, when you start a project, do you listen to a sound first, and then draw?

Yes, you listen to the site, you listen...

That's interesting because my work has a lot to do with listening, more than viewing. Do you know John Berger's book "Ways of Seeing"?

"Ways of Seeing," I know it.

So, can we speak about ways of listening too?

Absolutely! So, in listening to the site, you are putting your head, so to speak, into the ground, to be able to listen to the inaudible, which is inaudible in the normal range...

To listen to the inaudible. That's interesting.

Yes, what you cannot hear. Well, when I was in Berlin in the Jewish Museum, I really thought, you know, about people. I wasn't thinking of the shape of the building, that came later, but whose voices passed through that site?

People who are not there anymore...

Who are not there anymore, like it creates a kind of matrix around the star, the connected voices of people that intermarried, these couples that never would have met in Berlin. So, yes, there are different ways of looking at the void or...

And what is the difference, in your opinion, between what can be seen and what can be listened to?

Well, I think architecture has to provide a full experience. It's not just... you know, audible, or visual, or tactile. It's a full human experience. It's about our existence, an existence that consists of where you are, what you are looking at, so it does work on many levels. To define the gravity of the situation or the openness of the horizon or something that you can… You know, there would be no reason to construct memorials to the Holocaust or museums to world war, to violence, because it's retrospective… It doesn't mean anything, really, if you can't go beyond… and somehow touch on another nerve that came before. You know, the millions of deaths, to create something that means something. It's kind of nothing. So, there has to be some kind of other transformation that makes it worthwhile to build such a thing. You can call it hope, you can call it a glimmer of understanding, but I have always thought about it. What would it mean to build with tragedies or catastrophes? But in a way, as I say, even in a house in Connecticut, there's a catastrophic event that's in it, the displacement of the native people who used to live there.

And here, near here, at Ground Zero, because I've read in this work there are two… there are many parts, but you've thought about placing different big holes there, like the shadows of the Twin Towers. Those holes have touched me deeply and now you are remembering with sound. But there is also another tower, taller than the previous one. There are two different movements…

Six Tower is 1776 feet tall…

But it's taller than the Twin Towers.

Yes, but it wasn't about how tall… it was the height… the numerical height, which is 1776.

Referring to the constitution…

It's a date, you know. They might not know and some people may find out that it is that height. I thought… really, that was the idea… not being the tallest tower.

The idea, the date

The date, the date.

That's very nice but, I'm sorry, just an idea that your work triggered in me…, because you are a cosmopolitan person, you are not only American. You have lived in many…

I have many different passports (*laughter*).

You are a citizen of the world. But the idea of the holes has a lot to do with your experience from many parts of the world; and to build a tower, a taller tower once the previous ones were destroyed, that's so American…

Well, my idea was not to build a taller tower. It was about composed powers, in a certain emblematic way around emptiness. I was the only architect who suggested not to build the towers in the center, as you remember. All the other architects suggested building megastructures in the middle of the site. I put the towers as far away as I could from the center where people perished, to the periphery of the site. They are as far away as possible in order to bring light in, and also not to bring… not to build anything where people perished. By the way, nobody considered it a sacred site. It's a piece of river real estate, owned by the port authorities; private developers, architects, everybody built in the center, it is the obvious place, where the old building used to be. But I decided very early on that nothing should be built where people had perished, and not only that, I struggled to go all the way to bedrock, you know, not just the surface but going underground, to where the tragedy really happened, you know, where the people really disappeared. And that bedrock is—to me—the whole site is really a three dimensional site. It's not just a surface, or just the holes. It's a bigger hole, which is vast… beyond the footprints of the building.

How can you deal with emptiness?

That's the art of architecture! In general, the thing is, when you build… you know, there's an E. T. Hoffman story where the character builds a house from the inside, without any windows and doors. He builds it, and then tries to figure out where you could put a hole in the building to see something. But architecture is kind of like that, in a way, because you need holes, as you said, and you know even the most primordial place today, something like a home, is penetrated by millions of holes, never mind plumbing, but new technology and everything… so it's hardly more than a hole. The hole, that intimate space that we think is our abode, is just completely open. There are no walls, it's just a leakage of space.

You spoke about E. T. Hoffman. Do you know the story that Freud took?

Olympia. Olympia, yes.

Yes, yes. And "The Uncanny." Because that is very present in your work, the idea of the uncanny, which is slightly different from the familiar, the familiar turns into uncanny with a slight… a very, very… subtle movement.

Well… the uncanny is the moment of estrangement from your expectation, and that's a very… that's the definition of art, generally. Freud used it in a very peculiar way to define a survey, a mode, rather that the norm, but there is no norm. Even the most industrialized, cubic, steel, glass thing is uncanny.

In what way?

Well, when you really think about the idea of neutralizing space, and making it sort of isomorphic, and so on. It's much more strange than some of the expressionist things that people have thought about in the past, like… neutrality itself, I would say, is uncanny.

I think you are more influenced by psychoanalysis than you think. I'm listening to you and there is... your discourse is very close to psychoanalysis, you know?

But the truth is that you can't separate it from philosophy, from literature, criticism itself or politics. To me it's almost a synchronous field. And I have read fantastic things in relation to architecture. It's very interesting that in the case of major thinkers like Derrida, major philosophers like Chomsky, major philosophers like Harper Moss, or Heidegger, how little consciousness there is of architecture in their work.

They don't think of architecture as a human science, a human practice.

No... Yeah, they don't think... and they don't see that right there, in it, is the most profound change that's going on.

But also, many architects don't think of architecture in the social field, as a social discipline.

Oh, no, because architecture has now, you know, departed from its origin, which is humanistic. It's a humanistic discipline. Architecture is a liberal art, which is freedom of thought, you know, poetry and mathematics are freedom of thought. Architecture is becoming much more of a commodity, a set of commodities.

There is some truth in fragments in some way, as opposed to totality, and in your work, the fragment experience is very impressive. Is there something to that?

Oh, yes, of course, because we are fragments, people, our souls.

But many people think in totalities, in an imaginary way and... it's a delusion but they think that way.

Everything is to be completed and totalized. And we see what a catastrophe that kind of thinking is, and where it has led: nowhere. But, you know, it's hard... this is where the subconscious of architecture comes in, because we can't think about it; it's hard to think about it. It's not just an architectural thought. It's hard to think about how we wound up accepting that corner, that window and that street, why we feel we are not able to be free of it. It's metamorphosis. It's Gregor Samsa. How do you escape? But architecture can provide something really fantastic also, if it is true to the existential experience, if it confronts what it means, in this street or this place or this... you know, house, what does it mean for people who live there? And how do you design something that has a future?

You think with many different references, from different fields. I agree with that way of thinking, but not many architects think the same way, not many architects work with so many books around.

And this is just a fragment. I have the best books at home (*laughter*). Yes. Let me tell you something... architecture today is more like a menial profession. Like a manual, you know. It doesn't attract interesting people for the most part. I always wondered why, in the Baroque or in the Renaissance, architecture attracted the most intelligent people, scientists and artists... Where are the interesting people going today? I don't know, they are going somewhere else. It's interesting, you know, how professions attract people. Often I wonder why architecture does not attract that kind of explorers, adventurers, any more.

Explorers... that's a lovely word. And how did become an architect?

Actually, I didn't, did you know that? I'm an architect because of—and this is really true—how I grew up in Poland, and this is the story: I grew up in an era of anti-Semitism and I wanted to play the piano, and my parents were too afraid, because of the neighbors, to bring the piano into the courtyard, they were just too scared. So they brought me a piano in a suitcase, which is an accordion, and I kind of played this instrument and became a *virtuoso*. When I came to Israel, somebody said to me "You should compete in America... For music prizes," you know. I was the only person with a suitcase that I couldn't even carry. It was too heavy for me. So my father carried it to the jury room, and the jury was Mrs. Kusevitski, who was the wife of Serge Kusevistki, Frances Cary, a very fine violinist, and Isaac Stern. And when I came into the room, I still remember how they looked at me like, you know, like I was in the wrong place. This was a classical music competition but, anyway, I played. I played only classical music, I played Bach, and so on. There were five winners; Isaac P. was the winner along with me and three other people, but I was the only person to receive this award who didn't become a figure in music. Isaac Stern came up to me right after I finished, he put his hand on my head and said, "You have already exhausted the instrument, you know. There's nothing more you can do. You have to play the piano." But he didn't realize the difficulty of going from a vertical to a horizontal keyboard so, yeah, I became an architect as a result of that. So, architecture is all vertical anyway, it's not horizontal. I would have never been an architect otherwise. I drifted into it and, by the way, I never worked for another architect. I tried once or twice to work with some famous people and I resigned after two days. That is not for me. And I really pursued a different path altogether, through drawings. Through drawings not of fantasies, but sort of a different kind of drawings. And my first building is the Jewish Museum. I never built even a small building, nor did I even propose a small building. I never drew a building before. Also, at the school of architecture, I refused to make imaginary buildings. Usually you are taught, you know, "make a school, make a house," and I refused, because I thought if you don't have a client, you don't have a political setting, a society, a budget, a reality, you know, it's only a game! One that I would not want to play. So I did something completely different. So how I became an architect is a mystery to me. It really is, because it was just a totally different path.

And do you feel like a foreigner in some way? Is foreignness present in your way of looking, in your way of designing, in your way of living?

For sure, but I think that's a characteristic of being Jewish.

It's also a characteristic of being an artist, in a way, to be not all that aligned with society. But not many architects occupy this place...

It's probably because architecture depends so much on business links, and networks, and being in a place and playing a game. I'm very lucky, because most architects work very hard to carve out certain jobs that they can have, you know. It's hard to be an architect, because you have to sit in one place and go and ask to work for them, and form a relation with capital, with money. But I was lucky enough to avoid that, really very lucky, because my career was based, actually, in the beginning, only on competitions. I won several competitions in a row, you know, for different kind of projects. And then I was lucky enough to work in different countries. We've lived in eight different cities.

You are a kind of nomad architect.

It's definitely true. We've lived in eight different cities, in many countries.

Last question. From your outsider's point of view, what do you think about psychoanalysis, the truth, about psychoanalysis' place, psychoanalysis' future, the value of psychoanalysis, if it has any?

It has, absolutely has. You know a lot about it. I've never been attracted to it in terms of personally undergoing it, but I know many people around me, most people around me who do...

Most people?

Most people, including my children. But I guess the myth of the psyche, the mind, that is so present in psychoanalysis, has never attracted me. To me, it was a kind of story, you know, a likely story that could be told that way, but I found out that the likely story could be better told in other ways. You could access that sort of depth of understanding from completely other angles.

Chapter 18

Caetano Veloso, the man who dreamed psychoanalysis

Any way you look at him, Caetano Veloso is mestizo. A glance at his home library suffices to confirm that we are in the presence of a true intellectual. He is also a poet, for whom words' music counts. And of course, a tremendous artist, an icon of Brazilian music who has sustained a spirit that is *avant garde* and yet popular at the same time. He is also a political man, aware of the weight his voice carries in contemporary discussions. He is a local artist, loyal to the landscape of Bahia and Rio de Janeiro where he has been educated and now lives, while simultaneously a global star.

Another perhaps less well-known side of him involves his passion for psychoanalysis. He is someone who has made psychoanalysis part of his life, to the point of deciding his place of residence according to whether or not psychoanalysts are available there. He is a person whose perception is sufficiently fine-tuned to be able to discuss psychoanalysis as if he were a psychoanalyst, and yet at the same time, has been able to take advantage of what analytical practice has to offer. As is the case with many recognized artists and intellectuals, Caetano's life can be traced along the lines of the itinerary of his analysis.

And in some way, I have been able to do the same in this interview, a long conversation in Portuguese and Spanish that we had at his triplex in Ipanema, in Rio de Janeiro. As opposed to the delays and hurdles that generally have to be overcome to obtain an interview with an artist of his caliber, Caetano had responded immediately to my invitation, with a warm e-mail written from the Northern part of the world while on tour.

You have had a number of experiences with psychoanalysis over the course of your life, haven't you?

Four. The first was in London. I may have told the prehistory of my relationship to psychoanalysis elsewhere, but basically when I was a child, I had a lot of health problems. I was sickly, and the skinniest of the children in my family. My throat was always red and swollen, and I was so skinny, they were always taking me to the doctor. One time they took me to a doctor in Santo Amaro. He talked to me—and that was uncommon. And I liked him, I liked how he treated me. He asked me a bit

DOI: 10.4324/9781032708591-18

about my life while examining me. "Stick out your tongue. Do you sleep well?" I liked the feeling I took away from that appointment, and it stuck with me. It got me thinking that I should have a doctor like that, someone who treated people's emotional states, you know what I mean? Someone to talk to. I literally dreamt that there might be a doctor like that, one who through conversation could work out the knots inside a person, work on a person's structure.

Sometime later, I saw a North American movie where one character, a girl, tells another that she should talk to a psychologist, or something like that. Anyway, the other girl asks her, "What is a psychologist anyway?" "It is someone who treats your emotional problems," the first girl replied. And I thought, "So there is such a thing! How funny, as a kid in Santo Amaro I always imagined that there was!" Then, as a teenager, I learned what psychoanalysis was, and I was sure I would find it fascinating.

Then I read a little Freud, but I did not go into psychoanalysis. I grew up, came to Rio—my cousin brought me—and spent a year here taking care of my health problems. That was when I was thirteen, and I stayed until I was fourteen. I lived in the north, the poorest section of the city... At the age of fourteen you start to really grow up, leaving childhood behind. I didn't like childhood very much. Now I do, but it took me a long time. When I was young, I was sure I would never have kids. I felt sorry for my friends with kids. I mean, for God's sake, what could be more trouble than having kids, to say nothing of being a kid? A child is born in the dark and then he can't remember it, and then it gets clearer.

My impression of adolescence is... very different from most people's. There is a myth that the adolescent is a person in the throes of anguish and that adolescence is the time when your troubles begin... I think it is the other way around... [laughter]. I understand that a lot of teenagers have problems, but I think that is because they are in a better place, they are freer... It is a much more joyful and interesting time. There might be conflicts, but that is another issue. In fact, the conflicts arise because the person is up to it, you know what I mean? I didn't have a bad childhood. My parents were wonderful, and so were my siblings. But I found being a child... a drawback... There is a certain happiness that comes with leaving childhood behind... And that is strange, I guess, since the myth is that childhood is wonderful. And then you have to put up with all the responsibilities of adult life, which is annoying and difficult—but the idea that childhood is a delight... I didn't want to have kids because I wasn't interested in raising children. But when I turned thirty, I felt... a need... a desire to have kids.

A need and desire to have kids.

Need and desire... It was as if... as if I were a woman who started to feel her biological clock ticking... You start feeling the desire to have kids. I am a man and I felt that. I was very curious and I had a lot of respect for female sexuality, because it almost seemed as if it didn't exist. At school, all the boys would talk about masturbation... That was where I learned about it, and it was an amazing discovery for me. There were tips, sayings... I started to understand masturbation, and it was a revelation... I think that masturbation and orgasm were the most important discoveries of my life. It was as if life now had meaning, as if I now knew why life was worth living.

But the girls didn't talk about that. I have been with many women in my life, and I have talked to them a great deal... And I learnt a lot, right? I have been married twice—two long marriages—but I have been with many other women, just casual encounters or short affairs, but I talked a lot with all those women, and they confirmed that people don't talk about that. Some of them were familiar with masturbation—they had discovered it on their own, but they didn't dare to talk about it...

And having had so many partners, what have you discovered about the mysteries of women?

I lost my virginity at the age of twenty... I mean really lost it, right? I messed around with a girl in Salvador, but no penetration because she was Jewish. She was very pretty and a virgin, and she didn't want to... She didn't want to lose her virginity. Girls never went to bars or out alone at night... It was so hard. And the girl I was crazy for... Having sex with girls like her was unthinkable. It would have been a complete lack of respect, a disaster for her own life and for her family. So there were none of the freedoms there are today, right? That has, happily, changed for the better.

Have you learnt things from women?

I learnt from Simone de Beauvoir's books [laughter], from her Memoirs of a Dutiful Daughter and The Second Sex. Certain things led me to learn. One of them was French films, because in North American films there was no sex. But in French films there was... There were two movie theatres in Santo Amaro, and they showed each movie for two days so that you could see them in either of the theatres. I saw every film. I was mad for movies, and French films had scenes of men kissing women in bed and you could see breasts. Everybody at school commented that a French film was playing. The boys found them a bit boring, but they loved some of the scenes and they would eagerly wait for a breast or a naked woman to appear on the screen. And the women seemed aroused, you know what I mean? Pleasure! I didn't know anything about that, since girls never talked about it, and you had to show respect for mothers and sisters, and women were raised to... The topic of sex was not even considered, you know what I mean? In those French films I saw female sexuality—and it was like a revelation. I was fascinated. So that meant that women also had... It was a mystery. And then I understood that it was question of cultural repression, and I became a bit of a feminist. I believed that women should have more freedom to express themselves in the world, more freedom to just be. I thought it was sad that they didn't. I had some cousins who lived in Salvador. They were older than me, they read a lot—it was a pretty intellectual family—and I heard them talking about all this. One of my female cousins talked about the existentialism which was in fashion; she talked about Sartre and Simone de Beauvoir, and so I got my hands on Memoirs of a Dutiful Daughter and The Second Sex.

I started wondering if women also had sexual feelings, if they had orgasms too. Judging from the French movies, it appeared that they did [laughter]. And then I read it in Simone de Beauvoir. Finally, in Salvador, I met a very pretty girl. She took the initiative and asked me to the movies. I thought the idea was to see a film… The movie didn't matter much, and it was a wonderful discovery. Then we went to the beach.

I had some experiences with guys as well—more like boys, really—during that same period in Salvador. Mutual masturbation or group masturbation. That has to do with psychoanalysis as well, because it is sex.

The discovery of sexuality.

I was fascinated by Freud because it was relevant to my own experience, with sex in such a central place.

That is a source of affinity with Freud.

For me, that affinity was total. I still feel it, because I think that Freud's intuition about the importance of sex is very profound. It is what makes Freud so powerful.

There was always a lot going on in my mind, a lot of angst and fear. I was a hypochondriac. I was afraid of having a disease that would kill me or… I was terrified of being sick. I had seen a woman have an epileptic seizure; I thought she was possessed by a Candomblé orixá, or spirit, but it was at a Catholic mass. For a long time, I was scared of that.

I have trouble falling asleep. My mother says I had insomnia as a baby. Everyone would go to sleep, but I didn't want to. Even when I was only two or three years old, I wanted to stay up and keep talking. I am the same way today. Sleeping—or the idea of sleeping—is always a bit problematic for me. I mean, I am here now, talking to you, thinking about things, and… in a little while I am supposed to just shut all that down? I cannot fathom that, and I have trouble giving myself over to sleep.

I lived a lot of experiences like that, and my vision of the world was quite peculiar, because my household was very peaceful. My parents loved each other so much, and they got along great. They were always together. They never fought, and they were both very decent people and very affectionate with one another. That led to an environment… But I also felt that my house was under a sort of bell jar. I would observe the world and hear news about what was going on. Our household was large because before my father married my mother he lived with the daughters of his older sisters. He was living with three sisters and six nieces when he and my mom got married. She became a part of that household of women. The odd thing is they never fought. We kids never saw a single fight.

You grew up surrounded by women.

The house was full of women, and my parent's first child was a daughter. Then they had another daughter, then came my brother Rodrigo, then another son, Roberto, and then me, a son, and then Bethânia. They raised two other girls, the oldest before their oldest daughter, and Irene, who came after Bethânia. Two more girls. The household was overwhelming feminine. My father was the only man in the house until the first son was born. I was not very masculine, because of that environment … at least in part. But my father was incredibly open. He just let things flow naturally. He respected us and was always by our side. The only thing he demanded of us was honesty. He didn't demand masculinity or a clear sexual definition. My father was amazing, a man of great humanity. He was the one who set the tone so that there was no strife between all the women in the house. This is very difficult to achieve.

There had to be a man to provide some order and structure…

It seems almost impossible that the household was not rife with conflict, but it was not. Bethânia, my sister, was the one who introduced me to popular music. She was quite famous when she was seventeen and eighteen years old, and my father asked me to look after her. Bethânia stood out in that conflict-free world because of her personality, something that came from within her. I found it charming, I still do. I would laugh. It was funny the way she dramatized relationships. Sometimes she would be upset with a member of the family, and none of us could understand why. Some people say it's because she is a Gemini (she is the only Gemini in the bunch). Later, when astrology became part of my imaginary, that did explain it.

So that was more or less how I got my start in music. I was curious about psychoanalysts, I was interested in it, but it was not until later that I felt the need to go into analysis.

And when was that?

It was in 1968. The military coup was in '64. Things got rough, but not so terrible. It was scary. I dropped out of the university because things got ugly. A professor of mine was detained, students were disappeared. Bethânia was invited to Rio to replace Nara Leão in a show. Since Bethânia came, I did too. She sang a song of mine, and it was a hit. So I got involved in popular music. I was already into it, but until then it was not my main focus.

I was into painting, I wanted to make films and write. I liked music—songs, really—and I did a few shows with some friends of mine in Salvador. Then Gilberto Gil's attitude toward popular music started to change, and that eventually led to Tropicália. What he needed from me was an intellectual contribution, and later a theory. He needed me to theorize and articulate what the movement meant. So I started thinking, "OK, I'll do this for now and then make a movie. That is what I really want to do." But then, in 1968, a coup happened within the coup: the AI-5[1] brought unlimited repression and a harshening of the regime. And in '68, Gil and I were arrested. We spent two months in prison. It was terrible, they didn't give any explanation for why we were being held. I was living in São Paulo, that was where my domicile was. I was married to Dedé, who had been my girlfriend since I lived in Salvador. We lived together and had agreed never to have kids.

And that's how I started making music. Tropicália, and the explosion of the counterculture the world over, coincided with what I was doing, right? 1969 was the year we created Tropicália, and in '68 I was arrested. It was really frightening, because there was no support on the left for what I was doing. On the contrary, the left scorned it: I admired The Beatles and was not opposed to electric guitars. In other words, I was open to rock music, so the leftist students thought we were all sellouts to imperialism [laughter]. That was literally what it was like, they reacted against us. I appealed to alienated kids who were looking for something different, kids who let their hair grow and got involved in the counterculture.

But the military government made up a charge. They claimed that at a show in Rio I had disrespected the flag and the national anthem—it was not at all true, but they arrested us. We were in jail for two months, and I was not interrogated until the middle of the second month. The first week I was in solitary confinement, as was Gil. I didn't see anyone. Nobody asked me anything. There was no explanation. I would sleep on the floor. I couldn't bring myself to eat. I felt terrible and so upset because I didn't know… I had the feeling that this was life, and that everything I remembered from the outside was a fantasy of mine, a dream.

I was in bad shape mentally for about two months. Then they flew us up to Salvador in military planes. They told us they would let us go there—which was pretty arbitrary, since we lived in São Paulo. When they arrested me at my house, they told me I wasn't going to jail but to an interrogation. The police car came here to Rio, and then they took me to the federal police headquarters, and from there to the army barracks, and from there to the military police barracks in the Tijuca compound, and from there to another military compound, and from there to a paratrooper base. All of that over the course of two months, and then we would be released in Salvador because we are from Bahía. But when the military plane landed in Salvador, the local division of the air force arrested me; a guy from the federal police argued with a guy from the air force, and I was back in custody. I nearly dropped dead, because in Bahía they had a warrant for my arrest from two months prior in case I tried to flee there. They had never informed the forces in Bahia that we had been arrested—the whole thing was a big mess.

That is so Latin American…

Very Latin American—complete chaos. Anyway, the military officer took me away, and the guys from the federal police argued and stormed out. And I was under arrest. I was devastated. I looked over at Gil and said, "Gil, what's going to become of us now?" They held me at the air force base, and the whole thing started all over again. It was awful. Meanwhile, the guys from the federal police were calling Rio and Brasilia to try to get things straight. They finally sorted it out, and that night they came over and released us. But the release went like this: the police officers took us to chief of the federal police in Salvador, who was an army colonel. He looked us over and said, "You have come this far, but there are no charges or any-thing against you," deriding the chaos that beset his own organization [laughter]. "Anyway, this is the situation: you two have to come here every day; you cannot go outside the limits of the city of Salvador." So we settled on a time, and he said, "Be here tomorrow." And we went every day for four months. We couldn't give interviews, do public performances, nothing like that for four months.

Gil had two daughters, and he started to complain that he had not been able to work for six months. I didn't have any kids. The only solution was exile. We bought the tickets.

And you ended up in London?

We ended up in London, but first we went to Lisbon. But at that time Portugal was under Salazar [laughter].

From one hell to another...

From one hell to another, and all of it in Portuguese! And from there we went to Paris. Guilherme Araújo, our agent in Europe, was there because Gil's concert would be the first one by a modern Brazilian artist, a Tropicália artist, ever held outside of Brazil; the show would be at the Midem Festival, in Cannes. When they let us go, we went into exile. One of the guys from the federal police who was putting me on the plane even said to me, "Don't come back. And if you do, turn yourself in immediately to save us the trouble of having to look for you—it won't take more than a day." That was exactly what he said. So I was bitter when I left Brazil. The idea of living anywhere else horrified me; Brazil is the only place I like living. That was where strange things happened to me. I had taken ayahuasca, a very power hallucinogenic drink, in 1968. It ended up being harrowing for me. The visions during my trip were lovely, but after a few hours my mind was at its limit. I wanted to get out of it, and I went mad. It was awful, and I was terrified, but it subsided. It was not long after that I got arrested, and then went into exile. The day they let us go, Gil and I went to my house in Bahia. When I saw the house, the photos in the living room, I went mad again, just as I had with the ayahuasca. I thought that I had gone crazy for good, no turning back, because this time I hadn't taken anything. I was totally desperate. When Gil saw me like that, he started to cry. I looked over at him. I saw he was crying, but I no longer recognized him. I wanted to look at myself in the mirror to see if I could get back to myself, and it was horrible. It wasn't that I didn't know who I was; it was that I didn't know what it was I was seeing. My father took one look at me and said, "Don't tell me that those sons of bitches have taken your wits!" But I recovered.

Your father's word was what calmed you down...

He said "sons of bitches" in front of my mother. He had never sworn in her com-pany before. That was when I started to cry. All of that informed our decision to leave. We went from Lisbon to Paris. It was 1969, so the events of Paris in '68 were recent. It was sweet, but it also ended up... De Gaulle returned and took over... The streets were full of police. The atmosphere was oppressive.

Going to London was the sensible thing to do, our agent told us. London was peaceful, there was music... Music was what mattered most, and there were no policemen arresting people... But in London, despite all that, I felt awful. I was pretty depressed. I tried to find a psychoanalyst... They told me there was a Brazilian psychoanalyst who saw patients in London—a very pleasant Jewish guy. And that was the first time...

Did he help you?

I liked him a lot. He was very laconic, one of those analysts who listens a lot and says next to nothing; the sessions never went over. But that worked for me... it helped me. But my expectations regarding psychoanalysis... it was strange. When I dreamt. I thought that in psychoanalysis you would come to the office and... that whole idea of free association... I imagined things would be very free... But that's not what it was like at all. You walk in, and there is another person there, you know what I mean? There is another person and there is you. And you have to talk, and you don't know where to begin, and... all the social codes are at play as you build a relationship, albeit a very special one, a relationship different from other relationships, right? You open yourself up so much to a person who is not a part of your life—and that is a unique situation. And I saw all that, but I felt disappointed that things did not happen as I had dreamt, it was as if... But I know he liked me. His name was Abrahão Brafman, and I have warm feelings for him.

Was it when you came back to Brazil that you thought about going back into analysis?

When I first went back to Bahia, I was so happy that, for a while, I didn't give psychoanalysis a thought. I had stayed in London for three years. And it was during that time—that time when I was in analysis—that I started to want to have a child (I just made that connection!). That desire began in London, but grew when I began to feel a depression coming on because I didn't know when, or even if, I would be able to go back to Brazil. At first, I was totally consumed by angst. I remember meeting Cabrera Infante, the Cuban writer. We became friends. He feared—and with good reason—dying without ever going back to Cuba, and he did. That possibility was, for me, unbearable.

When there was the first glimmer of hope that I could come back to Brazil, the desire to have a child began to set in. That was when I started psychoanalysis. The promise of returning to Brazil was so important. I had barely begun to tell my wife that I wanted to have a child when she said, "What's this about?" After all, I had made a firm decision never to have kids so that I would not be tied down. I wanted to be free. Besides, I didn't like children.

But when I came back to Brazil and Bahia, she was so happy to have me back. I have had some affairs while I was away, and two trips to Brazil before returning for good. As soon as I got back, Dedé said, "Caetano, I have something to tell you. I am willing to have a child, but here in Bahia." We lived in Bahía for three years. Moreno's birth was the most important thing that ever happened to me as an adult. And even today I love having children. I have three. It's an amazing experience.

But after three years in Salvador, and when Moreno was three, I felt the need to go back into analysis. I wanted to work things through, to go deeper, to deal with myself within psychoanalysis. But there were no psychoanalysts in Salvador at that time. I remember I even talked to João Gilberto about it. I told him that in Salvador there were no psychoanalysts. "No need for them, Caetas…" [laughter]. I wanted to go to São Paulo, but Dedé said she wouldn't go there. "If you go to Rio, I'll come along," she said. So we did, and I am still in Rio today.

Were there psychoanalysts in Rio?

Yes, there were. I was looking for someone specific: Inês Besouchet. Clarice Lispector had dedicated a book to her. She is one of the most important figures in psychoanalysis in Brazil. By that time, she was already an older woman.

She must have had something special.

I went to talk to her. We had two meetings, and she told me she didn't have time to see me, but that she would find someone for me. She gave me three names. The first one didn't work out. I didn't like where the second one's office was (I was superstitious and his street ran by the cemetery). She smiled and sent to me a young analyst. "I think it'll work well for you," she said. So I went to see that third person. and I loved it. From the get-go, I felt a real affinity. The famed transference took place! It had in London too, but this time all the more so, and it lasted for the entire treatment. He was the psychoanalyst with whom I felt I went deepest… I stayed with him for many years, and he was about to terminate my therapy. I was getting ready for that when he had a change of heart. He was becoming interested in a group with Lacanian roots that had broken away from the more traditional strains. It was the group run by MD Magno. Today MD Magno is my analyst. The analyst I was talking about… I was in analysis with him for years, and he started to get really involved in Magno's group. And he started to change. That was when he told me… Actually, I was going to start analysis all over again, change everything, or at least do something different. Then one day Inês Besouchet showed up at a show. She came back into the dressing room. She had such a particular manner, she was almost evanescent, ethereal. She was fascinating and so pleasant. She came over and said, "I liked the concert very much… I think the time has come, don't you agree?" I didn't get what she meant. She clarified, "The time has come for you to come see me"—that is, for me to do analysis with her. She was my analyst's supervisor, right? So she had ushered in that change in him. I think it coincided—no, it wasn't that it coincided. I think she was supervising him as we moved toward termination, when he suddenly went through that change. And he really changed a lot, quite suddenly. He became fascinated with Magno's neo-Lacanianism, which was Magno's big thing.

He was not an orthodox Lacanian, right? What he was doing was something new…

He was the one who brought Lacan to Brazil—a very important figure—but he veered his work in another direction, you know what I mean? He developed his own theory and his own perspective. His work is very interesting. A friend of mine went to some of Magno's classes and invited me to go along and check it out. There was, I thought, something interesting in what he was doing, but I didn't really respond all that much on a personal level because of something I see in Lacan as well, which is… a sort of mystification. And that is a whole question in psychoanalysis, right? I love psychoanalysis for all the reasons I've told you, from the question of dreams to Freud's choice to put sex at the center of the human experience. For me all of that… is enormously valuable. Then there are those terrible critiques of the history of the psychoanalytic movement and what psychoanalysis is today… Popper's idea that psychoanalysis is a modern form of superstition.

But one of your analysts defended superstition, isn't that right? I mean, held it above religion at least.

The one I liked so much.

Yes. So is it so bad that psychoanalysis is a twentieth-century superstition?

Not necessarily. After all, my analyst would say that superstition is better than religion.

You had four analysts, right? Abrahão Brafman, Rubens Molina…

I was still in treatment with him when Inês Besuchet came to tell me that the time had come to go see her. When I told him I was going "to talk to the lady," he said, "Inês is wonderful. Go see her." And I saw them both.

At the same time?

Yes, for a while. And I would tell each one what was going on in my process with the other.

 Something strange happened to me in the middle of all that—it's worth telling you about. The great Brazilian artist Lygia Clark believed that art should not only go beyond the limits of the painting, but even be experienced by both the author and the viewer—the viewer and the art, and sometimes the artist, right? She was a pioneer. She believed that her art would ultimately become a form of therapy—she turned it into therapy. She stopped making objects and started doing therapy. And she invited me [to participate in one of her therapeutic events]. I was in analysis with Rubens Molina and also with Lygia Clark. She was my friend, and I admired her a great deal, so I went. It was very interesting and peculiar. I mean, it was Lygia Clark and she used things that had to do with her art: bags with different textures inside, sand, pieces of stones, coarse and soft things, water… she also had some tubes she would blow through. The air would hit certain parts of your body. I was sitting there in my underwear, and she would do those things; she didn't talk or ask much. She would concentrate on certain parts of my body and... But I didn't experience any specific change after the experience.

Did you prefer traditional analysis? Or another form of psychoanalysis?

I preferred talk-based psychoanalysis, but I was curious. It is odd that an artist radicalizes the meaning of her art to the point that it becomes interaction with the viewer. She discovered an actual form of therapy, and she continued to practice that therapy to the end of her days. One day, as we were finishing up, she said to me, "Look, Caetano," that was how she talked, "we're going to call it quits here. You are not responding. But that's fine, we can still be friends" [laughter]. We didn't see each other all that much, but she liked me and I respected her a great deal. Until the time she died, she did that form of therapy. She believed that art—or at least her art—would, if taken to its logical conclusion, turn into a form of therapy.

To what extent do you think that your various experiences with psychoanalysis have made you who you are? Is there a common thread? What mark has psychoanalysis left on your life?

After Inês died, I didn't go back into analysis for fourteen years, you see? I had gradually been leaving Rubens behind because he was changing and I was not able to change along with him. But I did continue my analysis with Inês. I adored her, but my analysis with her was not very productive. It's odd, very odd.

That analysis didn't help you much?

It was not very productive.

Because there was something there... She came for you... She went to your dressing room for you.

Yes, she came for me.

That can't work.

She came to me because I had first gone for her. "I think the time has come. You came to me, and I think now is the time," do you understand?

I do. I understand that it did not work.

But it did! The whole thing with her was lovely and pleasant. And the fact that she was a woman was a bit strange and interesting. She was very old by that time, but I had sexual fantasies about her. It is a bit strange, because I wouldn't say I consider myself or experience myself as one-hundred-percent heterosexual. But the men I have been in analysis with, the one I am in analysis with now, never appear in my sexual fantasies…that never comes to my mind. With her… every time I was there, sitting there, with her sitting there listening to me… There was an atmosphere… and I would have fantasies… I never mustered the courage to tell her… It's odd… I was ashamed because she was elderly and well respected and all. And I started hinting at it one day, but she cut it short, and I didn't… I tried to tell her, but couldn't say it straight. It's odd—something to take note of. Sexual fantasies, or even love fantasies, could easily be a part of transference, but it didn't happen with any of my male analysts, just with her. But the part of analysis that has to do with understanding my issues, with clarifying things—that did not happen with her. She was almost supernatural… It was amazing! She ended up getting involved with a Brazilian guy who worked miracles and he saved her. She was very frail. They had expected her to die from the time she was very young because of her heart—she lived on the verge of death. But she made it to a very old age. She would have episodes, and this guy came into her life when she was on the verge of death and he saved her. Thanks to him, she was suddenly fine… and that had an enormous impact on her. Anyway… [laughter] Things…

Have you read more recent psychoanalysts?

I have read Klein, who is very clever, and a little Bion. I've read some Lacan, but I find the whole Lacan thing a bit annoying, which is odd because I love word plays, I just love them. I adore concrete poetry and Joyce… I think they are great, but at a certain point people get caught up in a sort of fascination with him… I have seen the videos of him that are on the Internet, but to me he seems very mystifying. Some of his thinking is fascinating, right? Of everything of his on the Internet, the nicest one I have seen is a television program where he starts by saying, "Je ne dis que la vérité: pas toute…" Something like that, right?

Not the whole truth, because there's no way to say it all…

Yes, I always speak the truth… but not the whole truth [laughter].

Listening to you makes me think one cannot say the whole truth. Only half truths, like Lacan says, but that is quite a bit, Caetano, wouldn't you say? A lot of truth.

Yes, a lot can be said.

Note

1 Acto Institucional N° 5, a decree issued by de facto president General Costa e Silva on December 13, 1968. In effect until 1978, the decree sanctioned a series of arbitrary actions with lasting effects, including the ability to detain those considered enemies of the regime without due process.

Chapter 19

Slavoj Žižek, the tender agitator

Some encounters only come about through insistence. In response to every one of my requests, the Slovenian philosopher, one of our most incisive contemporary thinkers, would stall, saying that he was old and in ill health. As if he had decided to test my mettle, he responded to each new invitation with a new postponement. When he finally agreed—maybe just to get me off his back—he said that it didn't make sense to travel to Ljubljana for an interview that was bound to disappoint me.

The uniform soviet architecture didn't manage to entirely ruin the lovely capital of a country that may lack the scale needed to be one. Walking along its streets— where Žižek is a celebrity, with posters featuring his photograph everywhere—I think that it doesn't seem so far off that he had ventured to present himself as a candidate for president in such a place.

We meet where he had indicated, at SEM, a cafe located in the heart of the city's cultural district, a large, old, relaxed house where people engage in lively conversation in the courtyard. When Žižek appeared as an agitated whirlwind, dressed in jeans and a Fred Perry t-shirt and received like a regular, the image was far from what one would have in mind for a man who was finished and in bad health. He ordered a Coke Zero and began to talk before I asked him anything, as if there were no time to lose, his ideas falling over one another to come out as if flooding him. He spoke in his English, with a strong Eastern European accent, in a kind of torrent of free association, alternating between erudite references and fascinating gossip. Something that is, on the other hand, quite related to psychoanalysis, which holds him as one of its most original thinkers, apart from the traditional clinical realm.

I love your way of thinking.

Well, don't be so sure. I am now getting old and very strange. Not that I'm less leftist, but I hate this blind sympathy for immigrants. I hate this masochist attitude, you know, by Europe: "We are guilty. We are guilty for everything. We were the colonizers so we should open our borders..." and so on. We are all paying a price for it now. You know, the left is so hypocritical here. On the one hand, the left wants to open the borders to the refugees and so on, and at the same time the left wants democracy. Those in government do not listen to the people, and so on.

DOI: 10.4324/9781032708591-19

Make a referendum in practically all European countries now about "Should we allow refugees or not?" The answer in all countries would have now been: no. If you look at the left which succeeded, and sorry, if you still call it a left, there's only one genuine success story: China. I mean, one has to be honest here. I don't think that in all the history of humanity there was ever such a period of just forty-fifty years when so much new wealth, the whole new middle class, was created. I think that leftists traditionally hate two things. They hate, on the one hand, this wild rule of capital, cruel competition, anonymous financial movements, all this capitalist stuff; and on the other hand, leftists hate the authoritarian state. But in China we have exactly the combination of these two. They worked perfectly. And it's not only China now, it's also Vietnam. Vietnam is another miracle now, developing in an absolutely incredible way.

In the beginning of the Soviet Union, Luria was fond of psychoanalysis, before the coming of behaviorism.

Absolutely. Even until the end you find traces of this. Did you read a wonderful book by Luria, a short one, on a mnemonist, a guy…? It's like 30 or 40 pages. But he asks… it's not simply these brain sciences and behaviorism; he asks a wonderfully correct question: what did it mean, subjectively, for this guy to have a perfect memory? And he provides a wonderful, almost Lacanian, answer. He says how, to be able to live with it, how he had to change, to reorganize his entire subjective economy. It was the only way for him to survive. Because first, he had to apply techniques not to remember, but to forget things. Because you can function normally only by forgetting things. I once had a wonderful debate in America with some cognitive scientists, and they're not all total idiots. We agreed that if you compare humans with apes, what we humans can do is not more complex, it's less so. We know how to abstract. We know how to erase the unimportant. So this is why the only way for him to survive is first to learn through rituals to forget. But the second point was much more interesting, very Lacanian: the only way for him to survive was to experience his situation as temporary. And the most interesting attitudes with today's psychoanalysts and brain scientists… and the intelligent brain scientists know that this is a question. So you can, in some sense, prove that when you think you are making a free decision, you are just registering something that already took place in your mind. Ok. Now there are big problems with how this affects your self-experience. Is it that once you know this you accept the fact that you lose your free will? I know… But can you accept this? And the majority thinks that you cannot, that we live in a necessary illusion of free will. Then there are others who are more radical. What I'm saying is that this is what interests me immensely. Here, we Freudians or Lacanians, I repeat it all the time, not just what is so fashionable to say now, that we are controlled by digital machineries, that everything is registered… but this is, I think, where things are happening. The Chinese are doing it like crazy, but the Americans also, this direct digitalization of our brain. They've already made pretty good progress. How you link your brain to a computer, and a computer can already discern your basic thoughts. So they can control your thoughts. What does it mean? I think the whole notion, our notion of being a human person, implies this gap: I'm here, reality is out there, I can think freely, out of control. If this basic gap between inherent outer life is closed, then I'm more and more convinced that maybe something new is emerging. We will no longer be humans. What I don't believe is that we will just turn into automata and so on. But what will happen without subjective identity if we really can directly link our mind to a machine? We still must subjectivize this fact.

Do you think that in that sort of post-human future that you are imagining, there will be a place for psychoanalysis? Will psychoanalysis be needed?

Of course, maybe not the same psychoanalysis... First, I don't believe in this simple determinism, that we will be simply objectivized. Because the resource of our freedom, again, is not free will in a simple, positive sense. It's negativity. You can abstract, you can withdraw... You can say no... A guy called Benjamin Libet, you should read him, he is the famous scientist who discovered this, that when you make a free decision, a second earlier your brain already knows it, so you are not free. But then he says, it's wrong to conclude from this that there is no free will. He says, all positive decisions are determined, we are not free. But avoid them, and there is the freedom. I have spoken to intelligent scientists who told me you shouldn't compare men with apes at the level of complexity. Apes are much more rational. But precisely things like death drive, self-sabotaging and so on... that's where human freedom begins. Human freedom is not I'm doing what I want to be happy. Human freedom is: I could be happy but why don't I screw it up. Here things are so interesting. Here I see a space for dialogue with really intelligent cognitive scientists who are well aware that things are not as simple as that. Again, I think that, precisely, of all these open questions, the unconscious, and with it, psychoanalysis, will persist because... We should just establish these old divisions. People speak about digital unconscious in the sense of things that are out there, but this is not the unconscious, this is still simple external mechanical unconscious. The Freudian unconscious is purely virtual, it's outside, it's in the symbolic. It's not part of your deep brain. The moment you take these old Freudian notions seriously, elaborated by Lacan, of split, divided subjects and so on, it all gets complicated. Here we need a dialogue. If you ask me, again, I think that we live in an era—I always repeat this because now it's fashionable all around the world to say psychoanalysis is out, and so on—... No, it's never been as needed as it is today, because today we... Freud was never this simplistic idiot who thought: because we have certain desires, but social morality prohibits us to follow these desires, we need a psychoanalyst to be able to leave behind these paternal prohibitions and follow our desires. No, Freud was much more refined already. He knew, to put it in very simple terms, as I often say, the problem with the father is not that, let's say, you want a certain sexual practice, the father prohibits it, then you rebel against the father. No, the problem is why, precisely, with a permissive father, self-sabotage is even stronger. Today we live in permissive societies and we have more impotence and frigidity than ever. We encounter precisely all these paradoxes today and here, I think, psychoanalysis is needed. Lacan says that the subject of psychoanalysis is the subject of modern science. What I want to say is that—how to put it?—the topic of psychoanalysis is precisely when this simple, direct logic no longer functions. I have good connections with some people from China, who are now trying to develop psychoanalysis. And you know what they all tell me? At least in the generations that are a little bit older, you always fall back to the trauma of the cultural revolution. All the family traumas are still that. It's their Holocaust. That's why I disagree a little bit with Badiou who still celebrates cultural revolution. Yeah, but for all intellectuals and so on, you know what an absolute trauma this was. I mean, you were physically beaten, red guards broke into your apartment, if they found a foreign book there, they were not interested if it was a Marxist book or whatever, a book, they beat you and so on. It was such a nightmare! So I wouldn't be as keen as Badiou to celebrate…

Are you finishing a book now?

I'm always finishing a book. A big fat one, where in one chapter I try to recapitulate—because I have already read it, he sent it to me in PDF before it appeared—his third volume: *L'immanence des vérités, The Immanence of Truth.* This is why Badiou is not a Freudian: he doesn't believe in what I call, following Hegel, radical negativity or Freud's death drive. For him, death drive negativity is just some kind of pathological perversion or whatever… He believes in the positive, you begin with a project, of the good, truth event, fidelity. My whole vision is different. I think that in this duality, there is simply no space for psychoanalysis. And I think that in order for the space that Badiou calls "truth" to be opened, you need what Lacan calls "traversing the fantasy experience of radical negativity," and so on and so on. This is a big debate. It's not just me, my friend Alenka Zupančič also wrote many things… We are now working very hard on this, on what is missing in Badiou.

What is missing in Badiou?

Missing in the sense that in him, there is simply no real Freudian unconscious, or what he calls the death drive. It's neither what Badiou calls the order of being, where we are individuals just searching for happiness, whatever; nor it is directly a truth event. It's something much more… it's something in between. That's what I don't see in Badiou, and this then also brings us to political differences, and so on. But let me tell you another thing: I think—and this brings me a lot of problems—that if you read Lacan closely, although he pathetically proclaims all the time, "I was raised against philosophy, I'm an anti-philosopher."

So do you think that psychoanalysis is a kind of philosophy?

No, but if I may, I put it like this: I agree with Lacan that philosophy emerges by repressing something. But this something is not something pre-philosophical in the sense of primitive wisdom, or science or whatever... It's some much more radical insight... What Lacan would have called... there is no big A, there is no sexual relationship, and so on. So that psychoanalysis deals with what was *Urverdrängt*, the primordial, repressed by philosophy. But it's still, if you want, the unconscious of philosophy. There is no psychoanalysis without philosophy. Psychoanalysis just looks deeper into what philosophy had to repress. And this is clear in Lacan. He's in debate with philosophers all the time.

There is also no philosophy without psychoanalysis in your opinion...

In some sense, yes. Not literally, but in the sense that what psychoanalysis brings out is some crack in the order of being. But this means a very precise reading of Freud. That in this sense, psychoanalysis, as Lacan always insisted, is not just another science about psychic trouble and so on.

Freud wrote something that...

Yes, but Freud was often an idiot. As Lacan put it—sorry—Freud didn't know what he discovered.

But he also wrote that in his opinion psychoanalysis wasn't a Weltanschaüung.

Yes, but he meant this in a more scientific way.

Not in a philosophical way?

Freud was not consistent. That's the basic fact. But he was always tempted to propose some scientific reductionism. At some point Freud even writes in a very cognitive, neuronal way that when we really know how our mind works we will no longer need psychoanalysis. That we will directly be able... Many neuronal scientists quote him, Freud. Freud knew that this, psychoanalysis, is temporary. Now that we know how our mind works we no longer need Freud and we no longer need psychoanalysis.

Do you think that psychoanalysis has lost a kind of provocation...

Yes and no. That's a good point. Lacan put it very nicely. What was the provocation of psychoanalysis? It was not, as we thought, those unfortunate metaphors, you know... our mind is like... our rational ego is just the tip of the iceberg, then there is, submerged, the unconscious; it's not the irrationality of the human mind, but it is... Freud's big discovery is how even our unconscious is integrated with discourse, with a certain strange rationality. So this is the big news. Psychoanalysis is not *lebens* philosophy, the philosophy of life, where you justify: oh, we are irrational, passionate beings. No, our passions are artificial, constructed, and so on and so on. That's where psychoanalysis is more current than ever, today. But not the existing one.

Which one do you imagine?

Maybe it will fail. Lacan, towards the end of his life, was a pessimist. He said maybe psychoanalysis will simply disappear with this new stage of new capitalism. I think the situation is very much open, in the sense that the greatest danger to psychoanalysis comes from psychoanalysis itself. From all those revisionist traditional psychoanalysts who are totally at a loss today. I can give you a metaphor that I like. I often quote the story when Napoleon was crowned emperor. He ordered the Pope to crown him. The Pope approached Napoleon with the crown, and Napoleon took the crown out of the Pope's hands and put it on his head himself. And then the Pope gave him a wonderful answer. He told Napoleon, "I know why you did this, you wanted to destroy and humiliate Christianity. But believe me—he said to Napoleon—you will fail. We, the Church, have been trying to do this for two thousand years, and we failed." In this sense, and Lacan saw this very clearly, all of psychoanalysis is fighting against is its own subversive from…

The psychoanalytic institutions?

Yes. They fight what is really subversive in psychoanalysis. And maybe it will disappear.

Perhaps the problem is with psychoanalysis as a profession. Because it's different as a theory and as a practice.

Yes, but that's the problem. Critics of mine often claim that I'm just a philosopher, and that every psychoanalyst must be based in practice.

You have never had a clinical practice?

No! No, I must admit it, I have a problem here. And my answer is very simple: look at me, I'm a nervous wreck. Imagine yourself in trouble; can you even imagine taking me on as an analyst? But what I want to say is that with Freud, it's clear that psychoanalytic theory is not just the theory of praxis, but at the same time, it's the theory of why the practice ultimately had to fail. Freud put it in very precise terms when he said that psychoanalysis as a practice would have really only been possible in a society which would no longer need psychoanalysis. Psychoanalysis is literally, in this sense, an impossible profession. You work in conditions that basically condemn you to fail. And this is what theory explains. Theory does not just explain how to do a good psychoanalysis. Theory also explains why ultimately, you will fail. I always quote Beckett…

Oh, I love that… "failure is the truth, fail again, fail better"…

Yes. That's why I think that to be a true psychoanalyst, you have to also know theory, at least at a certain level. If you abandon theory, you change psychoanalysis into a simple clinic. Some people don't work well, let's try to accommodate them so that they will function better. The meaning of what Freud called, they translated it wrongly, the "Unbehagen in der Kultur."

Discontent, in English.

Yes, ultimately you need psychoanalysis, not simply because you didn't fully, successfully socialize yourself; you have to recognize that your private problems are reactions to what is wrong and pathological in society as such. If you tell me these translations, I must tell this dirty story that I like. When I visit a country I always ask for obscenities, differences in languages. You know which one is my favorite from Argentina? One of the big differences with Spain, in your Spanish, is the verb "coger"; in Spain it's simply to grab something... But with you it's the "f" word. And there's a wonderful story, you must know it, all Argentineans know it. A Spanish idiot comes to Argentina and says, "¿Dónde puedo coger un taxi?," that is, Where can I get a taxi? Do you know the Argentinean answer? "You can try in the exhaust pipe, but it would not be very clever..." I like this! This is the spirit of psychoanalysis.

Humor is very important in your theorizations.

Yes, but my point is that all great dialecticians, like Hegel already and so on, are full of humor. Even Lenin, the late Lenin, was obsessed by this. He wrote about how there is not enough humor in the central committee, and he even said that we need another special Board that will control the central committee, and he's really describing some kind of—ok, it's not the correct term—collective psychoanalysis and acting with humorous remarks, with jokes and so on. You know what fascinates me? Hegel has a wonderful notion of—it's extremely subversive—what he calls objective humor. He said there's subjective humor, which is irony: British arrogance, I laugh at you and you're the idiot. Hegel opposes this. He said that this is subjective vanity; you just think you are brighter. He says that a true dialectician discerns objective humor, where things are already in themselves so hilarious that you don't have to be brighter than reality. You just register the madness of reality.

Reality makes the jokes.

Yes! That's why I think, for example... I don't trust those liberal critics of Trump who just make fun of Trump; Trump is already his own joke. Auschwitz, at its most horrible, you have humorous moments there. Not in the sense that you laugh, but in the sense of this madness which has a humorous ethic. Tragedy underestimates the horror of the Holocaust. A tragic hero still retains a certain dignity, like you're a Nazi torturer and I say torture me but I will never speak! When things are really horrible it's obscene to designate them as tragic. Tragedy is the story of a hero who confronts the enemy but discovers that he is... This is the tragic recognition, I'm fighting an enemy but—my God!—I'm really fighting myself! Like Oedipus.

But you cannot analyze Auschwitz in this way. The tragic experience of the Jews which we loved, they were really responsible for Holocaust... No! The Holocaust was terrifying. It was not a tragedy, because it was a comedy, totally contingent. You did nothing, you were put there, what happened to you had no deeper meaning. That's the truth. Tragedy is always a tragedy of meaning. In this sense, I even go to the end here, and claim that we return to Lacan. Tragedy is Antigona. Again, I'm not downplaying the pain, the horror; I'm claiming that tragedy, the notion of tragedy works only at a certain, still moderate, level, where you have a tragic conflict. And it's an obscenity to designate the Holocaust a tragedy.

You like to provoke.

Yes, but you know what my answer would be? My pedagogic aim would be to establish that the real provocation is reality itself. People like Putin, Trump and so on... They are true provocateurs. I make fun, I provoke them, but my aim is to make people see that they are the true provocation.

Do you think that psychoanalysis needs to be more amusing, less tragic?

I like this desperate humor, which it's not a humor of, "oh, now it's easy, we can laugh," but is a humor of despair. Humor means it's too traumatic; we cannot yet confront it as a tragedy. You know, you are too young to know, but you've heard about the Bosnian massacre at Srebrenica. I've written about it. But now I have some new, even better jokes. In Bosnia, around Srebrenica, in order to confront that horror, where almost all the men were killed and so on by Serbs, people have developed an extremely obscene humor. The victims! The joke, for example, a classic joke—I warn you, it's very vulgar—you have Mujo and Fatah, a Bosnian couple from jokes, a married couple. And they establish that Mujo, the husband, is probably among those found in a mass grave, and the problem is that their faces, bodies, are distorted. The only part that remains safe is the penis. So they collect some fifty penises from the bodies and ask Fatah, "Please go through them, and see if any of them is Mujo's." So she goes through them and she says, "Not Mujo's, not Mujo's," and then she finds one penis and says, "This one is not even from Srebrenica!" That she fucked them all is a beautiful Lacanian ambiguity. It can be read, she fucked them all and she knows that this is not... Or, it can be read like she fucked maybe only two men, Mujo and this other penis that she recognized. But you know what is so interesting? I know the guy, we'll publish something by him. His name is Damier Arsenievich, a Muslim Bosnian linguist who studies this, and he told me that these jokes are not meant as making fun, like "it's over." It's still too painful for them to confront it in a tragic way. The only thing they can do is make jokes about it. It's a kind of recognition of defeat. They cannot yet do the work of mourning, they cannot do it yet. So that's why the only thing that remains are jokes. So, I would say, let's have jokes, but not in order to make it easier, but to recognize, to admit, that we cannot yet confront it.

Do you think that this kind of massacres, like Srebrenica, the Holocaust, are unthinkable in a way?

No, no, I don't believe that. It takes time, look at the Holocaust! You need time to understand. You cannot go directly to it. Time is needed to confront it. And in the time in between, you need humor. The only authentic thing is humor in that time.

What is your place in relation to psychoanalysis?

I prefer not to think about it. My place is very simple. I think that we philosophers, even psychoanalysts… we cannot provide answers. We can ask the right questions. That's all we can do. People ask me, what about ecology? What to do politically? I cannot do. I can only tell you, or the people—I hope I can—where they make a mistake already in the way they ask questions.

What is your place in relation to the psychoanalytic community?

I'm a little bit arrogant here, and at the same time isolationist. I do what I do, it's their problem to decide that. I don't focus on them. I don't care if I'm marginal or not.

You have done something that I appreciate a lot. You have found a way to speak to huge communities of people.

Yes, but I'm reaching a limit there. I'm progressing more and more into writing two different types of books. On the one hand, these fat philosophical books, nothing less than a thousand pages or so, and on the other hand, shorter political books. I don't like this. I'm basically a pessimist. I don't believe in this really popular intellectual. It's always a misunderstanding. People, the broad majority—I'm a pessimist here—cannot really follow all this, and so on. But they can follow what you call provocations. That's enough for me. To provoke, to make them think.

Chapter 20

In few words (a shared epilogue with J. M. Coetzee and Joseph Kosuth)

The twenty-odd testimonies I have compiled here are just a sample of a larger group, part of an ongoing project that offers me the unusual privilege of accessing—with a greater degree of intimacy than most everyday mortals—the emotional kitchen, as it were, of the thinking process of the most advanced of our species.

But this selection also emerges from another group, that of the interviews that didn't take place, where at times, an exchange of e-mails that sustained a negative answer—as in the case of Bernardo Bertolucci—wound up being as interesting, or even more so, as an interview that never happened. Like everything we do, this book is also the result of a race against the absolute master: death, since some of my interviewees, such as Abbas Kiarostami, passed away when our encounter—almost always involving lengthy planning and consisting of different stages—had barely begun, or shortly after we had met. Others were already quite infirm when I proposed the conversation. There were some—as happened with Hanif Kureishi, Christian Boltanski, Ernesto Laclau, or Sudhir Kakar—who became gravely ill or passed away after our encounter.

The interviews I have carried out have, in fact, often become intertwined in a mute dialogue with my interviewees' novels, films, essays, or other artistic works—at times beginning before or continuing after—where I would find answers to questions that circled around in my head, or I would track down leads and reconstruct genealogies like a detective.

It may be worthwhile to include a pair of additional testimonies in this collection, even in a fragmentary manner. One of them is that of J. M. Coetzee, who was awarded a Nobel Prize in Literature for his stories, which are every bit as lucid and austere as his conversation. Perhaps my desire to interview him was due to having read, in a letter from the South African to Paul Auster, that if it wasn't for Freud, he would not be who he is. It took me forever to lay hands on his e-mail address and to overcome several hurdles. When I finally did get it, I wrote to him, proposing to travel to Adelaide, Australia. He has lived there for years, as an exile, because—as he wrote to say later—"the demographics of South Africa, where I was born, and of Australia, where I have lived since I've retired from the academic world at the age of 62, are very different. South Africa is a country of young people with little regard for the old." Having chosen a remote corner of the world as where to spend

DOI: 10.4324/9781032708591-20

his advanced age could imply—I think—something more than he was alleging. For this reason, I also asked him about another choice he had made, one with political consequences for the Spanish language, since I was aware that Coetzee had decided that the Spanish translations—in a foreign language, that is—of his latest novels were to be considered their original versions. In other words, that their translation into other languages would be done on the basis of the Spanish version. He wrote to me: "The three books *The Childhood of Jesus*, *The Schooldays of Jesus* and *The Death of Jesus* are set in a different time and place—a different kind of time and place—to the time and place you and I know. They are not unique in this respect. There is plenty of speculative fiction that takes place in what we can loosely call 'another world'. Most writers of speculative fiction use the convention that the language spoken in this other world will be the language they and their readers use. I do not subscribe to this convention. When the two main characters of *The Childhood of Jesus* step off the boat, they find themselves in a world where Spanish is spoken—not English—and where they have to learn Spanish before they can make themselves understood. Clearly there is a certain anomaly in presenting the story of these two persons in the English language. But I am not competent to write their story in Spanish. So the first two books were presented to the world in English. By the time I wrote the third book, I had discovered a Spanish-language publisher and a translator who were prepared to assist with the transmutation and publication of an English-language text into a Spanish-language text. *La muerte de Jesús* accordingly appeared in Spanish a year before *The Death of Jesus* in English. There are further, subsidiary reasons why I have grown indifferent to being positioned as a writer who belongs to the English-speaking world. Among these reasons are my opposition to the spread of English across the world at the expense of smaller languages and the fact that the kind of books I write no longer find much favor in the English-speaking world."

Shortly before the outbreak of the pandemic made it impossible to travel, Coetzee finally—in a style that was amiable but curt, foreign to those of us like myself whose cultural upbringing has been in the Latin tradition—turned down the encounter in person that I was proposing, and said that he preferred a written exchange instead. And so we conversed that way, with immediate responses on his part, as opposed to my e-mails with barrages of questions which took months to be sent and were reduced in the return e-mails as though having passed through a still, transmuted into the few he chose to answer.

Perhaps it isn't a bad idea to conclude this book of meetings in person and sometimes intimate conversations with fragments of a dialogue with someone whom I have never seen face to face; someone who cultivates distance—both in his writing and as an interviewee—as few others do, but has great ability when it comes to constructing a "good story," an area in which literature and psychoanalysis converge.

When I asked him about the importance of Freud and psychoanalysis in his life, about the cultural legacy of psychoanalysis in the West and the marks it has left, Coetzee answered: "To my reading of Freud I attribute, in part, a certain ethical outlook of mine. Specifically, I see the creature we call homo sapiens as an unstable moment in the evolution of the mammal—unstable in the sense that he/she/it is under the control of two incompatible masters, the basic drives (*Trieben*) on the one hand and reason on the other. The fundamental and ineradicable discontent (*Unbehagen*) of the human condition results from being tugged continually in opposing directions. If you see human beings in this way, it is hard to be too judgmental about them."

And regarding the connection between psychoanalysis and literature, and even whether psychoanalysis could be a form of literature, the Nobel posed the question: "What is literature, after all, as distinct from writing? The question can be made more interesting if one asks what the status is of the texts of Freud's case histories. To a certain extent these case histories preserve the monologues of Freud's patients; to a certain extent they mold them according to Freud's own desires, as advocate of his pioneering method of interpretation. The status of the 'raw' monologues of his patients interests me the most. In them I see the patient elaborating a life-story for himself or herself, a fiction in which he or she can believe."

Keeping in mind what Walter Benjamin had written about a certain "spirit of narration" which has long since been lost, I asked Coetzee if psychoanalysis might contribute to its restoration. And he said that "in the eyes of Walter Benjamin, narration (story-telling) belongs to a pre-industrial age, an age when people were rooted in the place of their birth and the wider world was a source of wonder to them—hence their appetite for tales of strange places. This appetite still exists: one has only to think of the immensely popular fantasies that Hollywood churns out, based on comic-book stories written for children. I doubt that the discipline of psychoanalysis, which at least in its classical, Freudian form conceives of itself as a science, is either able or willing to restore the spirit of the pre-industrial storyteller. But perhaps psychoanalysis can help us to understand the strange phenomenon of adult audiences absorbed in childish fantasies of omnipotence."

When we finished our conversation, we were still in the middle of a pandemic, the consequences of which were beyond calibration. I wanted to ask him if he thought that the difficult times we were facing needed "good stories" in order to be understood. There he changed his direct, incisive tone to respond to me in an allusive manner, telling me that actually, "two alternative ways of dealing with hard times are offered by Boccaccio and Defoe. Boccaccio suggests that we seek refuge in a safe space, with a group of friends, and amuse ourselves telling stories while we wait for the plague to pass. Defoe suggests that we make a record of how human beings behave when threatened by the plague."

It isn't difficult to imagine with which of these two ways of confronting this unprecedented era Coetzee identified. From his island, he himself—like Defoe's Robinson—sustained his isolation, while the rest of us entertained ourselves by telling stories. Many of them even took the form of interviews, much like the ones compiled in this book.

At this point, it hardly seems strange that Coetzee himself, who undoubtedly has a strong interest in psychoanalysis as a cultural discipline, has never actually been in analysis. That may well be, as he said to me, because "I treat psychoanalysis as a means of understanding oneself rather than as a therapy." Or it may simply be because he does not need it, because his writing serves as analysis for him. Reading his autobiographical texts suffices to give you an idea of how that might materialize. I have come to think that one clue to figuring out how it is that someone with Coetzee's talent and ability for introspection, someone who is incapable of contemplating himself without Freud, has never laid down on any couch resides in his position as a subject.

Because toward the end of his life, Coetzee would seem to be in a place that is not all that different from the place one reaches following a laborious analysis. Far removed from any arrogance or conceit, when I asked him in what way he would like to be remembered, he answered by telling me a story, a family anecdote with which it might be time to bring things to a close; at least for now.

The great South African writer, the ephemeral correspondent who answered my questions from the other side of the world, had been going through a process of reduction before my eyes, a distillation in keeping with his extremely laconic manner, evident even in his signature. He who a year and a half ago had signed his immediate response to my first e-mail "John Coetzee," sometime later would do so with "John" to finally wind up with no more than "J." And this is what "J" wrote to me:

"My great-uncle Albert du Biel was a novelist writing in the 1920s, when a corpus of literature in the young Afrikaans language barely existed. In the most recent history of Afrikaans literature, published in the present century, Albert du Biel's contribution to the literature of his nation is regarded as so slight that he is mentioned only in a footnote. If, in the histories of literature published in the 22nd century, I am still present, even if only in a footnote, I will be content."

The other testimony that interests me in order to conclude is from Joseph Kosuth, the conceptual art pioneer and legendary artist who would initiate a collection of contemporary art in the very place—Berggasse 19, Vienna—where Freud lived, analyzed, and wrote.

I spent two years tracking him down. I spoke with half a dozen assistants in order to set up the interview, and every time we were about to meet—in London, Miami, or New York—something would happen to make the encounter impossible. Finally, having given up all hope, one day in the midst of the pandemic I received an e-mail from him, when it was no longer possible to set up a meeting in person. I sent him questions, and he sent me answers. Then, just as suddenly as he had appeared he disappeared, almost as if he himself were a work dealing with time, with death, with the pulsating and evanescent nature of the unconscious, which had engaged him with so many questions.

As opposed to Coetzee, Kosuth's approximation to psychoanalysis had not been through reading alone. When I asked him about it, he wrote: "My approach has been based on both theory and experience. I was in psychoanalysis in my early twenties for about three years. However, my primary interest in the thinking of Sigmund Freud has concerned its impact on the culture in general."

Kosuth explained that Freud's influence on his work "is a result of my coming to understand that my project as an artist is one which concerns the construction of meaning. To this end it I felt that psychoanalysis was a valuable tool in the process of understanding how meaning is constructed in culture."

Perhaps this is why he decided to put together the collection of contemporary art at the Freud Museum in Vienna, a place that is empty because Freud's furniture, objects, and books are in the museum of the same name in London. I also asked him about this, and he said: "It seemed to me that Freud's working process shared many characteristics with that of an artist. For Freud, of course the value of his activity was in science as a medical value, but the nature of his investigations, as well as Freud personally, shared much with the artistic endeavor as in a cultural investigation as well."

There in Vienna, in that place of memory, within that emptiness where the echoes of the Nazi barbarity that would obligate Freud to migrate can still be heard, art is now the field from which the questions emerge. As Kosuth told me: "Art doesn't need explanations if you understand that an artwork is that rare occurrence of a problem and its solution as being both found at the moment of exposition simultaneously."

When I asked him about how the analytical framework might be conceived from an aesthetic perspective, he answered with an enigma that returned the question back to me: "This is probably clarified most simply in viewing the aesthetic point of view from a psychoanalytical one." So I insisted. Throughout the entire length of this book, in which scientists, writers, and artists talk about psychoanalysis, the question of whether our discipline is closer to science or to art functions like a red thread. I also asked Kosuth about this, and he replied: "Perhaps one is the balcony from which the other can be best viewed." Like Coetzee, Kosuth was as laconic in his words as he is in his work, and he answered as only a Zen master could.

At a certain point, I asked him about Duchamp, and how art history can be considered before and after his apparition (where his work is undoubtedly possible due to the advent of Duchamp). His response, a perfectly Duchampian gesture, led me further yet, to think about how we produce knowledge in our discipline. He said: "I think that the creative approach to problem-solving in science shares much with an artistic approach. If we consider the observations of Thomas S. Kuhn in *The Structure of Scientific Revolutions,* and you consider his concept of paradigm shifts, some parallels with Duchamp's approach are apparent."

At another point, I wrote to him: "You have traveled a lot, lived here and there, even in places visited only by anthropologists... I can imagine that you—much like Montesquieu in his Persian letters—, more than doing so in order to know more about the others, i. e. the natives, you traveled all that way in order to know more about your own cultural background... Is that true? How do you manage to remain a foreigner to yourself?" Always using fewer words in his answers than I did in my questions, he quite succinctly said: "By acknowledging as much as possible the dual relationship between the foreigner and the guest that lurks, most often uncritically, within all of us."

Another of the concerns that runs throughout this book has to do with the current state of psychoanalysis, and for that reason, I asked him about Freud's contemporaneity. He replied: "In the sense that the contemporary is by definition an activity by the living for the living, any use of anything is vulnerable to a contemporary judgment and use. There has been much use of Freud's thinking in the field formed by his activity, and its practical application always remains an open question. Outside as well as inside of that field, the influence of Freud is ubiquitous."

Now, at the end of this book, I think about the truth distilled—more in their form than in their content—in the fragmentary testimonies from Coetzee and Kosuth. Coming as they both do from the world of words and images, the concise nature of their phrases and their generosity between the lines make for a stark contrast, like a minimalist postcard compared to the jumble of words poured out in all the preceding interviews. It is as if in one way or another, they each testify to a limit.

My encounter with both of them also contrasted with the meetings in person for the other interviews because of the virtual mode imposed, evidencing something that does nevertheless inhabit the other encounters also, and that is the undercurrent of discord that is reached sooner or later. This is replicated, naturally, in every analytical encounter. There, sooner or later a certain structural mismatch will manifest itself, a degree of discord, where words reach their limit. It is this radical discord that invites us, time and time again, to invent new encounters. This limit in the face of what can be said is what obligates us, time and time again, to try out new words.

Index

Printed in the United States
by Baker & Taylor Publisher Services